To Jill & Joey

Love

Pam

12/3/03

THE SOURCEBOOK OF ARCHITECTURAL & INTERIOR ART 18

THE SOURCEBOOK
OF ARCHITECTURAL
& INTERIOR ART 18

GUILD Sourcebooks

Madison, Wisconsin

USA

THE SOURCEBOOK OF ARCHITECTURAL & INTERIOR ART 18

GUILD Sourcebooks
An imprint of GUILD, LLC
931 E. Main Street
Madison, Wisconsin 53703
TEL 608-257-2590 • TEL 877-284-8453

ADMINISTRATION
Toni Sikes, CEO and Founder
Reed McMillan, Vice President of Sales

DESIGN, PRODUCTION AND EDITORIAL
Georgene Pomplun, Art Director
Sue Englund, Production Artist
Katie Kazan, Chief Editorial Officer
Jill Schaefer, Editorial/Production Coordinator
Jill Schaefer, Writer (Interviews)
Amy Stengel, Production Intern

ARTIST CONSULTANTS
Nicole Carroll • Carla Dillman • Lori Dumm
Amy Lambright • Laura Marth • Mike Mitchell

Copyright ©2003 GUILD, LLC
ISBN (hardcover) 1-880140-52-7 • ISBN (softcover) 1-880140-51-9

Printed in China

COVER ART: Martha Pettigrew, *Gossip,* 2002, bronze, 78"H. Photograph: Jafe Parsons.
PAGE 1: Arthur Stern, *Frozen Music,* leaded glass, 5.8' x 5.2'.
PAGE 3: Gwenn Connolly, *Ascending,* bronze, 12'H x 8'W x 5.8'D. Photograph: Arthur Stern.
FACING PAGE: Linda Leviton, *Pick Up Stix,*
copper, oil and patina, 36" x 36" x 2". Photograph: Jerry Anthony.

GUILD.com is the Internet's leading retailer of original art and fine craft.
Visit www.guild.com.

LUST

It is accepted wisdom that we should not be materialistic, that "less is more." I never bought it. Remember Jimmy Carter's confessing lust in his heart? Well, let me confess that there is lust in my heart…for hefty doorknobs and stair railings that make my hand want to linger. For colored glass windows that change the atmosphere of a room, and murals that transport me out of the room to somewhere else entirely. For handmade tiles and mosaics, paintings and photographs, sculpture and objects, and oh so much more. These things have power. Throughout the ages, art has been used in churches, mosques and synagogues for inspiration and transformation. Those church elders were wise; they knew that art was good for the soul. Well, I'm here to say that our homes, workplaces and public spaces—where we spend most of our time—deserve at least the same attention to the visual environment as our places of worship. As we compiled the latest edition of the *GUILD Sourcebook,* I found myself agog at the bounty of talent available to design and art professionals. We take great pride in presenting the work of these artists, with confidence that you and your clients will covet what they have to offer. And if you, too, find lust in your heart, call the artist and commission an original work of art. It's guaranteed to bring you great satisfaction *and* make the world a better place for all of us.

Toni Sikes
Publisher

Opposite: *Hemisphere 18 Twist,* Brian F. Russell, cast glass and forged steel, 12" x 11" x 9".

TABLE OF CONTENTS

TABLE OF CONTENTS

The Sourcebook of Architectural & Interior Art shows artwork of enduring value; we think you'll refer to it for years to come.
If, at any time, you're unable to reach an artist through contact information included in this book, call GUILD at 1-877-284-8453.
We keep track of updated phone numbers and the like, and are glad to share our most current information.

Using the Sourcebook

The Sourcebook of Architectural & Interior Art 18 is designed specifically for individuals and trade professionals seeking artists to create large- or small-scale commissioned artwork. In addition to each artist's display of images, listings in the back of the book describe the artist's range of work, commissions and recent projects. These listings are organized in alphabetical order by the heading on each artist's page. They contain all the information necessary to contact the artist about your project, thus making the sourcebook a unique direct-call resource.

PRODUCT SEARCH

If you already know what type of work your project calls for, a search by section will help you find results quickly. Artists in the sourcebook are arranged in sections covering work as varied as large-scale glass in the Architectural Glass section to art quilts and tapestries in Art for the Wall: Fiber. Check the Table of Contents for a list of sections.

When paging through a particular section, keep in mind that the photos presented on each of the artists' pages are representative of the work that they do, not the full extent of their capabilities. If you like an artist's style but are interested in having him or her take on a different type of project than the ones pictured, contact the artist and see if it's a good fit. Likewise, you can broaden your searches to several different sections to find an even wider variety of choices. If you are searching for freestanding sculpture, for example, you might want to look through not only the Representational Sculpture and Non-Representational Sculpture sections, but the Public Art section as well.

13

ARTIST SEARCH

If you know the name of the artist you want to work with, you can easily search using the Artist Information section or the Index of Artists & Companies, both found in the gray pages at the back of the sourcebook. The Artist Information section provides a wealth of detail about each artist, including the materials and techniques they use, examples of their commissions and collections, and publications that feature photographs of their artwork (including previous GUILD sourcebooks). Both the Artist Information section and the Index of Artists and Companies include page references, so you can easily locate the artist's full-color page in the book.

Want to know more about an artist's work? Don't hesitate to call the artist directly for more information.

LOCATION SEARCH

Looking for an artist in your area or another specific region? Turn to the Location Index. Located in the back of the book, this index can help you find artists from across the United States, Canada and abroad.

INSPIRATIONAL BROWSING

Even if you don't have a specific project in mind, *The Sourcebook of Architectural & Interior Art 18* will prove an invaluable tool. It can be taken to client meetings to show a world of possibilities, browsed through for future inspiration and used to see the newest projects of artists you've collaborated with in the past.

Opposite: Architectural glass, Avalon Towers, Daniel Winterich.

The Commission Process

The nearly 250 artists featured in *The Sourcebook of Architectural & Interior Art 18* represent a remarkable spectrum of artistic talent and vision. Whether you're looking for a large-scale public sculpture or a residential accessory, this book can put you directly in touch with highly qualified artists throughout North America. Any one of these artists can be commissioned to create a unique work of art — but with so many exceptional artists to choose from, finding the right one for your specific project can be a challenge. Once the artist has been selected, careful planning and communication can help ensure a great outcome.

Having watched art commissions unfold since the first GUILD sourcebook was published in 1986, we can suggest steps to ensure successful partnerships between artists and trade professionals. We especially want to reassure those who have been reluctant to try such a collaboration because of questions about how the process works.

This article is a how-to guide to the art commissioning process. It suggests strategies to help selection and hiring go smoothly. It also describes steps that can help set common (and realistic) expectations on the part of artists and clients, and explains advantages of including the artist in the design team early in the planning process.

FINDING THE ARTIST

By far the most important step in a successful commission is choosing the right artist for your particular project and budget. This choice is the decision from which all others will flow, so it's worth investing time and energy in the selection process and seasoning the search with both wild artistic hopes and hard-nosed realism. The right choices at this early stage will make things go more smoothly later on.

Some clients will want to help select and work with the artist. Others will want only minimal involvement, leaving most of the decision-making to the design team. Regardless of who makes the decisions, there are several ways to find the right artist. Obviously, we recommend browsing through *The Sourcebook of Architectural & Interior Art 18*. Every artist featured on these pages is actively seeking commission projects; that's why they're included in the book. Many of these artists have already established strong track records working with designers, architects and art consultants; you will gain from their professionalism and experience. Others are newer in their field; their determination to prove themselves can fuel an exciting and successful collaboration.

15

NARROWING THE FIELD

Once your "A-list" is narrowed down to two or three names, it's time to schedule meetings, either face-to-face or by phone. As you talk, try to determine the artist's interest in your project, and pay attention to your own comfort level with the artist. Try to find out if the chemistry is right—whether you have the basis to build a working relationship. This is also the time to confirm that the artist has the necessary skills to undertake your project. Be thorough and specific when asking questions. Is the artist excited about the project? What does he or she see as the most important issues or considerations? Will

your needs be a major or minor concern? Evaluate the artist's style, approach and personality.

If it feels like you might have trouble working together, take heed. But if all goes well and it feels like a good fit, ask for a list of references. These are important calls; don't neglect to make them! Ask about the artist's work habits, communication style and, of course, the success of the artwork. You should also ask whether the project was delivered on time and within budget. If you like what you hear, you'll be one important step closer to hiring your artist.

EXPECT PROFESSIONALISM

If this is an expensive or complicated project, you may want to request preliminary designs. Since most artists charge a design fee whether or not they're ultimately hired for the project, start by asking for sketches from your top candidate. If you're unhappy with the designs submitted, you can go to your second choice. But if the design is what you'd hoped for, it's time to finalize your working agreement with this artist.

As you discuss contract details, be resolved that silence is not golden and ignorance is not bliss! Be frank. Discuss the budget and timetable, and tell the artist what you expect. Now is the time for possible misunderstandings to be brought up and resolved—not later, after the work is half done and deadlines loom.

16

WORKING WITH AN ART CONSULTANT

As your project gains definition, you'll need to pay attention to its technical aspects, including building codes, lighting specifications, and details related to zoning and installation. Most designers find the artist's knowledge and understanding of materials, code, safety and engineering complete and reassuring. However, complex projects may warrant hiring an art consultant to help with these details, as well as the

initial selection of art and artists. Just as you would when hiring any other professional, call references to be sure the consultant you hire is sophisticated and experienced enough to provide real guidance with your project. This means the ability to help negotiate the technical aspects of a very specific contract, including issues like installation, insurance, storage, transportation and engineering costs.

PUTTING IT IN WRITING

It is a truism in any kind of business that it is much cheaper to get the lawyers involved at the beginning of a process rather than after something goes wrong. A signed contract or letter of agreement commits the artist to completing his or her work on time and to specifications. It also assures the artist that he or she will get paid the right amount at the right time.

Contracts should be specific to the job. Customarily, artists are responsible for design, production, shipping and installation. If someone else will install the artwork, be sure you specify who will coordinate and pay for the installation; if

not the artist, it's usually the client. With a large project, it's helpful to identify the tasks that, if delayed for any reason, would set back completion of the project. These should be discussed up front to ensure that both parties agree on requirements and expectations.

Most trade professionals recognize that adequate compensation for artists ensures the level of service needed to fulfill the client's expectations. The more complex the project, the more you should budget for the artist's work and services.

PAYMENT SCHEDULE

Payments are usually tied to specific milestones in the process. These serve as check points and assure that work is progressing in a satisfactory manner, on time and on budget. Payment is customarily made in three stages, although this certainly depends on the circumstances, scope and complexity of the project.

The first payment is usually made when the contract is signed. It covers the artist's time and creativity in developing a detailed design specific to your needs. You can expect to go through several rounds of trial and error in the design process, but at the end of this stage you will have detailed drawings (and, for three-dimensional work, a maquette, or model) that everyone agrees upon. The cost of the maquette and the design time are usually factored into the artist's fee.

The second payment is generally set for a point midway through the project and is for work completed to date. If the materials are expensive, the client may be asked to advance money at this stage to cover costs. If the commission is canceled during this period, the artist keeps the money already paid for work performed.

Final payment is usually due when the work is installed. If the piece is finished on time but the building or project is delayed, the artist is customarily paid on delivery, but still has the obligation to oversee installation.

You will find that most artists keep tabs on the project budget. Be sure that the project scope does not deviate from what was agreed upon at the outset. If the scope changes, amend the agreement to reflect the changes.

THE ARTIST AS DESIGNER

Not every artist charges a design fee; some consider preliminary sketches a part of their marketing effort. But it's more common for an artist to require a design fee of 5% to 10% of the final project budget. In some cases, especially when the artist has a strong reputation in a specialized area, the design fee may be as high as 25% of the project budget; this is most common when an artist is asked for specific solutions to complicated architectural problems.

A few points about design are worth highlighting here:

1. Design Ideas Are the Artist's Property
It should go without saying that it is highly unethical, as well as possibly illegal, to take an artist's designs—even very preliminary or non-site-specific sketches—and use them without the artist's permission. Some artists may include specific language about ownership of ideas, models, sketches, etc., in their contracts or letters of agreement. Even if an artist does not use a written agreement, be sure you are clear at the outset about what you are paying for and what rights the artist retains.

2. Respect the Artist's Ideas and Vision
When you hire a doctor, you want a thoughtful, intelligent diagnosis, not just a course of treatment. The same should be true when you hire an artist to work with a design team. Most GUILD artists have become successful through many years of experience, and because of their excellence in both technique and aesthetic imagination. Take advantage of that expertise by bringing the artist into the project early, and by asking him or her for ideas.

3. Consider a Separate Design Budget for Your Project
A design budget is particularly helpful when you:
- want to get lots of ideas from an artist;
- need site-specific ideas that involve significant research;
- require a formal presentation with finished drawings, blueprints or maquettes.

To evaluate designs for a project from several artists, consider a competition with a small design fee for each artist.

4. Keep the Artist Informed of Changes
Tell the artist about changes—even seemingly minor details—which may have a significant impact on the project design. If the artist is working as a member of the design team, it's easier to include him or her in the ongoing dialog about the overall project.

It comes down to an issue of professionalism. Artists have the technical skills to and amazing things with simple materials. But they also have sophisticated conceptual and design talents. By paying for these talents, trade professionals add vision and variety to their creative products. In such a partnership, both parties gain, and the ultimate result is a client who is delighted by the outcome of the collaboration.

A COLLABORATIVE ATMOSPHERE

With most commission projects, it's best to bring the artist into the process at about the same time you hire a general contractor. By involving the artist at this early stage, the space will be designed with the art in mind, and the art will be designed to enhance the space. As a result, there will be no unpleasant surprises about size or suitability of artwork. Furthermore, when art is planned for early on and is a line item in the budget, it's far less likely to be cut at the end of the project, when money is running low.

Early inclusion of the artist also helps ensure that the collaborative effort will flow smoothly throughout all phases of the project. If the artist is respected as part of the team, his or her work can benefit the project's overall design.

Naturally, the scope of the project will determine the number of players to be involved with the artist. How will decisions be made? Who is the artist's primary liaison? Will a single person sign off on designs and recommendations? Are committees necessary? It's important that all individuals understand both their own responsibilities and the responsibilities of their collaborators.

SEEK TWO-WAY UNDERSTANDING

Be sure the artist understands the technical requirements of the job, including traffic flow, intended use of space, building structure, maintenance, lighting and environmental concerns. By fully explaining these details, you'll ensure that the artist's knowledge, experience and skills inform the project.

Keep the artist apprised of any changes that will affect the work in progress. Did you find a specified material unavailable and replace it with something else? Did the available space become bigger or smaller? These changes could have a profound impact on an artist's planning.

At the same time, the artist should let you know of any special requirements that his or her work will place on the space. Is it especially heavy? Does it need to be mounted in a specific way? Must it be protected from theft or vandalism? What kind of lighting is best? You may need to budget funds for these kinds of installation or maintenance expenses.

Most artists experienced with commissioned projects factor the expense of a continuing design dialog into their fee. There is an unfortunate belief harbored by some trade professionals (and yes, artists too) that a willingness to develop and adapt a design based on discussions with the client or design team somehow indicates a lack of commitment or creativity.

On the contrary. The ability to modify design or execution without compromising artistic quality is a mark of professionalism. We recommend looking for this quality in the artist you choose, and then respecting it by treating the artist as a partner in any decisions that will affect his or her work.

Of course, part of working together is making clear who is responsible for what. Since few designers and architects (and even fewer contractors) are used to working with artists, the relationship is ripe for misunderstanding. Without constant communication, things can easily fall through the cracks.

Above: Harriet Hyams, *Goddess I*, stained glass, 35" x 48".

FORGING A PARTNERSHIP

The partnership between artists and trade professionals is an old and honorable one. Many venerable blueprints indicate, for example, an architect's detail for a ceiling with the scrawled note: "Finish ceiling in this manner." The assumption, of course, is that the artisan working on the ceiling has both the technical mastery and the aesthetic skill to create a whole expanse of space based on a detail sketched by the architect's pen.

The artists whose work fills these pages — and with whom we work every day at GUILD — are capable of interactive relationships like those described here. We're delighted to see increasing numbers of trade professionals include artists on their design teams. After seeing the arts separated from architectural and interior design for too many years, we're happy to be part of a renewed interest in collaboration.

COMMISSION GUIDELINES

- Bring the artist into the project as early as possible.

- Be as specific as possible about the scope and range of the project, even in early meetings before the artist is selected.

- Be honest and realistic when discussing deadlines, responsibilities and specific project requirements—and expect the same from the artist. Don't avoid discussing the areas where there seem to be questions.

- For larger projects, use specific milestones to assure continuing consensus on project scope and budget. It may also be necessary to make adjustments at these points.

- Choose an artist based on a solid portfolio of previous work and excellent references. And remember that it's less risky to use an artist who has worked on projects of similar size and scope, who can handle the demands of your specific job.

- Consider hiring an art consultant if the commission is particularly large or complex. The consultant should help with complicated contract arrangements, and should make certain that communication between artists and support staff (including sub-contractors and engineers) is thoroughly understood.

- Trust your instincts when choosing an artist. Like selecting an advertising agency or an architect, choosing an artist is based partly on chemistry. You need to like the work and respect the artist, and you also need to be able to work together comfortably.

19

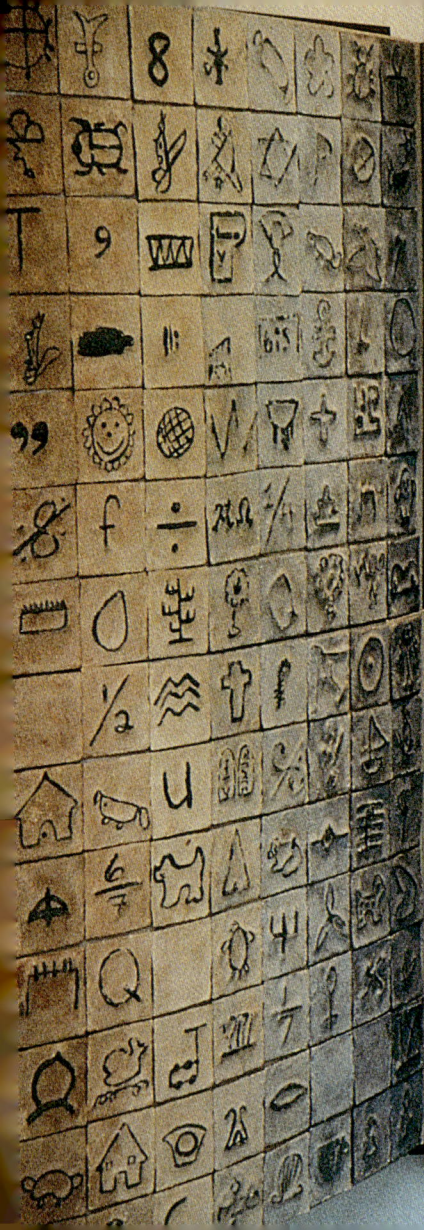

Architectural Ceramics, Mosaics and Wall Reliefs

MARY LOU ALBERETTI

ALBERETTI STUDIOS ■ 16 POSSUM DRIVE ■ NEW FAIRFIELD, CT 06812
TEL 203-746-1321 ■ E-MAIL MLALB@AOL.COM ■ WWW.SOUTHERNCT.EDU/~ALBERETT/

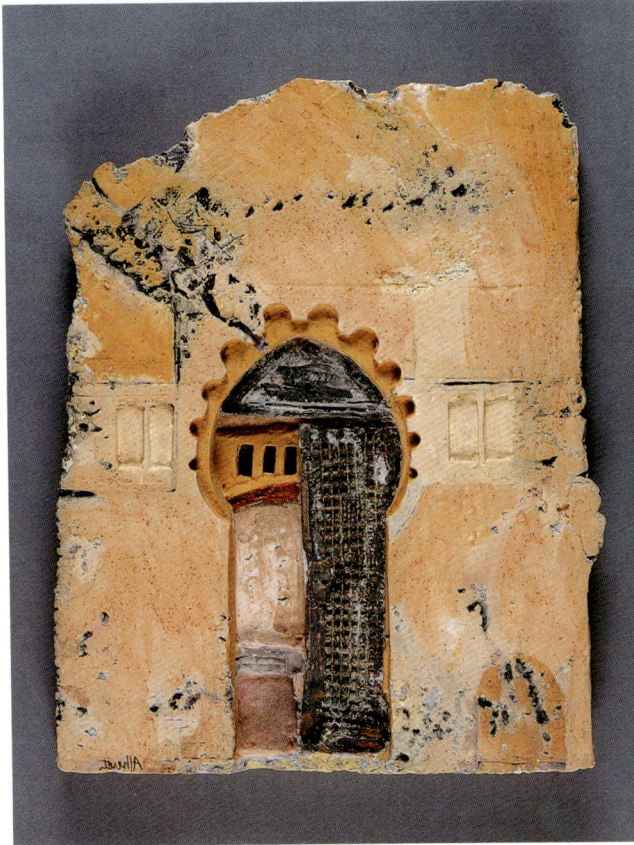

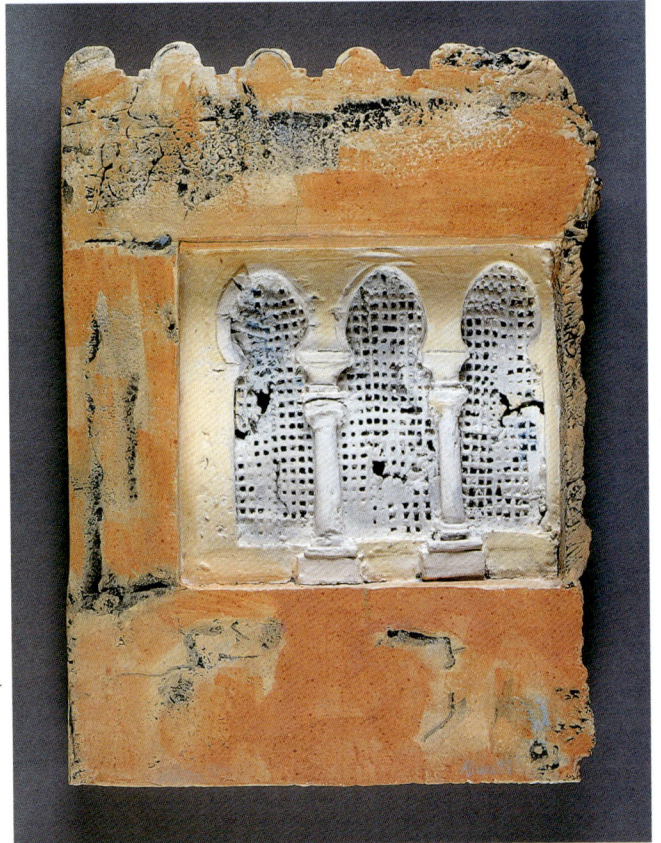

Top left: *Uccelli*, 2002, ceramic relief, 12" x 13" x 2". Top right: *Quattro*, 2002, ceramic relief, 14" x 15" x 3".
Bottom left: *Gateway*, 2002, ceramic relief, 21" x 18" x 2". Bottom right: *Tessoro*, 2002, ceramic relief, 22" x 17" x 2". Photographs: Bill Quinnell.

Printed in China ©2003 GUILD LLC The Sourcebook of Architectural & Interior Art

EARTH FIRE DESIGNS

FREDERICK MICHAEL KING ■ 740 METCALF SUITE #29 ■ ESCONDIDO, CA 92025 ■ TEL 760-747-3347 ■ FAX 760-871-3348
E-MAIL MICHAEL@EARTHFIREDESIGNS.COM ■ WWW.EARTHFIREDESIGNS.COM

23

Moroccan fireplace, clay with copper inlay, 68" x 65".

JOY BROWN

463 SEGAR MOUNTAIN ROAD ■ SOUTH KENT, CT 06785
TEL/FAX 860-927-4946 ■ E-MAIL JOY@ARTWITHIN.NET ■ WWW.ARTWITHIN.NET

24

Top: *One Earth, One Family* (two of three panels), 2002, ceramic relief, Hartford Hospital, CT, 4' × 12'. Photograph: Dan Lenore.
Bottom: *Eight-Figure Relief*, 2001, bronze, 30"H × 42"W. Photograph: Bobby Hansson.

JOSEPH DETWILER

13 RIVER RIDGE LANE ■ FREDERICKSBURG, VA 22406 ■ TEL 540-752-2656
E-MAIL JOE@JOSEPHDETWILER.COM ■ WWW.JOSEPHDETWILER.COM

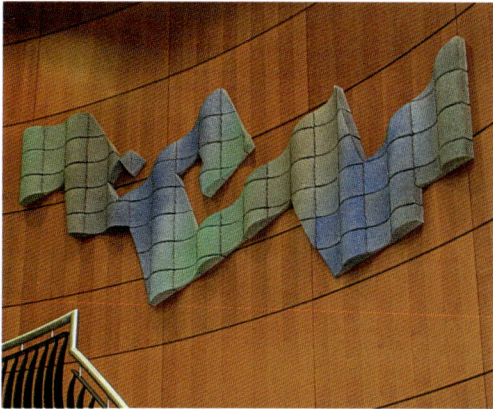

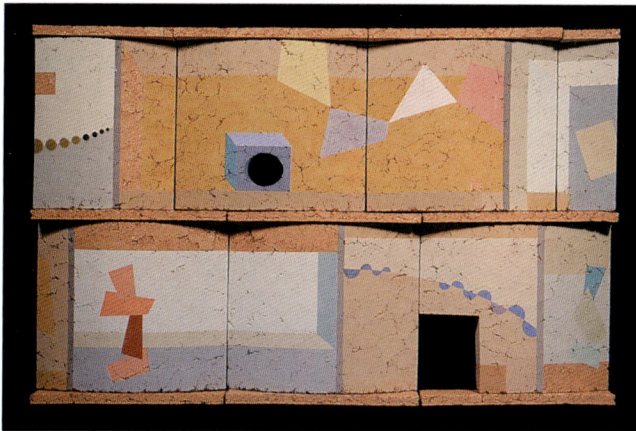

25

Top left: *Cool Force*, HealthSouth, Inc., Birmingham, AL, 7.5' × 15.5'. Top right: *Baroque Sequence*, 13" × 46" × 3".
Center left: *Concurrent Mystery II*, 25" × 40" × 2.5". Center right: *Still Life with Summer Landscape*, 15" × 24" × 2".
Bottom: *Orthogonal Landscape*, EGA, Inc., Washington, DC, 29" × 152" × 5".

TOM FAUGHT

TOM FAUGHT STUDIO & FOUNDRY ■ 200 KALUANUI ROAD ■ MAKAWAO, HI 96768
TEL 808-572-8904 ■ FAX 808-572-2642 ■ EMAIL FAUGHT@MAUI.NET ■ WWW.TOMFAUGHT.COM

26

Top: *Koi Fish Panel*, private residence, bronze and wood, 4' x 6'.
Bottom left: Lidded vessel, private residence, ceramic and bronze, 6'. Bottom right: *The Lady*, Hali'imaile General Store, Maui, bronze and wood, 8' x 4'.

JOAN ROTHCHILD HARDIN CERAMICS ■ 393 WEST BROADWAY #4 ■ NEW YORK, NY 10012
TEL 212 966-9433 ■ FAX 212 431-9196 ■ E-MAIL JOAN@HARDINTILES.COM ■ WWW.HARDINTILES.COM

27

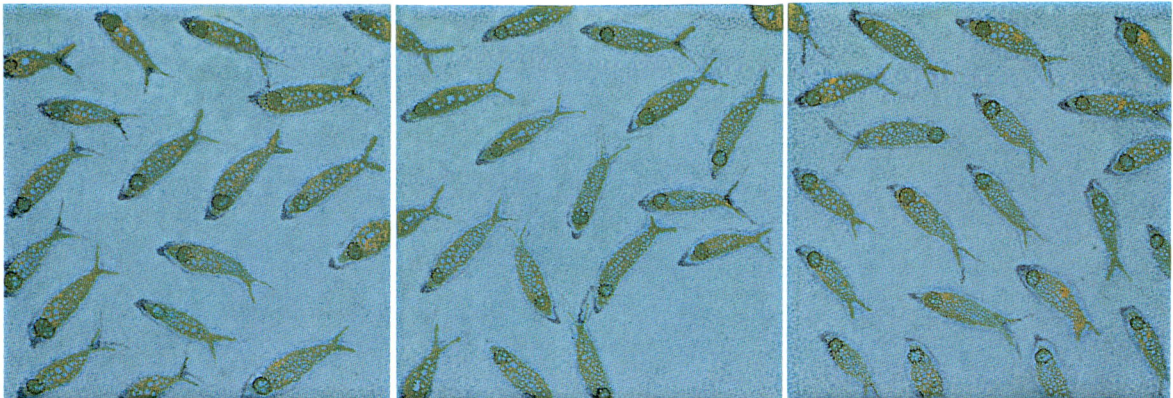

Top: *Woman on Orange with Fish*, 2002, ceramic tile, 12" x 12". Bottom: *Little Fish*, 2002, ceramic, each tile: 6" x 6". Photographs: D. James Dee.

KAREN HEYL

1310 PENDLETON STREET ML# 2 ■ CINCINNATI, OH 45202 ■ TEL 513-421-9791/760-489-7106
E-MAIL HEYLSTONE2@AOL.COM ■ WWW.KARENHEYL.COM

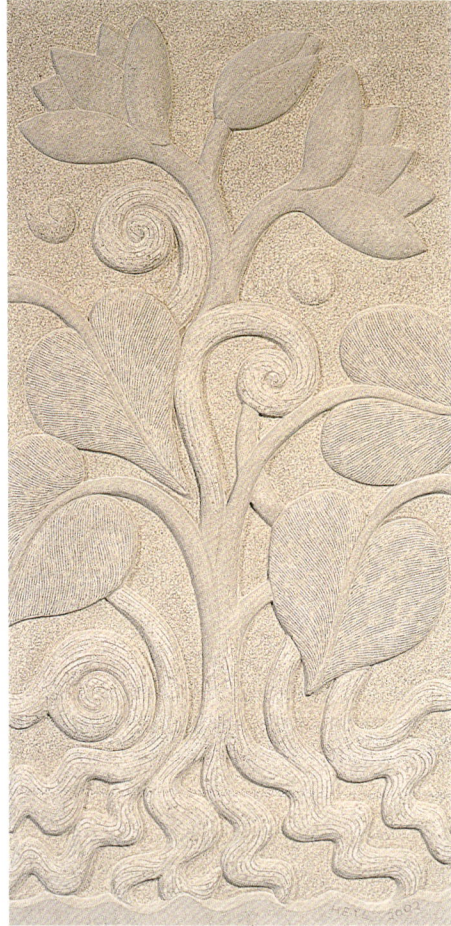

28

Top left: *Nature's Medicine*, 2002, Astra Zeneca Pharmaceutical Headquarters, Wilmington, DE,
limestone, 3 panels: 5' × 3.5' X 3", 2 panels: 5' × 2.3' × 3". Photographs: Sarah Bones Photography.

Top left: *Life is a Circus* (detail). Right: *Life is a Circus*, 2003, handbuilt porcelain, 72"H x 24"W x 2"D. Bottom left: *Life is a Circus* (detail). Photographs: Grace Weston.

HOWDLE STUDIO INC.

BRUCE HOWDLE ■ 225 COMMERCE STREET ■ MINERAL POINT, WI 53565 ■ TEL 608-987-3590
E-MAIL BHOWDLE@CHORUS.NET ■ WWW.BRUCEHOWDLE.CJB.NET

Top: Municipal Court Facility, 2002, Brighton, CO, 9' x 27'. Photograph: Frank Ooms. Bottom: *Peaceable Kingdom*, 2000, Mercy Hospital, Oshkosh, WI, 8' x 18'.

Summer Bouquet, 2002, ceramic, 48"H x 56"W.

TOM KENDALL

OAK LEAF POTTERY ■ 10936 THREE MILE ROAD ■ PLAINWELL, MI 49080
TEL/FAX 269-664-5430 ■ E-MAIL OAKLEAFPOTTERY@MEI.NET ■ MEI.NET/~OAKLEAFPOTTERY

Top: *Sun Dial*, 2000, Bronson Hospital, Kalamazoo, MI, ceramic and metal, 10' x 10'. Bottom: Tile panel, 2002, porcelain, each: 6" x 6".

THOMAS W. LOLLAR

41 CENTRAL PARK WEST, SUITE 8E ■ NEW YORK, NY 10023
TEL 212-362-9117 ■ FAX 212-875-5584

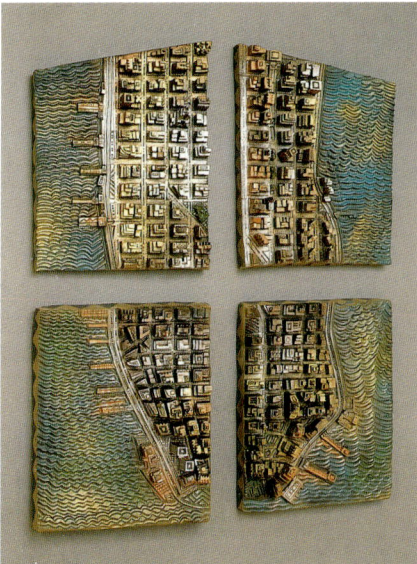

33

Top left: *New York City Mosaic* (commission), 5' × 14' × 3', client: Loeb & Loeb, Park Avenue. New York, NY. Top right: *New York City Mosaic* (detail).
Bottom left: *Manhattan I* (commission), 48" × 48" × 3". Photographs: D. James Dee.
Bottom right: *Viaduct* (commission), Levin College of Urban Affairs, Cleveland State University, Cleveland, OH, 50' × 9'. Photograph: Steve Zorc.

ELIZABETH MACDONALD

BOX 186 ■ BRIDGEWATER, CT 06752 ■ TEL 860-354-0594 ■ FAX 860-350-4052
E-MAIL EPMACD@EARTHLINK.NET ■ WWW.ELIZABETHMACDONALD.NET

34

Top left: *Book* (detail), 2002, St. Patrick's Episcopal Day School, Washington, DC, ceramic relief, 7' x 16' x 2'. Top right: *Book* (detail). Photographs: Marjory H. Train.
Bottom: *East Rock–Late Spring*, Wilbur Cross High School, New Haven, CT, 6' x 12'. Photograph: Robert Perron.

MILLERCLAY DESIGNS ■ 114 WALNUT ■ WASHINGTON, IL 61571
TEL 309-444-8608 ■ MILLERCLAY@ATT.NET ■ WWW.MILLERCLAY.COM

35

Top: *Little Tree with Birds*, 2002, Red Orchard Gallery, Bethesda, MD, stoneware, 7'H x 6.5'W.
Bottom: *Three Heads*, 2003, private residence, Morton, IL, stoneware, 34"H (tallest head). Photographs: John Beam.

JACOB JONES MOSAICS

CINDY D. JONES ■ LOUIS G. WEINER ■ 229 THIRD STREET ■ WAVELAND, MS 39576
TEL 888-365-1008 ■ FAX 228-466-0016 ■ E-MAIL CINDY@JACOBJONES.COM ■ WWW.JACOBJONES.COM

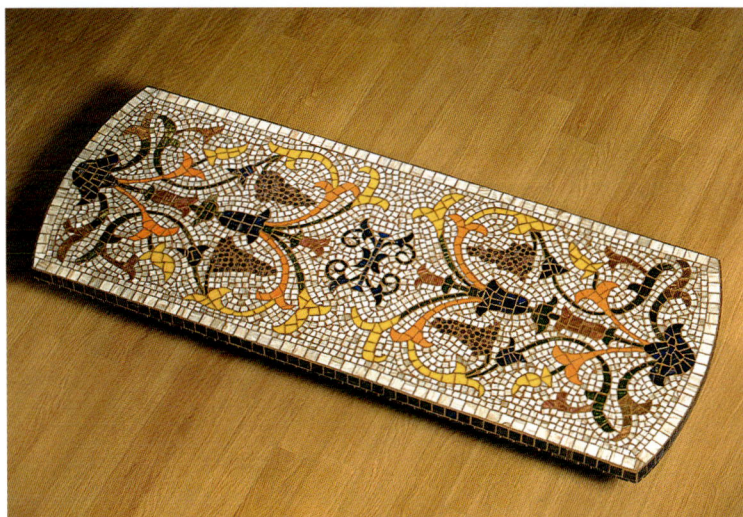

Top: *Night to Day Underwater Scene,* private residence, Key West, FL, 4' x 12'.
Bottom left: Arabesque Italian-design console table, 42" x 20" x 30"H. Bottom right: Tapestry-inspired dining table, 42"Dia.

Printed in China © 2003 GUILD, LLC: *The Sourcebook of Architectural & Interior Art*

CHARLES BROOKING TAUZER

NEW MOSAICS ■ 321 SOUTH MAIN STREET #19 ■ SEBASTOPOL, CA 95472
TEL 707-823-2297 ■ E-MAIL CTAUZER@NEWMOSAICS.COM ■ WWW.NEWMOSAICS.COM

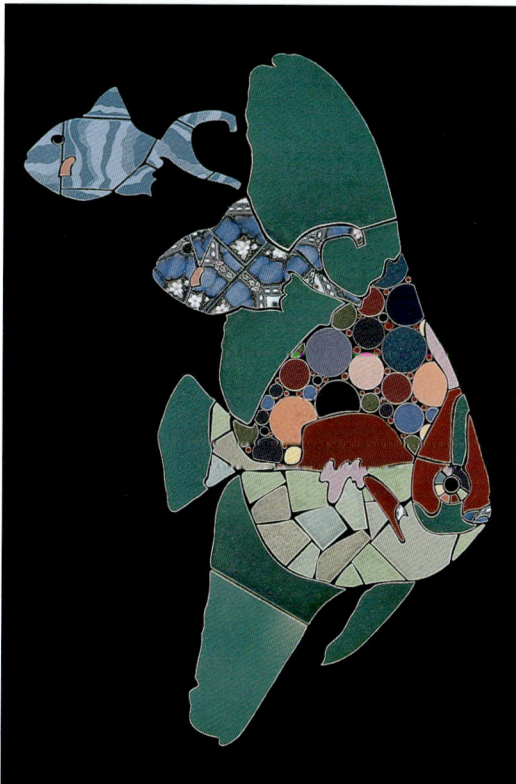

Top left: *Green Sea Turtle #3*, 2002, swimming pool mosaic, porcelain/ceramic tile, 42" x 32". Top right: *Green Sea Turtle #4*, 2002, wall hanging, porcelain/ceramic tile, birch, plywood and copper, 52" x 27" x 1.2" Bottom left: *Bat Fish Trio*, 2002, swimming pool mosaic, porcelain/ceramic tile, 26" x 27". Bottom right: *Octopus*, 2002, swimming pool mosaic, porcelain/ceramic tile, 53" x 47". Photographs: Rossen Townsend.

Architectural Metal

Custom Design: Public Art

ARTIST
Christopher Vespermann,
Kingston, New Hampshire;
design by The Butzer Design Partnership

PROJECT
Chairs for the Oklahoma
City National Memorial, 2000,
illuminated bronze, glass and stone;
glass fabrication by John Lewis

COMMISSIONED FOR
Oklahoma City National
Memorial Foundation, Oklahoma

TIMELINE
2 years

DIMENSIONS
Each adult chair: 60" × 16" × 16"
Each child chair: 48" × 12" × 12"

Christopher Vespermann had never completed a commission that was both so rewarding and so complicated. For one thing, the Oklahoma City National Memorial was a project of major significance, not only to a nation, but also to the individuals directly affected by the tragedy. "Creating a single, meaningful element was probably the most difficult part of the design process," Vespermann reports, "but when I met with members of the community—the survivors and family members of the victims—it added to the gravity and complexity for me." ■ The installation process was also very different for Vespermann. "Obviously the site was treated with great respect, and because the public had access, we were always working in front of an audience. No one talked—it was just understood by everyone that this was a kind of sanctuary." Vespermann says that despite a "crushing deadline," the artists would always stop working to help those onlookers who wanted to find the chair of a particular victim. The children's chairs, which were scaled at 80% of the adult chairs, were particularly haunting. ■ The dedication ceremony, which included President Bill Clinton, was very moving for everyone involved with the project. "Many tears were shed that day, and there was a common theme of survival that affected all of us. I think after working on that project, we all sort of felt like survivors ourselves."

FERROMOBIUS

ALLEN ROOT ■ DAVID CURRY ■ PO BOX 288 ■ SAN LUIS OBISPO, CA 93406
TEL/FAX 805-544-7960 ■ E-MAIL INFO@FERROMOBIUS.COM ■ WWW.FERROMOBIUS.COM

41

Windance Project, 2003, glass, steel, copper and cherry wood, 36" x 168". Photographs: Jo Jo Shaiken.

STEVE FONTANINI

STEVE FONTANINI ARCHITECTURAL & ORNAMENTAL BLACKSMITHING ■ PO BOX 2298 ■ 11400 SOUTH HOBACK JUNCTION ROAD
JACKSON, WY 83001 ■ TEL 307-733-7668 ■ FAX 307-734-8816 ■ E-MAIL SFONTANI@WYOMING.COM

42

Forged bronze railing of winter aspen trees and birds, Roney residence, Teton County, WY. Photograph: Florence McCall.

GREG LEAVITT / CAMILLE LEAVITT

914 POWDER MILL HOLLOW ROAD ■ BOYERTOWN, PA 19512 ■ TEL 610-367-8867 ■ FAX 610-473-8861
E-MAIL GREGORYALEAVITT@NETSCAPE.NET ■ WWW.GREGLEAVITT.COM

43

Top: Entrance arch sculpture, 2002, Lincoln Park Zoo, Chicago, IL, forged and fabricated steel, 75' × 21' × 12'. Photograph: Steven May.
Bottom left: Garden door, 2000, private residence, PA, hand-forged steel and redwood, 7' × 3' × 6".
Bottom right: *Dragon Sculptures* (detail), 1995, private residence, Tortola, BVI, hand-forged copper, 8' × 6' × 4'. Photograph: Joseph Pulcinella.

Architectural Glass

46

Top left and right: Gill residence windows, 2003, laminated beveled glass and 3D blown glass gesture elements, 6' × 10'.
Bottom left and right: Conference room entry doors, 2001, U.S. Voice and Data, sandblasted and laminated beveled glass, each: 2' × 5'.

ARCHITECTURAL GLASS ART, INC.

KENNETH F. vonROENN, JR. ■ 815 WEST MARKET STREET ■ LOUISVILLE, KY 40202
TEL 502-585-5421 ■ FAX 502-585-2808 ■ E-MAIL INFO@AGAINC.COM ■ WWW.AGAINC.COM

47

Suspended sculpture, 2002, Jewish Hospital Medical Center East, 30'H x 18'W. Photographs: David Harpe.

ART GLASS ENSEMBLES

CHRISTIE WOOD ■ 208 WEST OAK STREET ■ DENTON, TX 76201

TEL 940-591-3002 ■ FAX 940-591-7853 ■ E-MAIL ENSEMBLES@COMPUSERVE.COM

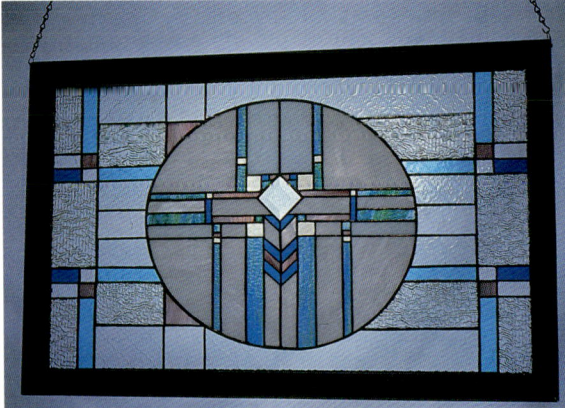

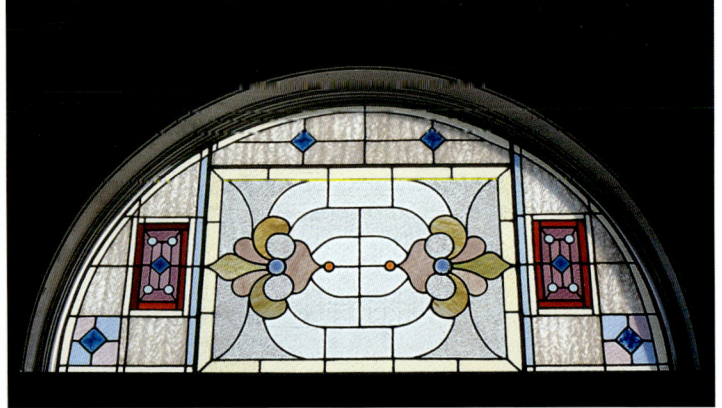

48

Top left: *Mission Statement*, 1997, private residence, Ambler, PA, 40" x 34". Top right: *French Half-Round*, 1998, private residence, Blue Bell, PA, 6' x 3.5'.
Bottom: *Cabernet Sauvignon in Summer*, 1998, private residence, North Wales, PA, 6' x 3.5'.

KATHY BRADFORD

NORTH STAR ART GLASS, INC. ■ 142 WICHITA ■ LYONS, CO 80540 ■ TEL/FAX 303-823-6511
E-MAIL KATHYBRADFORD@WEBTV.NET ■ KATHYBRADFORD.COM

49

Top left: *Faces of the Forest* (detail), 1997, multi-layered, sand-carved wall, Chicago, IL, 21' x 8' x 5". Top right: *Bamboo* (detail).
Bottom: *Bamboo*, 2001, sand-carved wall, Marriott Hotel, Anaheim, CA, 14' x 7' x 7".

WARREN CARTHER

CARTHER STUDIO INC. ■ 80 GEORGE AVENUE ■ WINNIPEG, MB R3B 0K1 ■ CANADA
TEL 204-956-1615 ■ FAX 204-942-1434 ■ E-MAIL WARREN@CARTHERSTUDIO.COM ■ WWW.CARTHERSTUDIO.COM

50

AstraZeneca Pharmaceuticals U.S. Corporate Headquarters, 2002, Wilmington, DE, carved glass, applied color and laminations with dichroic glass projection panel attached at rear (shown in detail), 25' x 15'. Photographs: Gerry Kopelow.

DAVID WILSON DESIGN

DAVID WILSON ■ 202 DARBY ROAD ■ SOUTH NEW BERLIN, NY 13843-2212 ■ TEL 607-334-3015 ■ FAX 607-334-7065
E-MAIL MAIL@DAVIDWILSONDESIGN.COM ■ WWW.DAVIDWILSONDESIGN.COM

51

Top left: *For Evelyn Smith* (west elevation), 2002, Stamford Courthouse, CT, glass, 24'H x 15'W.
Right: *For Evelyn Smith* (east elevation). Bottom left: *For Evelyn Smith* (detail).

JEROME R. DURR

JEROME R. DURR STUDIO ■ 206 MARCELLUS STREET ■ SYRACUSE, NY 13204
TEL 315-428-1322 ■ FAX 315-478-1767 ■ E-MAIL JRDURR0ART@AOL.COM ■ WWW.JEROMEDURR.COM

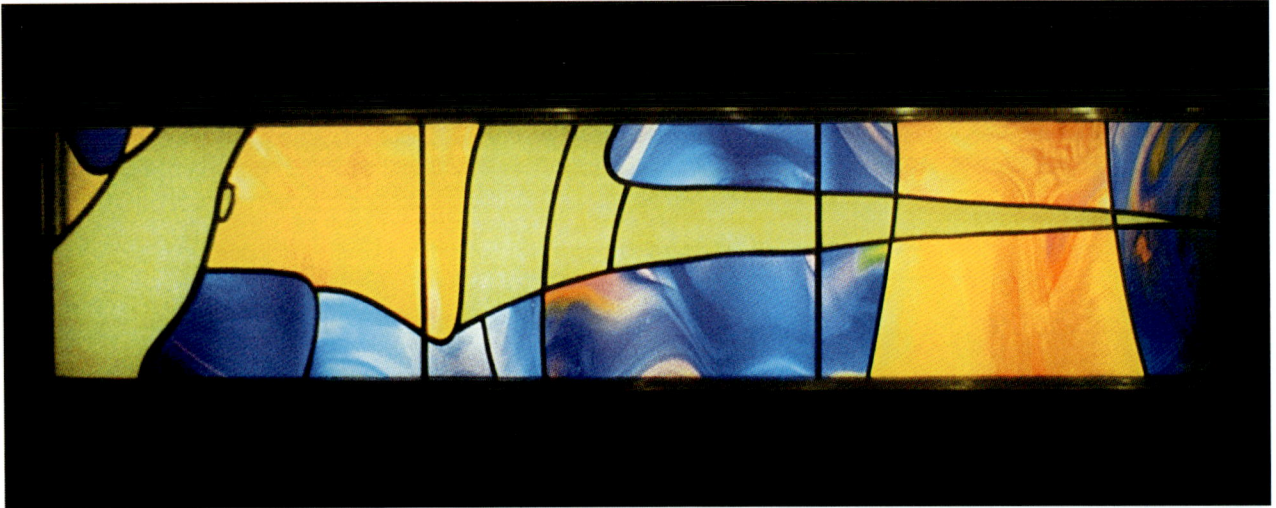

Stained, leaded glass panels, 2002, Lehman Brothers, New York, NY.

ELLEN MANDELBAUM GLASS ART

ELLEN MANDELBAUM ■ 39-49 46TH STREET ■ LONG ISLAND CITY, NY 11104-1407
TEL/FAX 718-361-8154 ■ EMGA@IX.NETCOM.COM ■ WWW.EMGLASSART.COM

53

Top left: *Glass Landscape*, 2000, South Carolina Aquarium, Charleston, leaded glass, silk screen and glass painting, 30' x 18'. Photograph: Timothy Hursley.
Top right: *Adath Jeshurun Synagogue Windows*, 1995, Minnetonka, MN, leaded glass and glass painting, up to 12'. Photograph: Saari & Forrai.
Bottom: *The Resurrection*, 2001, Marian Woods Chapel, Hartsdale, NY, leaded glass and glass painting, center window 13' x 4.5'; side panels 10.5' x 3.5'. Photograph: Stephen Ostrow.

FOX FIRE GLASS

LAUREL FYFE ■ 180 NORTH SAGINAW STREET ■ PONTIAC, MI 48342
TEL 248-332-2442 ■ FAX 248-332-2424 ■ WWW.FOXFIREGLASS.COM

54

Top: Passenger tunnel (detail), each panel 5' x 7'. Bottom: Passenger tunnel, 2002, Northwest World Gateway, McNamara Terminal, Detroit Metropolitan Airport, 700' continuous sand-carved glass mural. Photographs: Justin Maconochie Photography.

GLASSIC ART

LESLIE RANKIN ■ 5850 SOUTH POLARIS, SUITE 700 ■ LAS VEGAS, NV 89118
TEL 702-658-7588 ■ FAX 702-658-7342 ■ GLASSICART@GLASSICART.COM ■ WWW.GLASSICART.COM

Top: Carved backsplash; interior: Ron Nicola Interiors, Ltd.
Bottom left: Carved and welded entry doors. Bottom right: Carved and welded shower enclosure. Photographs: Chawla Associates.

Printed in China © 2003 GUILD, LLC: *The Sourcebook of Architectural & Interior Art*

NANCY GONG

GONG GLASS WORKS ■ 42 PARKVIEW DRIVE ■ ROCHESTER, NY 14625 ■ TEL 585-288-5520 ■ FAX 585-288-2503
E-MAIL NGONG@ROCHESTER.RR.COM ■ WWW.ARTSROCHESTER.ORG/ARTISTS/NGONG.HTM

56

For the Love of Life, 2001, Westchester County, NY, leaded glass, 12'W x 13'H.

Printed in China © 2003 GUILD LLC: *The Sourcebook of Architectural & Interior Art*

LYNN GOODPASTURE

10753 WEYBURN AVENUE ■ LOS ANGELES, CA 90024
TEL 310-470-2455 ■ FAX 310-470-4257 ■ E-MAIL LGOODPAST@AOL.COM

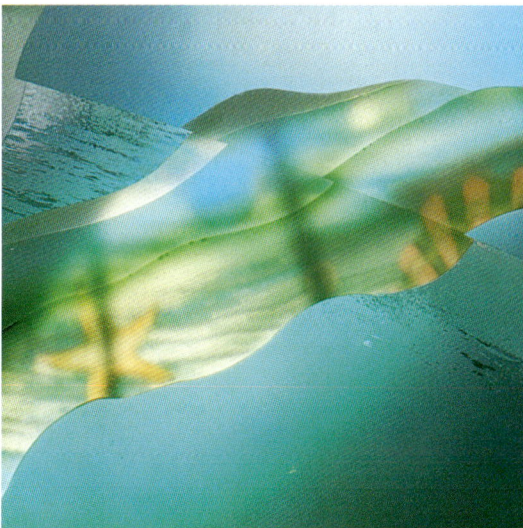

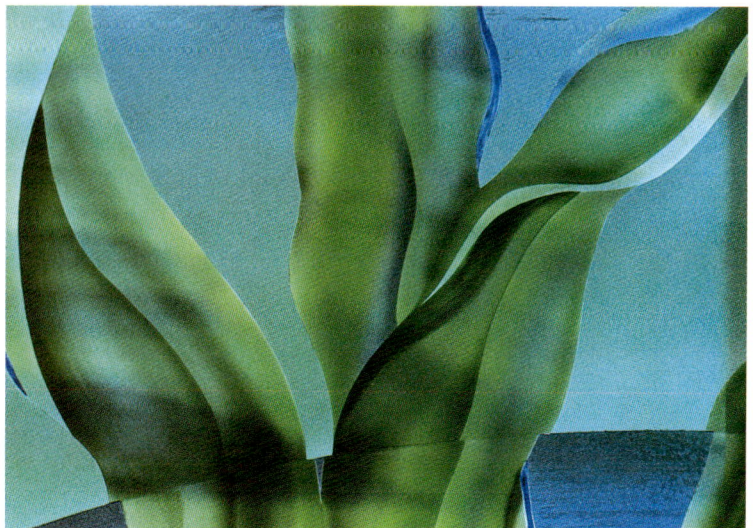

Top: *Beneath the Sea*, 2000, Mott Children's Center, Good Samaritan Hospital, Puyallup, WA, glass painting, 23' x 23'. Photograph: Eckert & Eckert Photography.
Bottom left: *Beneath the Sea* (detail). Bottom right: *Beneath the Sea* (detail).

MARK ERIC GULSRUD

ARCHITECTURAL GLASS/SCULPTURE ■ 3309 TAHOMA PLACE WEST ■ TACOMA, WA 98466
TEL 253-566-1720 ■ FAX 253-565-5981 ■ E-MAIL MARKGULSRUD@ATTBI.COM ■ WWW.MARKERICGULSRUD.COM

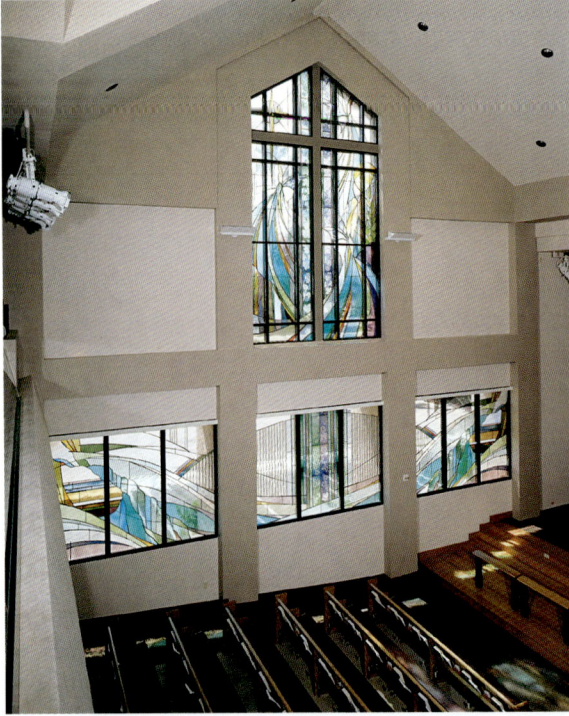

Top left: Window wall, 2002, Hope Lutheran Church, Palm Desert, CA, custom hand-blown leaded glass. Top right: Window wall (detail).
Bottom: Window wall (exterior view). Photographs: Greg Epstein.

Printed in China © 2003 GUILD, LLC: *The Sourcebook of Architectural & Interior Art*

PAUL HOUSBERG

GLASS PROJECT, INC. ■ 875 NORTH MAIN ROAD ■ JAMESTOWN, RI 02835
TEL 401-560-0880 ■ E-MAIL HOUSBERG@GLASSPROJECT.COM ■ WWW.GLASSPROJECT.COM

59

Untitled glass wall, 2001, The Peninsula Chicago Hotel, fused/cast glass, 12' x 9'. Photograph: Jon Miller/Hedrich Blessing (large photo).

HARRIET HYAMS

PO BOX 178 ■ PALISADES, NY 10964 ■ TEL 845-359-0061 ■ FAX 845-359-0062
E-MAIL HARRIART@ROCKLAND.NET ■ WWW.HARRIETHYAMS.COM

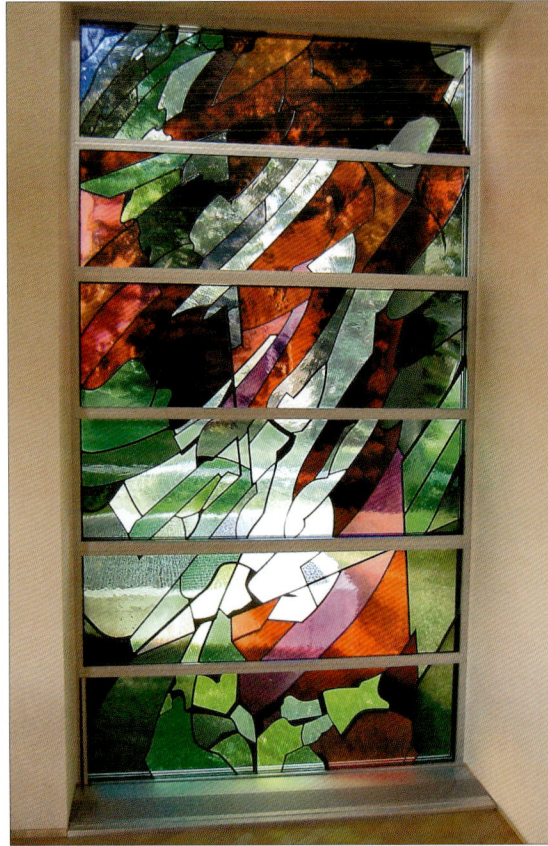

60

Top left: *Upper Eucharist Window* (detail), Dominican Chapel, Our Lady of the Rosary, Sparkill, NY. Top right: *Lower Eucharist Window*, Dominican Chapel, 9' × 5'.
Our Lady of the Rosary, Sparkill, NY. Bottom: *Resurrection Windows*, Dominican Chapel, Our Lady of the Rosary, Sparkill, NY, 6.75' × 6.5'. Photographs: Charles Shimel.

Printed in China © 2003 GUILD, LLC: *The Sourcebook of Architectural & Interior Art*

JOEL BERMAN GLASS STUDIOS LTD

JOEL BERMAN ■ 1.1244 CARTWRIGHT STREET ■ VANCOUVER, BC V6H 3R8 ■ CANADA
TEL 604-684-8332 ■ FAX 604-684-8373 ■ E-MAIL INFO@JBERMANGLASS.COM ■ WWW.JBERMANGLASS.COM

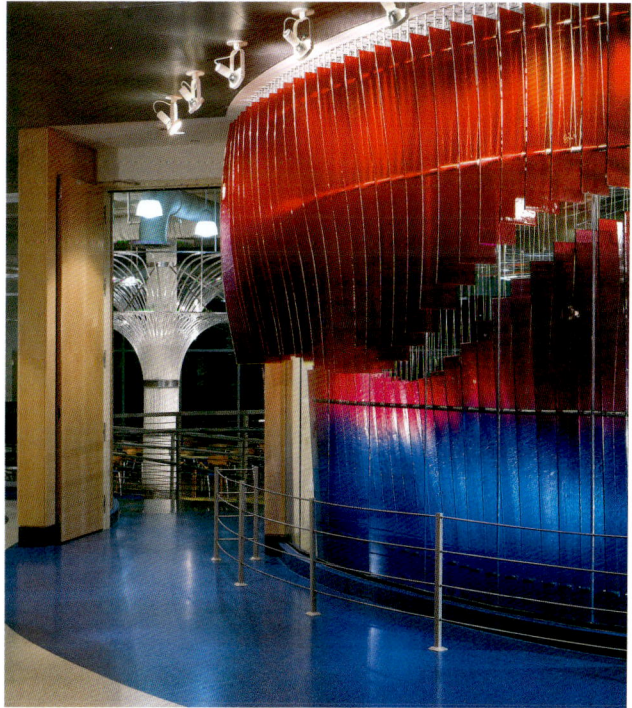

61

Top left: Cast glass collage sculpture, cantilevered with stainless steel posts and cables, hardware by Joel Berman Glass Studios Ltd, SMED International guest facility, Falkridge. Photograph: Jason Stang. Top right: Colored, cast, cable-suspended glass sculpture, Nortel Networks Headquarters, Atlanta, GA, hardware by Joel Berman Glass Studios Ltd. Photograph: Schilling Photography. Bottom: Architectural cast glass windscreens, corporate office, San Francisco, CA, 30'W x 9'H x 9'D. Photograph: Nic Lehoux Photography.

BJ KATZ

MELTDOWN GLASS ART & DESIGN LLC ■ PO BOX 3850 ■ CHANDLER, AZ 85244
TEL 480-633-3366 ■ FAX 480-633-3344 ■ E-MAIL BJKATZ@MELTDOWNGLASS.COM ■ WWW.MELTDOWNGLASS.COM

62

Sculptural glass wall, 2002, Maricopa County Forensic Science Center, cast glass with dichroic glass elements, 108"H x 220"W. Photographs: Richard Abrams.

GUY KEMPER

KEMPER STUDIO ■ 190 NORTH BROADWAY ■ LEXINGTON, KY 40507
TEL/FAX 859-254-3507 ■ E-MAIL KEMPERSTUDIO@JUNO.COM ■ WWW.KEMPERSTUDIO.COM

Sources (detail), Congregation of St. Agnes, Fond du Lac, WI. Fabricated by Derix Glasstudios, Taunusstein, Germany.

STEPHEN KNAPP

74 COMMODORE ROAD ■ WORCESTER, MA 01602-2792 ■ TEL 508-757-2507 ■ FAX 508-797-3228
E-MAIL SK@STEPHENKNAPP.COM ■ WWW.STEPHENKNAPP.COM

64

The Christ Doors, kiln-formed art glass entry with cast bronze handles, 10' x 6', client: The Solanus Casey Center, Detroit, MI 2002. Photograph: Stephen Knapp.

MASAOKA GLASS DESIGN

ALAN MASAOKA ■ 13766 CENTER STREET SUITE G-2 ■ CARMEL VALLEY, CA 93924 ■ TEL 831-659-4953 ■ FAX 831-659-3156
E-MAIL MASAOKA@MBAY.NET ■ WWW.ALANMASAOKA.COM

65

Bath glass, 1998, Timkins residence, lead with handblown glass and bevels. Photograph: Philip Harvey.

MELISSA PAXTON

COYOTE GLASS DESIGN ■ 907 MILL CREEK ROAD ■ SALADO, TX 76571 ■ TEL 254-947-0002 ■ FAX 254-947-0402
E-MAIL M.PAXTON@COYOTEGLASS.COM ■ WWW.COYOTEGLASS.COM

66

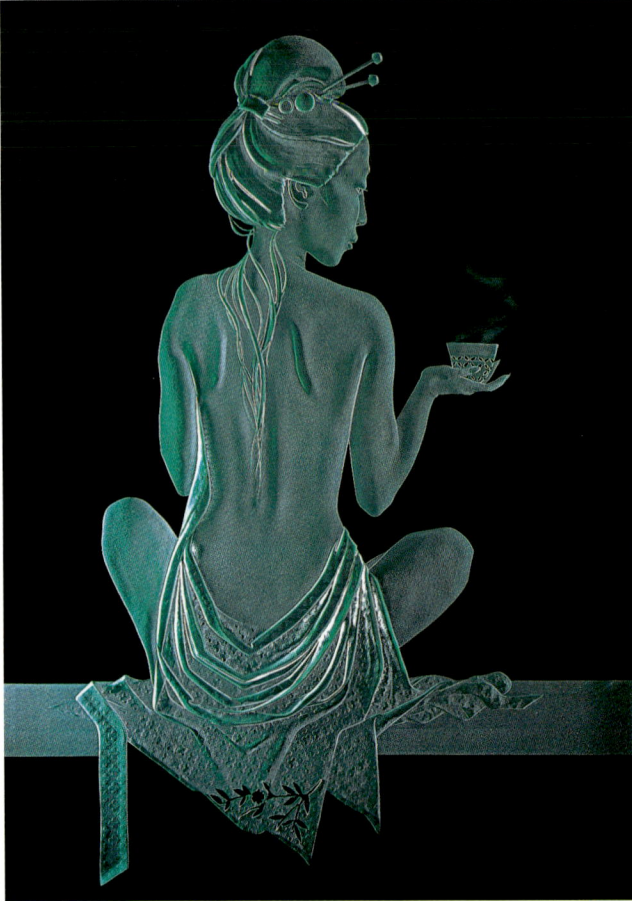

Top left: *Cup of Dreams*, Beverly Allen collection, Chichasha, OK, carved glass, 72" x 36". Right: *Glass Crystalscape*, Norm Elliot collection, Scottsdale, AZ, cast glass crystals in carved and copper-plated glass with backlight. Bottom left: *Giant Koi*, Norm Elliot collection, Scottsdale, AZ, carved and colored glass coffee table with powder-coated steel base and gold leaf. Photographs: Steve Thompson Photography.

PEARL RIVER GLASS STUDIO, INC.

ANDREW CARY YOUNG ■ 142 MILLSAPS AVENUE ■ JACKSON, MS 39202
TEL 601-353-2497 ■ FAX 601-969-9315 ■ E-MAIL AYOUNG@NETDOOR.COM ■ WWW.PRGS.COM

67

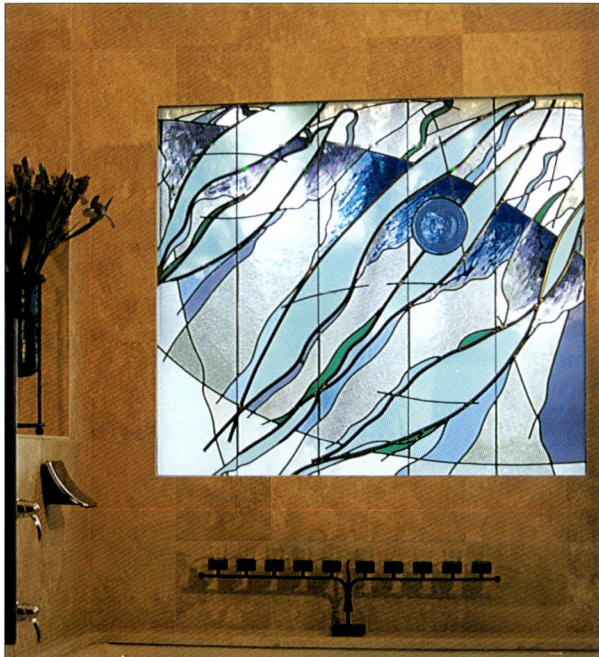

Top: Stained glass window (detail). Bottom left: Etched glass doors, 2001, private residence, Jackson, MS, glass, 40" x 66".
Bottom right: Stained glass window, 2001, private residence, Jackson, MS, antique glass and lead, 58" x 46".

68

Kat's Landscape, 2002, private commission, New York, NY, stained glass triptych, 93" x 93". Photograph: Thomas Daskam.

MAYA RADOCZY

CONTEMPORARY ART GLASS ■ PO BOX 31422 ■ SEATTLE, WA 98103
TEL 206-527-5022 ■ FAX 206-524-9226 ■ E-MAIL MAYA@SERV.NET ■ WWW.MAYAGLASS.COM

69

Perry residence, 2001, Medina, WA, bas-relief cast glass doors. Photograph: Dick Springgate.

JEFF G. SMITH

ARCHITECTURAL STAINED GLASS, INC. ■ PO BOX 1126 ■ FORT DAVIS, TX 79734-1126
TEL 432-426-3311 ■ FAX 432-426-3366 ■ E-MAIL INFO@ARCHSTGLASSINC.COM ■ WWW.ARCHSTGLASSINC.COM

70

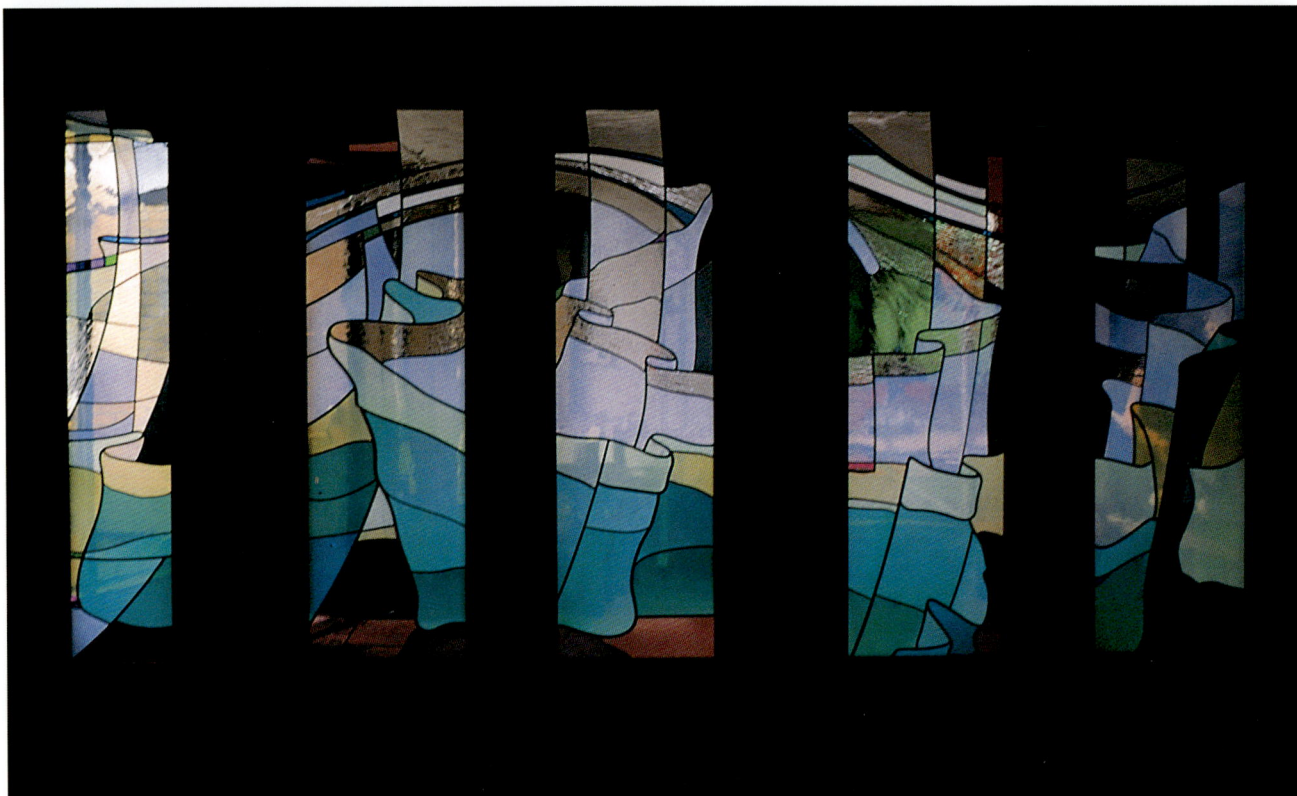

St. Bridget Catholic Church, Seattle, WA. Top left: *St. Bridget* window at main entrance, 5.6'H X 5.7'W'.
Top right: *Holy Spirit* window (4 of 8) at Reconciliation Chapel, 15.2'H x 21.6'W. Bottom: *St. Bridget's Cloak*, Narthex doors, each: 6.5'H x 18"-24"W.

DOUG SOELBERG

ARCHITECTURAL ART GLASS ■ 869 WEST 2000 NORTH ■ PROVO, UT 84604
TEL 801-224-6646 ■ FAX 801-223-9938 ■ E-MAIL AAG@AAGDESIGN.COM ■ WWW.AAGDESIGN.COM

71

Top: *Untitled*, leaded glass, 40" x 30". Bottom left: *I Just Forgot*, leaded glass with fired paint, 32" x 42".
Bottom right: *Deadly Virtues*, Justice Courts Building, Salt Lake City, UT, leaded glass, 14' x 13'. Photograph: Cheri Bailey.

ARTHUR STERN

ARTHUR STERN STUDIOS ■ 1075 JACKSON STREET ■ BENICIA, CA 94510
TEL/FAX 707-745-8480 ■ E-MAIL ARTHUR@ARTHURSTERN.COM ■ WWW.ARTHURSTERN.COM

72

Frozen Music, entrance window for private residence, Lafayette, CA, leaded glass with beveled glass prisms, 5.8' x 5.2'.

LARRY ZGODA

LARRY ZGODA STUDIO ■ 2117 WEST IRVING PARK ROAD ■ CHICAGO, IL 60618
TEL 773-463-3970 ■ FAX 773-463-3978 ■ E-MAIL LZ@LARRYZGODA.COM ■ WWW.LARRYZGODASTUDIO.COM

Entry, 1996, Chicago, IL, stainless glass with cut jewels. Photograph: Christopher Kean.

73

STUART REID ARCHITECTURAL GLASS

STUART REID ■ 364 ANNETTE STREET ■ TORONTO, ON M6P 1R5 ■ CANADA
TEL 416-762-7743 ■ FAX 416-762-8875 ■ E-MAIL STUARTREID@SYMPATICO.CA ■ WWW.STUARTREID.NET

74

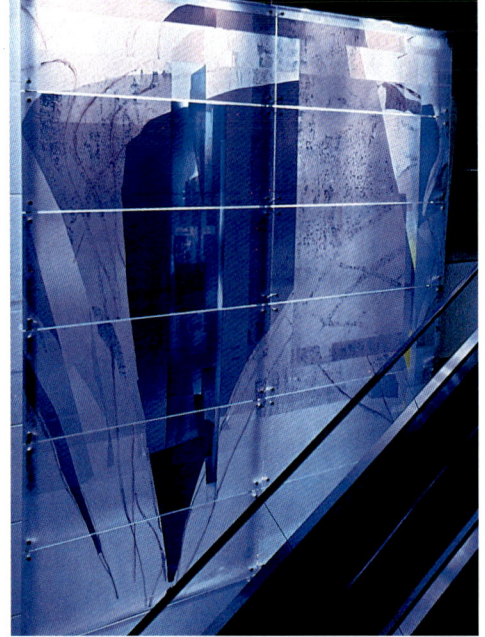

Left: *dance of Venus* (section one of four), Living Arts Centre main lobby, Mississauga, ON, Canada, 30'x 150'.
Right: *Homage to Mozart*, Salzburg Congress, Salzburg Austria, 20' × 40'. Top: Upper section. Bottom: Lower section.

SERANDA VESPERMANN

VESPERMANN GLASS GALLERY & STUDIO ■ 309 EAST PACES FERRY ROAD ■ ATLANTA, GA 30305 ■ TEL 404-206-0102/770-936-0633
FAX 404-266-0190/770-986-9101 ■ E-MAIL SERANDA@VESPERMANN.COM ■ WWW.VESPERMANN.COM

Top left: Meeting room door, Richmond Convention Center, VA, 92" x 11" and 28" x 11". Top right: Ballroom panels, Richmond Convention Center, VA, each: 90" x 30".
Bottom: Ballroom interior showing 8 of 16 panels, Richmond Convention Center, VA, each: 90" x 30". Photographs: James West.

DANIEL WINTERICH

STUDIO WINTERICH ■ 29 WELLER COURT ■ PLEASANT HILL, CA 94523
TEL 925-943-5755 ■ FAX 925-943-5455 ■ E-MAIL DW@WINTERICH.COM ■ WWW.WINTERICH.COM

76

Structural Mondrian, 2001, private offices, San Francisco, CA, painted tempered glass and stainless steel, 15' x 11', architect: Studios Architecture. Photograph: Tim Griffith.

VITRAMAX GROUP, INC.

FRED diFRENZI ■ 116 SOUTH 10TH STREET ■ LOUISVILLE, KY 40202 ■ TEL 502-589-3828 ■ FAX 502-589-3830
E-MAIL FRED@VITRAMAX.COM ■ WWW.VITRAMAX.COM

Top: Interior glass wall with floating glass panel, 2002, Jewish Hospital, Medical Center East, Louisville, KY, 7.25' × 23'. Bottom left: Interior glass wall (detail). Bottom right: Cast and formed glass basin with antiqued pewter wall bracket, 2002, ADA compliant. Photographs: Doug Decker, Decker Photographics.

77

Atrium Sculpture

JILL CASTY

JILL CASTY DESIGN ■ 494 ALVARADO STREET, SUITE D ■ MONTEREY, CA 93940
TEL 831-649-0923 ■ FAX 831-649-0713 ■ E-MAIL JILLCDESIGN@HOTMAIL.COM ■ WWW.JILLCASTYDESIGN.COM

80

One part of a three-part installation for Northwest Plaza, St. Louis, MO, layered Plexiglas and painted aluminum, 1' x 10.5' and 2' x 18', total width: 8'. Photograph: Trent Foltz.
Inset: *Sunrise/Sunset*, entry sculpture, City of Montclair, CA, painted aluminum, Plexiglas, 20'H x 13'W. Photograph: Jeremy Elliott.

CLOWES SCULPTURE

JONATHAN & EVELYN CLOWES ■ 98 MARCH HILL ROAD ■ WALPOLE, NH 03608 ■ TEL/FAX 603-756-9505
E-MAIL JON@CLOWESSCULPTURE.COM ■ WWW.CLOWESSCULPTURE.COM

To Life, 2002, Pfizer Drug Safety Technology Center, Groton, CT, mahogany, brass mesh and hangers, aluminum sphere with transparent and opaque paint, 15' x 9'. Photograph: Jeff Baird.

ROB FISHER

ROB FISHER SCULPTURE LLC ■ 228 NORTH ALLEGHENY STREET ■ BELLEFONTE, PA 16823
TEL 814-355-1458 ■ FAX 814-353-9060 ■ E-MAIL GLENUNION@AOL.COM ■ WWW.SCULPTURE.ORG/PORTFOLIO/FISHER

Slice of Life, 2002, AstraZeneca Pharmaceuticals Visitor Center, Wilmington, DE,
powder-coated perforated aluminum and stainless steel, 35' × 85' × 35'. Top photograph: Marcus Gardega.

ROBERT PFITZENMEIER

III FIRST STREET #1-3A ■ JERSEY CITY, NJ 07302
TEL 201-659-7629 ■ E-MAIL REPFITZ@YAHOO.COM ■ WWW.METALMORPHOSIS.ORG

83

Suspended Microcosm, 2002, Astra Zeneca, Wilmington, DE, anodized zirconium and stainless steel, 20'H x 24'W x 14'D. Photograph: Nancy Jo Johnson.

KORYN ROLSTAD STUDIOS

BANNERWORKS, INC. ■ 2610 WESTERN AVENUE ■ SEATTLE, WA 98121
TEL 206-448-1003 ■ FAX 206-448-1204 ■ E-MAIL KORYN@KRSTUDIOS.COM ■ WWW.KRSTUDIOS.COM

84

Left and top right: *Sheltering Tree*, 2002, University of Maryland Pediatric Emergency Center, Baltimore, enameled aluminum leaves, branches, rings, table base and digitally printed butterflies for two-story atrium and corridor. Photographs: Anne Gummerson. Center right: *Wind*, 2002, Glaxo Smith Kline, Pittsburgh, PA, anodized aluminum for three-story atrium lobby entry. Bottom right: *Swirling Vines*, 2002, Owatonna Clinic, Mayo Health System, Owatonna, MN; steel mesh leaves on enameled aluminum tubing for two-story atrium.

SABLE STUDIOS

PAUL SABLE ■ 2737 ROSEDALE AVENUE ■ SOQUEL, CA 95073
TEL 800-233-7309 ■ E-MAIL PAUL@SABLESTUDIOS.COM ■ WWW.SABLESTUDIOS.COM

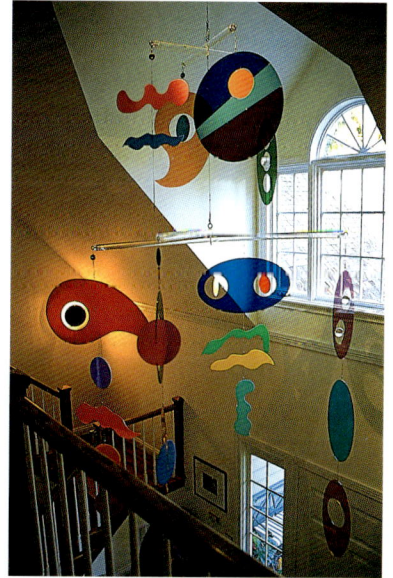

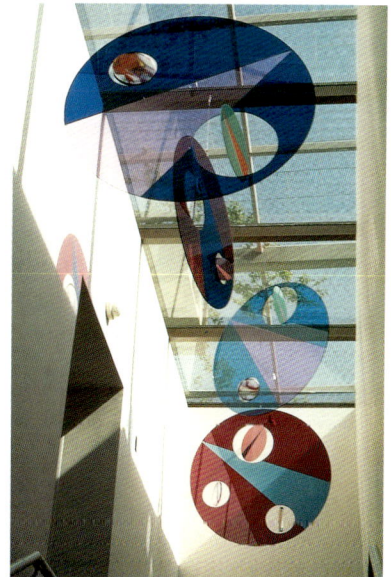

85

Left: *Dawn of Spring's Bouquet*, 2000, City Hall, Hayward, CA, acrylic, 15' × 15' × 18'. Top right: *A Mist of Fragrant Time*, 2000, private residence, acrylic, 10' × 12'.
Center right: *Sky Ballet*, Metro Plaza, San Jose, CA, acrylic, 4' × 6' × 17'. Bottom right: *Spectral Arc*, 1998, Lucent Technologies, FL, acrylic wall hanging, 4' × 5' × 11'.

Representational Sculpture

MARTHA PETTIGREW

PETTIGREW SCULPTURE STUDIO ■ 201 WEST 21ST STREET ■ KEARNEY, NE 68845
TEL/FAX 308-233-5504 ■ E-MAIL DPETTIMAR@AOL.COM ■ WWW.MARTHAPETTIGREW.COM

88

Gossip, 2002, bronze, 78"H, edition of five. Photograph: Jafe Parsons.

89

Leap of Faith, River City, Chicago, IL, 15'H x 15'W x 3'. Photograph: Arthur Stern.

ROBERT S. TOLL

3830 WILLAT AVENUE ■ CULVER CITY, CA 90232 ■ TEL 310-841-5050 ■ FAX 310-217-0859
E-MAIL ROBERT@TOLLSCULPTOR.COM ■ WWW.TOLLSCULPTOR.COM

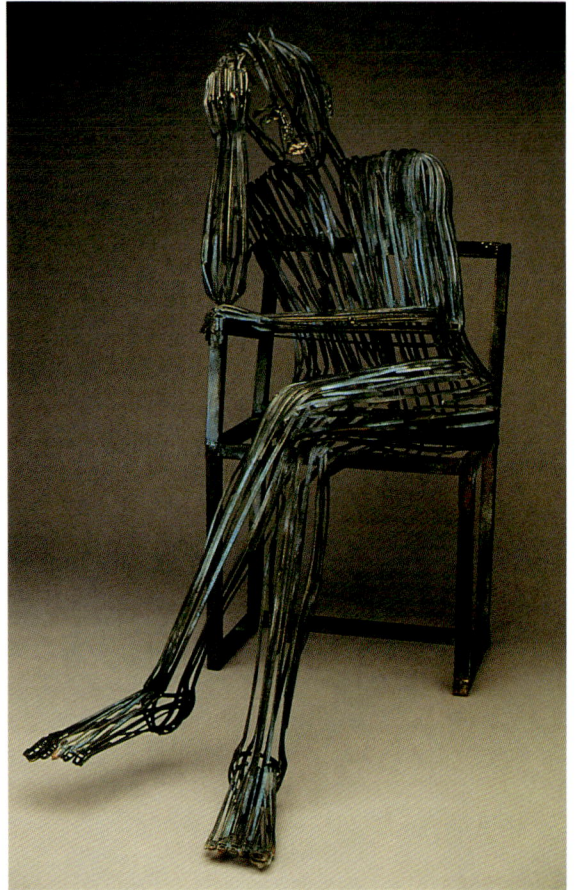

Left: *Increasing Doubt*, 2002, welded steel, 5.6'H x 20"W x 17"D.
Top right: *Second Chance*, 2000, private collector, welded steel. Bottom right: *Night After Night*, 1998, welded steel. Photographs: Gary Brod.

DIMITRY "DOMANI" SPIRIDON

DOMANI STUDIO ■ PO BOX 22717 ■ SANTA FE, NM 87502 ■ TEL/FAX 505-438-8388
E-MAIL DIMITRY@DOMANI-STUDIO.COM ■ WWW.DOMANI-STUDIO.COM

91

Top left: *Enigma,* 2002, bronze sculpture, 13"H × 15"W × 18"L, edition of 50. Right: *Anastasia,* 2002, bronze sculpture, 50"H × 20"W × 16"D, edition of 17.
Bottom left: *Donatela,* 2002, bronze sculpture, 22"H × 20"W × 16"D, edition of 35. Photographs: Hadley Harper.

ANN DELUTY

12 RANDOLPH STREET ■ BELMONT, MA 02478
TEL/FAX 617-484-0069 ■ E-MAIL ANNDEL@AOL.COM ■ WWW.ANN-DELUTY.WS

92

Top left: *Red Shell*, 1998, tiger-eye alabaster on marble base, 18"H x 8"W x 7"D. Top right: *Orange Delight*, 1999, translucent alabaster on marble base, 18"H x 11"W x 9"D.
Bottom: *Whales*, 1999, cockscomb alabaster on marble base, 10.5"H x 17.5"W x 10.5"D.

MARK YALE HARRIS

ARTWORK ■ 1701 SUITE A LENA STREET ■ SANTA FE, NM 87505 ■ TEL 505-982-7447 ■ FAX 505-982-7447
E-MAIL ARTWORKSFE@AOL.COM ■ WWW.MARKYALEHARRIS.COM

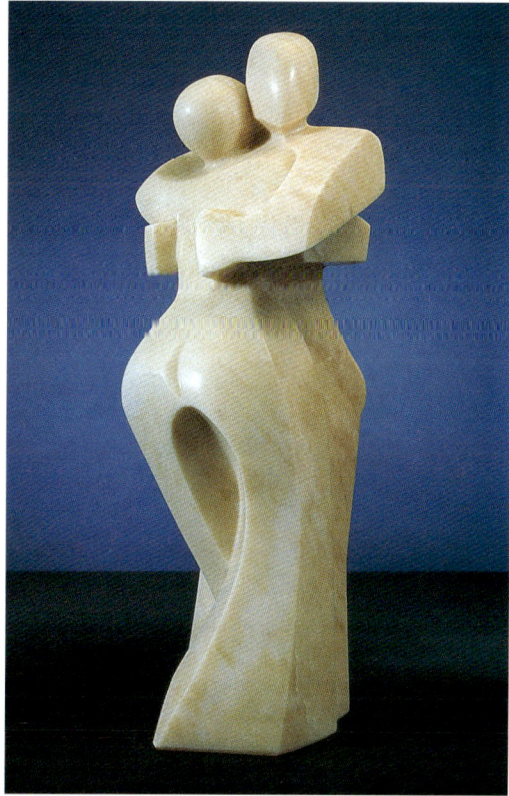

93

Top left: *Menage au Truchas*, 2001, Colorado white yule marble, 34" x 12" x 18". Photograph: Jamie Hart, Santa Fe, NM.
Top right: *Half Eaten Apple*, 2002, Portuguese rose marble, 32" x 10" x 7.5". Photograph: Stephen Yadzinski, Santa Fe, NM.
Bottom: *Tidbit*, 2002, bronze, 18" x 14" x 12", edition of 20. Photograph: Stephen Yadzinski, Santa Fe, NM.

KEN KALMAN

PO BOX 147 ■ CANYON, CA 94516 ■ TEL 925-376-0760 ■ E-MAIL KENKALMAN@EARTHLINK.NET

94

Top left: *Kangaroo,* 2003, aluminum sheet, cast aluminum and rivets, 60" x 84" x 24".
Top right: *Mule Deer,* 2001, aluminum sheet, cast aluminum and rivets, 60" x 64" x 18". Bottom: *Dog,* 2001, aluminum sheet, cast aluminum and rivets, 60" x 54" x 12".

Printed in China © 2003 GUILD.LLC: *The Sourcebook of Architectural & Interior Art*

RON LEEP

PO BOX 294 ■ REDMOND, OR 97756 ■ TEL 541-548-8644 ■ FAX 541-548-4744
E-MAIL RONLEEP@BENDNET.COM ■ WWW.RONLEEP.COM

95

Top: *Royal Surroundings*, bronze, 102" x 108" x 48", limited edition. Bottom left: *Lift Off*, bronze, 56" x 42" x 36", limited edition.
Bottom right: *Mule Deer*, bronze, 68" x 72" x 32", limited edition. Photographs: Karen Bridges-Findley.

CALI GOREVIC

377 LANE GATE ROAD ■ COLD SPRING, NY 10516
TEL 845-265-4625 ■ FAX 845-265-4620 ■ CALIG@MINDSPRING.COM ■ WWW.CALIGOREVIC.COM

96

Top left: *Tree Spirit*, bronze, 19" x 10" x 10". Top right: *Mother Tree*, bronze, 18.5" x 9" x 12".
Bottom left: *Hand of God*, bronze, 18" x 11" x 7". Bottom right: *Batchamatoo*, bronze, 21.5"H.

BIGBIRD-STUDIOS

PAT PAYNE ■ 2121 ALAMEDA AVENUE ■ ALAMEDA, CA 94501
TEL 510-521-9308 ■ E-MAIL PPBIGBIRD@AOL.COM ■ WWW.BIGBIRD-STUDIOS.COM

97

Top left: *Eagles Attack*, weathered welded steel, 58" x 68" x 40". Top right: *Sun Bird*, weathered welded steel, 93" x 60" x 42".
Bottom: *Intransitu*, weathered welded steel, 77" x 72" x 48".

AMY GRASSFIELD

PEAS-ON-EARTH ■ 901 WEST SAN MATEO ■ SANTA FE, NM 87505
TEL 505-982-9411 ■ E-MAIL AGRASSFIELD@YAHOO.COM

Top left: *Burpee's Pride* lamp, copper and steel, 12' x 6'. Top right: *Peace-ful Watering Fountain,* (detail), copper and steel, 6' x 7'.
Bottom: *Rest-in-Peas Bench,* copper, steel and mahogany, 7' x 7'. Photographs: Jamie Hart.

O.K. HARRIS

O.K. HARRIS STUDIO ■ 4417 11TH STREET NW ■ ALBUQUERQUE, NM 87107
TEL 505-344-1604 ■ FAX 505-880-8839 ■ E-MAIL OK@ARTISOK.COM ■ WWW.ARTISOK.COM

99

Sandhill Cranes – Life on the Rio, 2003, New Mexico, steel, each: 8'H x 6'W x 5'D. Photograph: Chuck Gallagher.

JERRY McKELLAR, SCULPTOR

JERRY McKELLAR ■ 195 MAY ROAD ■ COLVILLE, WA 99114 ■ TEL 509-684-2148 ■ FAX 509-685-9114
E-MAIL JDMCKELLAR@PLIX.COM ■ WWW.JERRYMCKELLAR.COM

Top left: *Indomitable Spirit*, bronze, 32"H × 27"L × 20"W, edition of 33, or 7.25'H × 6'L × 5'W, edition of 15.
Top right: *Flower Dancing in the Wind*, 5.5'H × 7'W × 5'D, edition of 15. Bottom: *Wary Greeting*, 38"H × 48"W, bronze mirror frame, 38", edition of 45.

ELLEN TYKESON

ELLEN TYKESON SCULPTURE ■ 1033 SHARON WAY ■ EUGENE, OR 97401
TEL 541-687-5731 ■ E-MAIL ETYKESON@YAHOO.COM

101

Left: *Luna,* 2002, Norwalk Furniture, Indian Wells, CA, bronze, 7'H, edition of 5. Photograph: David Simone. Top right: *Bird of Paradise,* 1999, bronze,
30"H, edition of 37. Photograph: Michael Smith. Bottom right: *Opal Whiteley,* 1999, city library, Cottage Grove, OR, 56" H, bronze, edition of 5. Photograph: Michael Smith.

ELIZABETH MacQUEEN

ELIZABETH MacQUEEN SCULPTURE & FINE ART ■ 58 FAIRWOOD BOULEVARD ■ FAIRHOPE, AL 36532
TEL 251-990-5995/805-234-0914 ■ E-MAIL MACQUEENSCULPTOR@AOL.COM ■ WWW.MACQUEENFINEART.COM

102

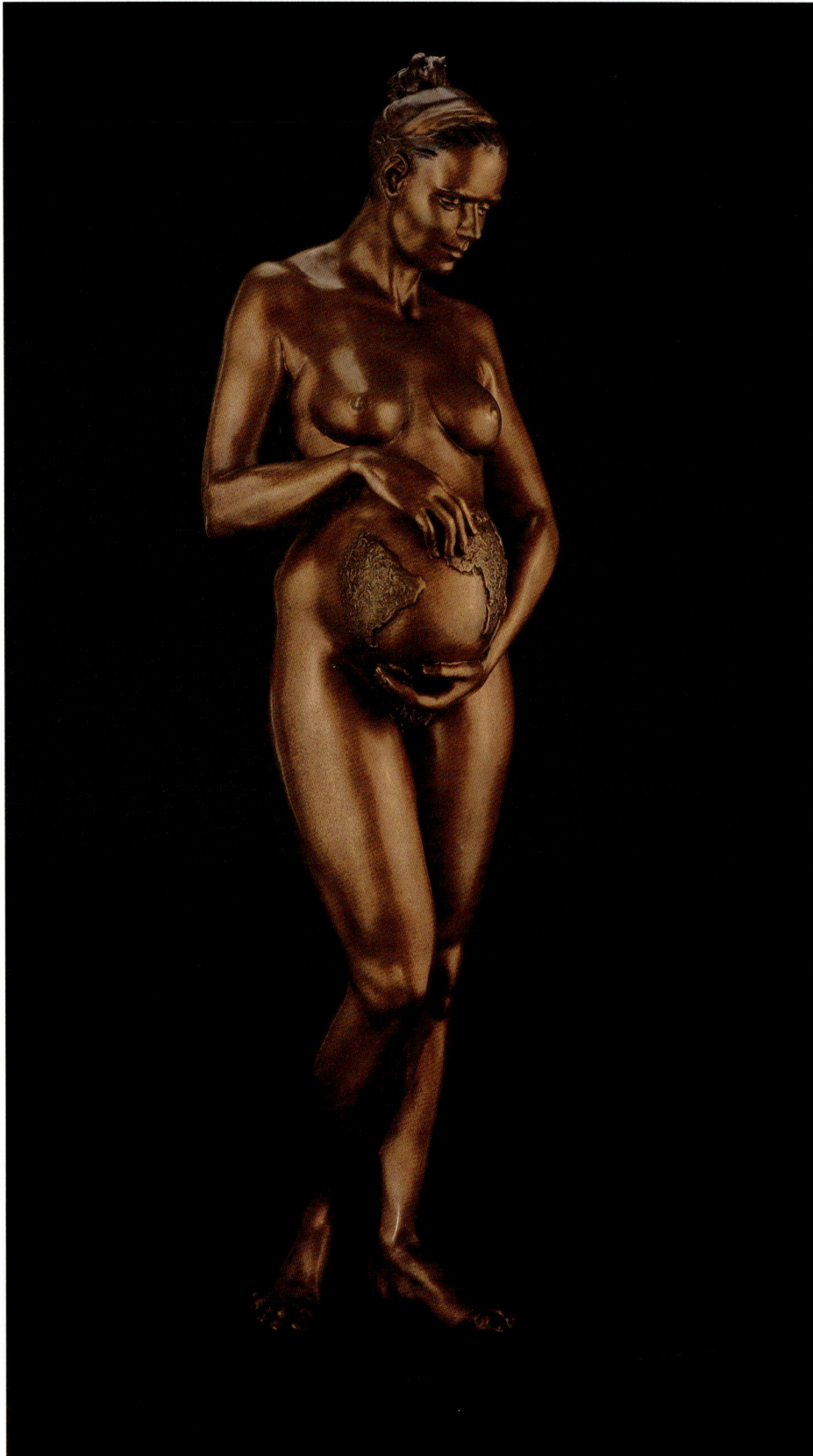

Gaea (Mother Earth), bronze, 6'H, edition of nine, casting by Artworks Foundry.

SABOROSCH

GLENN SABOROSCH ■ PO BOX 61 ■ FLETCHER, MO 63030 ■ TEL 314-974-3546

103

Top left: *Spring Fever*, 2001, welded steel, 11"H × 12"W × 6"D. Center left: *One Woman's Struggle*, 2002, welded steel and copper, 12"H × 10"W × 5"D.
Bottom left: *Spook'd*, welded steel, 22"H × 13"W × 9"D. Right: *Moondance*, 2000, welded steel, 25"H × 12"W × 12"D.

JEFF TRITEL

TRITEL STUDIOS ■ 19432 RICHMAR LANE ■ GRASS VALLEY, CA 95949
TEL 800-882-8098 ■ FAX 888-796-3776 ■ E-MAIL TRITEL@TRITELSTUDIOS.COM ■ WWW.TRITELSTUDIOS.COM

104

Left: *Hot Jazz*, bronze, 25"H, also available 50"H. Top right: *Violinist I*, bronze, 24"H.
Center: *Violinist II*, bronze, 25"H, also available 42"H. Bottom right: *Beethoven*, bronze, 12.5"H.

WINTER TEL 740-593-8180 ▪ SUMMER: HOSTETLER GALLERY ▪ #2 OLD SOUTH WHARF ▪ PO BOX 2222 ▪ NANTUCKET, MA 02584
TEL 508-228-3117/508-228-5152 ▪ E-MAIL HOSTETLER@EUREKANET.COM ▪ WWW.DAVIDHOSTETLER.COM

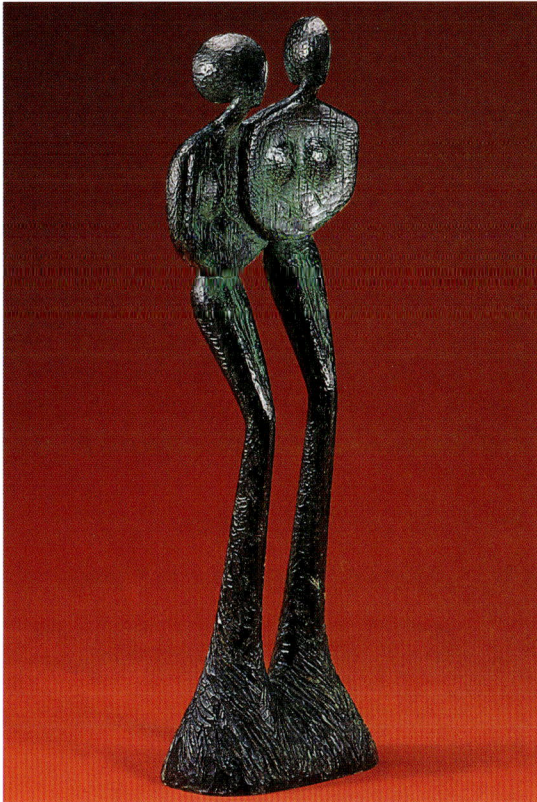

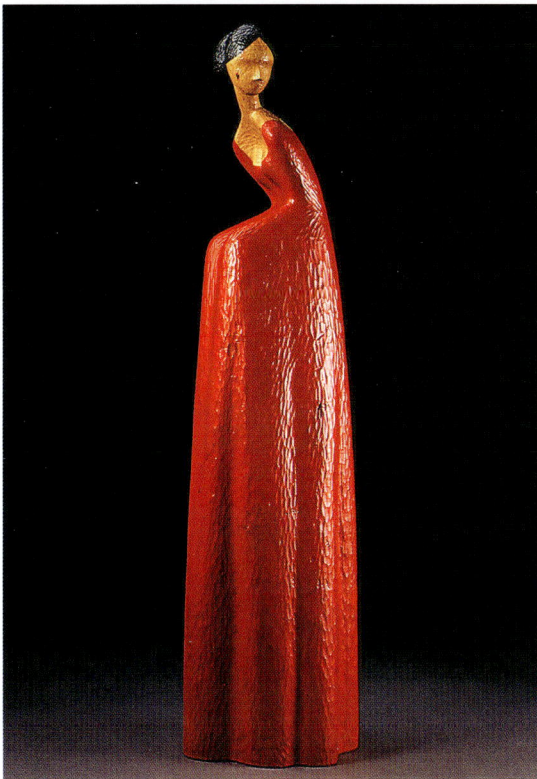

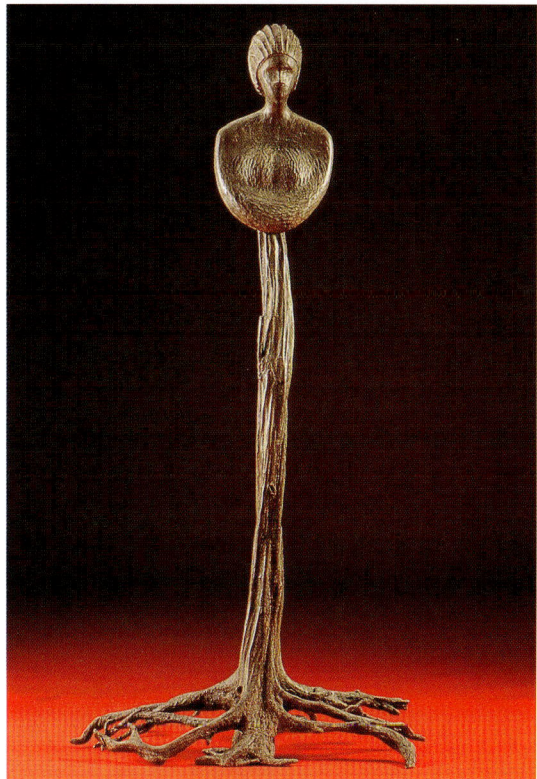

105

Top left: *Duo*, bronze with blue-green patina, 38.5" x 12" x 7", edition of 15.
Top right: *Sensuous Woman*, bronze with brown-gold patina, total: 65"H (base: 18"H), edition of 15. Bottom right: *Asherah Tree Goddess*,
bronze with pale gray-beige patina, 46"H, edition of 15. Bottom left: *Seated Woman*, ginko wood and paint, 49"H. Photographs: Lyntha Scott Eiler.

BARRY WOODS JOHNSTON

2423 PICKWICK ROAD ■ BALTIMORE, MD 21207 ■ TEL 410-448-1945 ■ FAX 410-448-2663

Faith, Hope and Love, clay to be cast in bronze, 16.5'H.

Printed in China © 2003 GUILD, LLC: *The Sourcebook of Architectural & Interior Art*

PATRICK MICHAEL BIRGE

REUNION STUDIOS ■ 1614 MANCHESTER LANE NW ■ WASHINGTON, DC 20011
TEL 202 352-4853 ■ FAX 202 882-9487 ■ E-MAIL PBIRGE@GWU.EDU

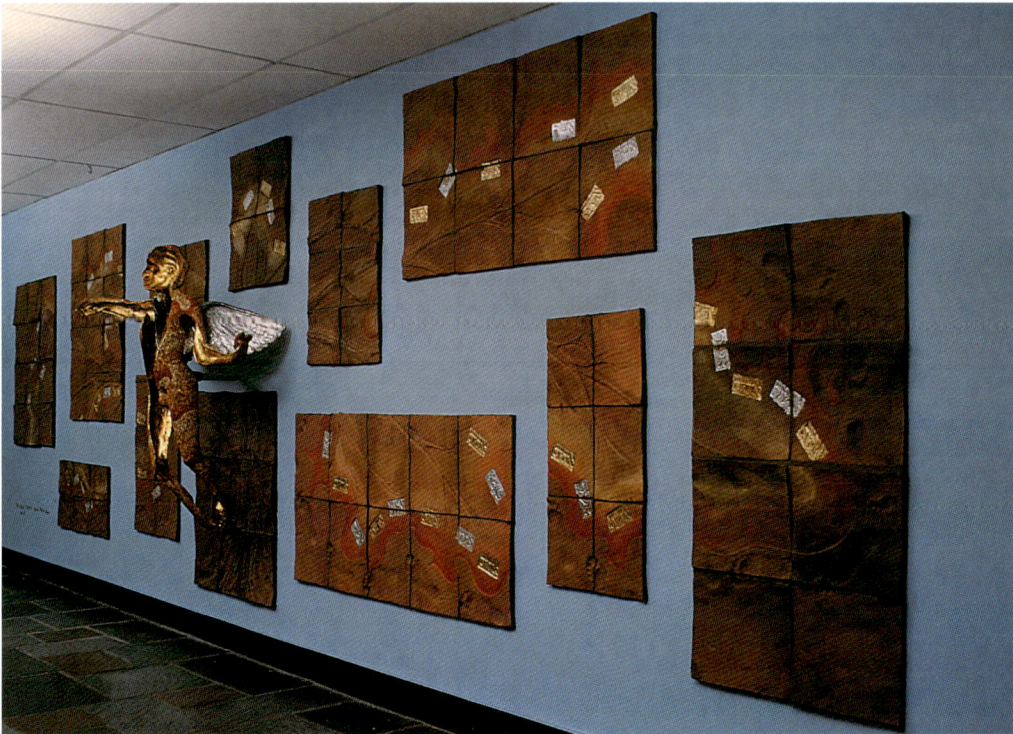

Top left: *The Burning Bush* (detail). Top right: *Joie de Vivre*, 2001, private collection, bronze with gold leaf, 37" × 22" × 13".
Bottom: *The Burning Bush*, 2000, Catholic Student Center, University of Maryland, terra cotta, mosaic and gold leaf, 25' × 8' × 2'. Photographs: John Woo.

NORBERT OHNMACHT

NORBERT OHNMACHT FINE ART ▪ 24544 ROAD 51 ▪ BURLINGTON, CO 80807
TEL 719-346-7586 ▪ FAX 719-346-5657 ▪ E-MAIL NPOHNMACHT@PLAINS.NET

108

Moments to Remember, 2002, Burlington, CO, 26"H x 21"W x 19"D. Photograph: Mel Schockner.

JANE RANKIN

19335 GREENWOOD DRIVE ■ MONUMENT, CO 80132
TEL 719-488-9223 ■ FAX 719-488-1650 ■ E-MAIL JRANKIN@MAGPIEHILL.COM

Top: *Sack Race*, 2002, bronze, life size. Bottom left: *Le Jeune Femmes*, 2000, bronze, 18" x 12" x 12".
Bottom right: *My Book*, 2001, bronze, 18" x 22" x 23".

MARIANNE CAROSELLI

8511 ALYDAR CIRCLE ■ FAIR OAKS RANCH, TX 78015 ■ TEL/FAX 830-981-4544
E-MAIL ARTIST@GVTC.COM ■ WWW.MCAROSELLI.COM

110

Left: *Free to Be*, bronze, 5'H, edition of 50. Right: *Earth Angel*, 36"H.

CYNTHIA SPARRENBERGER

SPARRENBERGER STUDIO ▪ 5975 EAST OTERO DRIVE ▪ ENGLEWOOD, CO 80112
TEL 303-741-3031 (STUDIO) ▪ TEL 303-618-8974 (CELL) ▪ E-MAIL CYNTHIA6@MAC.COM ▪ WWW.SPARRENBERGERSTUDIO.COM

Top: *Late for School*, 2002, bronze, 11.5' × 5' × 4.5'.
Bottom left: *A Wing and a Prayer* (back), 2000, bronze, 63"H.   Bottom right: *A Wing and a Prayer* (front).   Photographs: Marcia Ward/The Imagemaker.

111

ARMANDO HINOJOSA

ASD ART, INC. ■ 2702 GUSTAVUS STREET ■ LAREDO, TX 78043
TEL 956-722-6678 ■ FAX 956-722-4120 ■ E-MAIL ASD_ART_INC@YAHOO.COM ■ WWW.ARMANDOHINOJOSA.COM

112

Top: *Among Friends There Are No Borders*, Laredo International Airport, TX. Bottom left: *Sister and Friends*, Mercy Regional Medical Center, Laredo, TX.
Bottom right: *Cry of the Rain Forest*, artist's collection, Laredo, TX. Photographs: Guillermo Sosa.

GARY LEE PRICE

GARY LEE PRICE STUDIOS, INC. ■ 38 WEST 200 SOUTH ■ SPRINGVILLE, UT 84663
TEL 877-457-7423 ■ FAX 801-489-9588 ■ E-MAIL INFO@GARYLEEPRICE.COM ■ WWW.GARYLEEPRICE.COM

113

Top: *Circle of Peace*, life size, edition of 50, available in smaller sizes. Bottom left: *Journey II*, 73" x 74", edition of 50.
Bottom right: *Mark Twain Bench*, life size, edition of 40, also available in 17" x 18". Photographs: Craig Young.

ALAN LeQUIRE

ALAN LeQUIRE, SCULPTOR ■ 4304 CHARLOTTE AVENUE SUITE C ■ NASHVILLE, TN 37209 ■ TEL/FAX 615-298-4611
E-MAIL LEQUIRE@MINDSPRING.COM ■ WWW.ALANLEQUIRE.COM

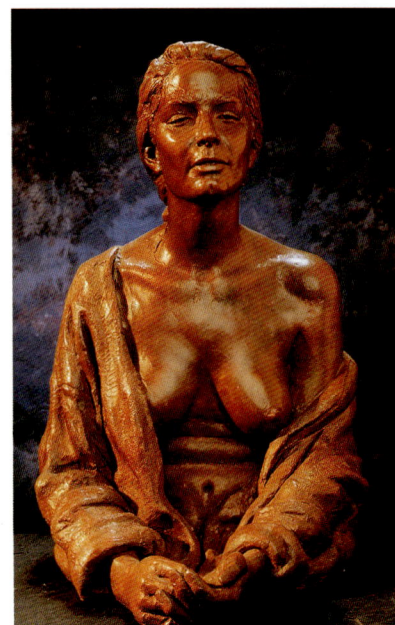

114

Left: *Athena Parthenos,* 1982-2002, Nashville, TN, gypsum, fiberglass and steel, 42'H. Top right: *Timothy Demontbrun,* 1996, Nashville, TN, bronze, heroic scale.
Bottom right: *Jess,* 1997, bronze, life size. Photograph: John Guider.

MARTIN EICHINGER

EICHINGER SCULPTURE STUDIO ■ 1302 NW KEARNEY STREET ■ PORTLAND, OR 97209
TEL 503-223-0626 ■ FAX 503-223-0454 ■ E-MAIL STUDIO@EICHINGERSCULPTURE.COM ■ WWW.EICHINGERSCULPTURE.COM

115

Left: *Gaia's Breath*, near life-size, cast bronze, 5.4'H, edition of 25. Right: *Dance of Yes and No*, cast bronze, 41"H, edition of 50.

EUGENE L. DAUB

295 WEST 15TH STREET ■ SAN PEDRO, CA 90731 ■ TEL/FAX 310-548-0817 ■ E-MAIL ELDAUB@EARTHLINK.NET

116

Left: *Corps of Discovery*, monument to Lewis and Clark, Kansas City, MO, bronze, 18'H on 21' granite base.
Top right: Meriwether Lewis (detail). Center right: Sacagawea (detail). Bottom right: York, Lewis, Seaman (detail). Photographs: Michael Michalavich.

FARRELL ART STUDIO

KATHLEEN FARRELL ■ 350 NORTH RAYNOR AVENUE ■ JOLIET, IL 60435 ■ TEL 815-723-6430 ■ FAX 815-722-9007
E-MAIL FARRELLARTSTUDIO@CS.COM ■ WWW.FCPAONLINE.ORG

117

Left: *Underground Railroad Hero*, 2002, South Chicago Street, Joliet, IL, cold-cast bronze, 4'H × 2.3'W × 2'D. Top right: *Mother Nature*, 1999, cold-cast bronze, 4'H × 2'W × 2'D. Bottom right: *Sator Sanchez*, 2000, cold cast-bronze, 8'H × 4'W × 3'. All works shown also available in tabletop size.

VICTOR ISSA

VICTOR ISSA STUDIOS ■ 3950 NORTH COUNTY ROAD 27 ■ LOVELAND, CO 80538
TEL 970-663-4805 ■ FAX 970-962-6780 ■ E-MAIL INFO@VICTORISSA.COM ■ WWW.VICTORISSA.COM

118

Left: *Spring*, bronze, life size, edition of 12. Top right: *Daddy's Home*, Miner's memorial, Frederick, CO, bronze, life size, limited edition.
Bottom right: *Eden Restored*, Centura Hospitals, Denver and Boulder, CO, bronze, life size.

TUCK LANGLAND

12632 ANDERSON ◼ GRANGER, IN 46530 ◼ TEL/FAX 574-272-2708 ◼ E-MAIL TUCKANDJAN@AOL.COM

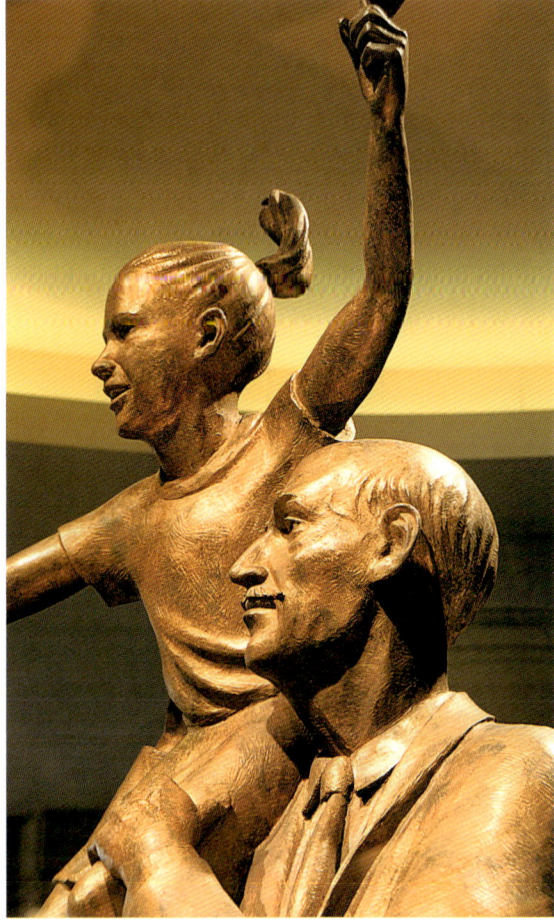

Top left: *Dancer*, from the *Circle of Care* sculpture, bronze, 7'H. Top right: *Generations* (detail), 2002, from the *Circle of Care* sculpture, bronze, 8.25'H.
Bottom: *Circle of Care*, Hillman Cancer Center, Pittsburgh, PA, bronze, 40'Dia.

BRUCE WOLFE

BRUCE WOLFE LTD. ■ 206 EL CERRITO AVENUE ■ PIEDMONT, CA 94611
TEL 510-655-7871 ■ FAX 510-601-7200 ■ E-MAIL LANDBWOLFE@EARTHLINK.NET ■ WWW.BRUCEWOLFE.COM

120

Printed in China © 2003 GUILD LLC: The Sourcebook of Architectural & Interior Art

Top left: *Chong-Moon Lee*, bronze, 16"H. Top right: *Barbara Jordan*, bronze, 7.2'H × 4.6'W.
Bottom left: *St. Clare*, bronze, 7.6'H × 4.2'W. Bottom right: *Christ* (detail).

121

Christ, bronze, 7.2'H.

Non-Representational Sculpture

ANAHATA ARTS

ERIC DAVID LAXMAN ▪ 478 MOUNTAINVIEW AVENUE ▪ VALLEY COTTAGE, NY 10989 ▪ TEL 845-353-8521 ▪ FAX 845-348-3687
E-MAIL ERIC@ANAHATA.COM ▪ WWW.ANAHATA.COM

124

Top left: *Anahata Fountain*, 2000, private collection, welded silicon bronze, 96" × 36" × 36". Photograph: Stuart Sachs.
Top right: Custom stair railing, 2001, patinated welded steel, 36" × 120"; *Sunflower Lingam* (landing), 1998, marble and steel, 48" × 10" × 10"; *The Inner "I"*, 1997, marble and steel, 60" × 15" × 15". Photographs: Sal Cordaro. Bottom: *Serpiente Grande*, 2002, private collection, welded stainless steel, 50' × 27" × 15". Photograph: Eric David Laxman.

DOUGLAS BRETT

MODERN LIFE DESIGNS ■ 668 POST STREET ■ SAN FRANCISCO, CA 94109 ■ TEL 415-441-7118
E-MAIL DOUG@MODERNLIFEDESIGNS.COM ■ WWW.MODERNLIFEDESIGNS.COM

125

Top left: *Speedskater* or *The Wings of Mercury,* ©2001, bronze, 22"H × 21"W × 7"D. Right: *Daddy Long Leggs* or *Clown on Long Leggs,* ©2001, bronze, 34"H × 13.5"W × 9"D.
Bottom: *3-Point Stand,* ©1999, bronze, 15"H × 17"L × 8.5"D.

GARY ALLEN BROWN

5420 WEST DEL RIO STREET ■ CHANDLER, AZ 85226
TEL 480-705-8300 ■ FAX 480-785-7577 ■ E-MAIL BAFFIN@COX.NET ■ WWW.GABSCULPTURE.COM

126

Left: *Sarah*, 2003, Baltic birch and mahogany, 57"H x 18"W x 12"D. Top right: *New Hair*, 2002, aluminum, Baltic birch and walnut, 16"H x 6"W x 20"D.
Bottom right: *Hook*, 2003, Baltic birch, jatoba and mahogany, 22"H x 15"W x 12"D. Photographs: Wilson Graham.

Printed in China © 2003 GUILD, LLC: *The Sourcebook of Architectural & Interior Art*

RUTH BURINK

BURINK SCULPTURE STUDIO ■ 1550 WOODMOOR DRIVE, MONUMENT, CO 80132 ■ TEL/FAX 719-481-0513
E-MAIL RUTH@BURINKSCULPTURE.COM ■ WWW.BURINKSCULPTURE.COM

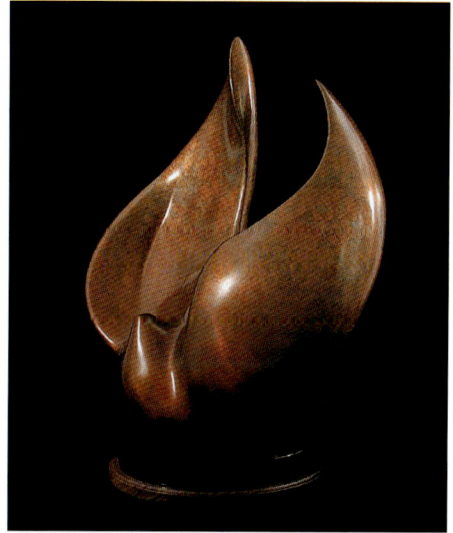

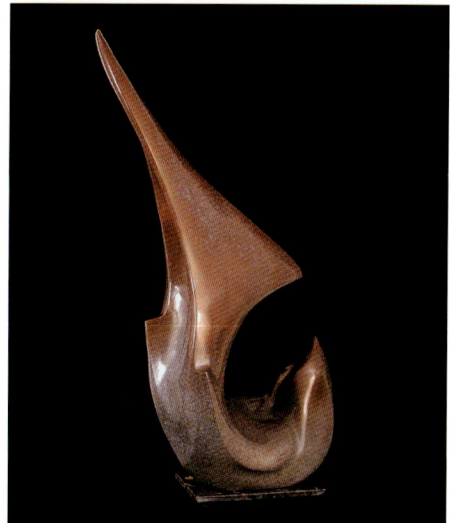

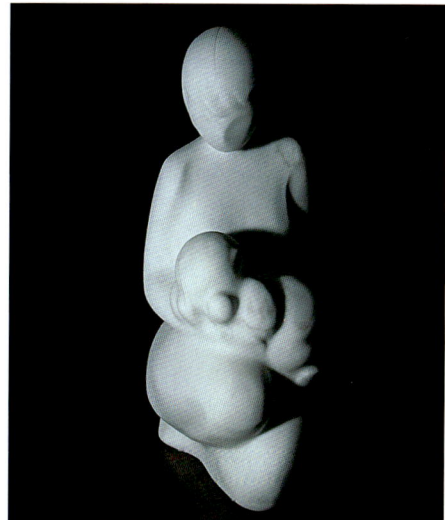

127

Left: *Come, Holy Spirit*, 2002, St. Peter Catholic Church Education Center, marble on granite pedestal, 8.5'H. Photograph: Casey Chinn, Colorado Springs, CO.
Top right: *Encircling Dove*, 2002, bronze, 2'H. Center right: *Peace*, 2002, bronze, 3'H. Bottom right: *Guardian*, 2000, Colorado Springs Health Partners, marble, 2.5'H.

RIIS BURWELL

RIIS BURWELL STUDIO ■ 3815 CALISTOGA ROAD ■ SANTA ROSA, CA 95404
TEL/FAX 707-538-2676 ■ E-MAIL RIISBURWELL@AOL.COM

128

Left: *Spirit Form: Emerging*, 2002, bronze, 12' × 6' × 4'. Top right: *Synergetic #2*, 2002, bronze, 26" × 8" × 8". Bottom right: *Spirit Form: Becoming*, 2003, bronze, 18" × 10" × 8".

RENO CAROLLO

1562 SOUTH PARKER ROAD, SUITE 336 ■ DENVER, CO 80231
TEL 303-695-6396 ■ FAX 303-695-8560 ■ E-MAIL RCAR173278@AOL.COM ■ WWW.RENOCAROLLO.COM

129

Left: *Sensual Lady*, bronze, 24" x 5" x 4". Right: *Grace*, bronze, 24" x 5" x 4". Photographs: Jeff Uhrlaub.

CASTLE SCULPTURE, LLC

JOSEPH L. CASTLE III ▪ 331 BAY HORSE ROAD ▪ BELLEVUE, ID 83313
TEL 208-788-1305 ▪ FAX 208-788-2519 ▪ E-MAIL JOSCASTLE@AOL.COM

130

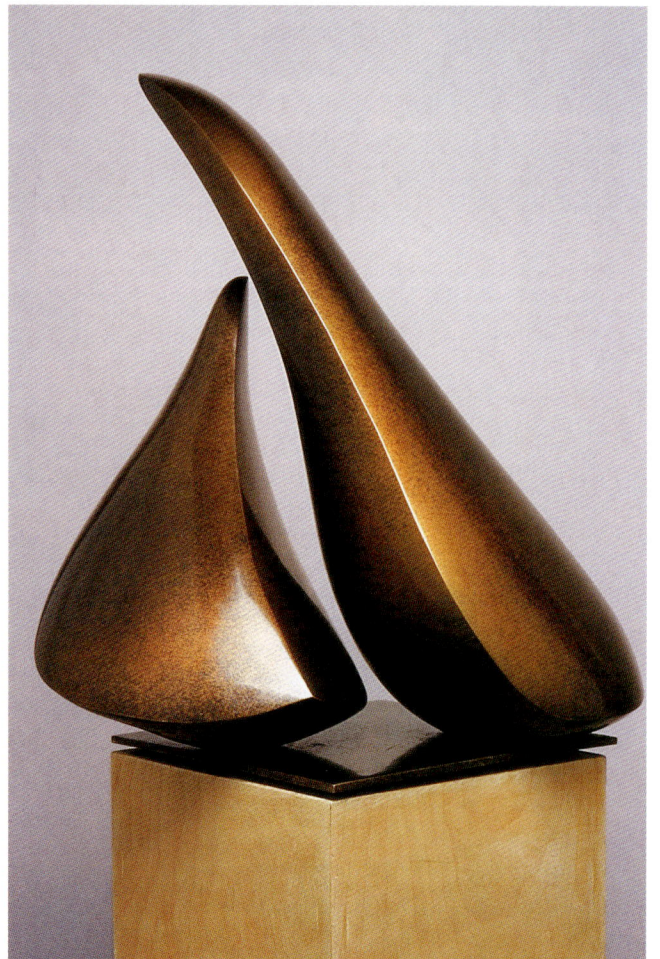

Top: *Relationship series*, VII, VIII and VI. Bottom left: *Relationship series*, VII. Bottom right: *Relationship series*, VI. Photographs: Andrew Kent.

RAIN KIERNAN

249 FAIRVIEW AVENUE ■ FAIRFIELD, CT 06824 ■ TEL 203-259-1910 ■ FAX 203-259-1933
E-MAIL RAIN@RAINKIERNAN.COM ■ WWW.RAINKIERNAN.COM

131

Top left: *Dea*, 2002, bronze, 24" x 41" x 31". Top right: *Unity II*, 2002, bronze, 31" x 26" x 26".
Bottom: *Maya*, 2001, marble and brushed stainless steel, 40" x 60" x 41". Photographs: Erin Kiernan.

DEMETRIOS & EAMES

PO BOX 870 ■ PETALUMA, CA 94953 ■ TEL 707-769-1777 ■ FAX 707-769-1780

132

Top left: *Generations,* from the *Lunar Asparagus People Series,* 2000, bronze, 10.25"H, artist: Llisa Demetrios. Top right: *Bronze Bench,* 1995, 18"H × 18"W × 6.6'L, artist: Llisa Demetrios. Bottom left: *Bollard,* 1986, powder-coated steel, 4' × 10"Dia., artist: Lucia Eames. Bottom right: *Lotus,* 1989, bronze, 11"H × 14.5"Dia., artist: Lucia Eames. Photographs: M. Lee Fatherree.

ANDY DUFFORD & CHRISTIAN MULLER

ARTSCAPES, LLC ■ 4441 WEST 30TH AVENUE ■ DENVER, CO 80212 ■ TEL 303-477-3780 ■ FAX 303-477-0737
E-MAIL ANDY@ARTSCAPESLLC.COM ■ CHRISTIAN@ARTSCAPESLLC.COM ■ WWW.ARTSCAPESLLC.COM

133

Top left: *Totem Circle*, 2002, private residence, Colorado buff sandstone, 16' x 16' x 13'. Photograph: James Stayton. Top right: *Moon Phase Floor*, 2002, private residence, granite, marble, sandstone and bronze, 15'Dia. Photograph: James Stayton. Bottom left: *Skyquilt*, 2000, Greenleaf Park, Colorado buff sandstone, steel and copper, 14' x 12' x 5'. Photograph: Jessica Westbrook. Bottom right: *Ability*, 2002, Pinnacol Assurance, Washington basalt and bronze, 8' x 3' x 3'. Photograph: James Stayton.

CHRISTIANSEN-ARNER

CHERIE CHRISTIANSEN ■ FRANZ ARNER ■ PO BOX 770 ■ MENDOCINO, CA 95460
TEL 707-937-3309 ■ WWW.CHRISARNSCULPTURE.COM

Left: *Meridian*, water sculpture, black granite on blue schist, 8' × 4' × 4'.
Top right: *Open to Love*, serpentine on black granite, 3' × 5" × 6". Bottom right: *Black Spring*, water sculpture, black granite, 48" × 24" × 24".

Torch to Lana'i's Youth, 2002, Lana'i, HI, cast bronze, copper, aluminum and fiberglass, 18.5' × 6'Dia.

RON FOSTER AND MICHAEL LINSLEY

KALEIDOSCULPTURE ■ 379 LA PERLE PLACE ■ COSTA MESA, CA 92627 ■ TEL 949-650-0662 ■ FAX 949-650-6890
E-MAIL RON@KALEIDOSCULPTURE.COM ■ E-MAIL MICHAEL@KALEIDOSCULPTURE.COM ■ WWW.KALEIDOSCULPTURE.COM

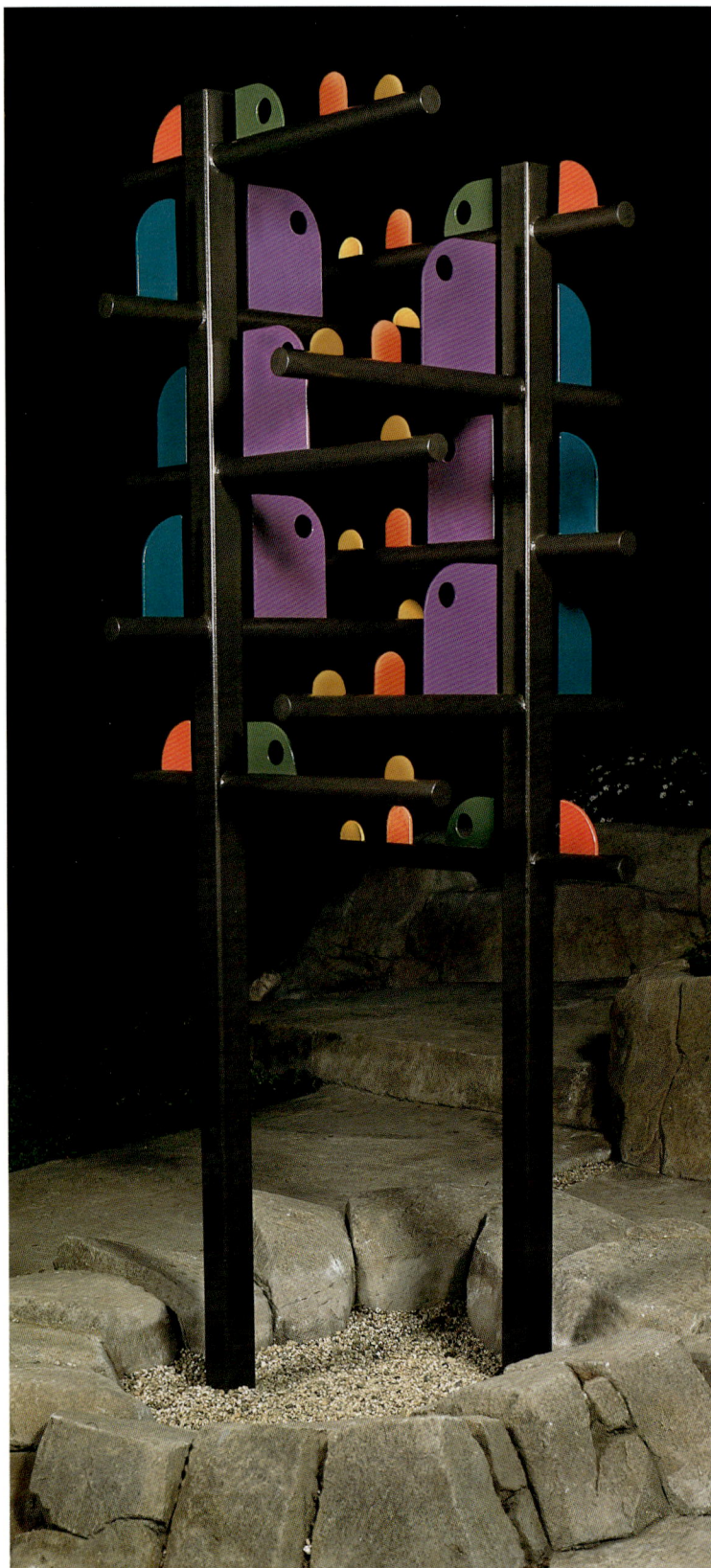

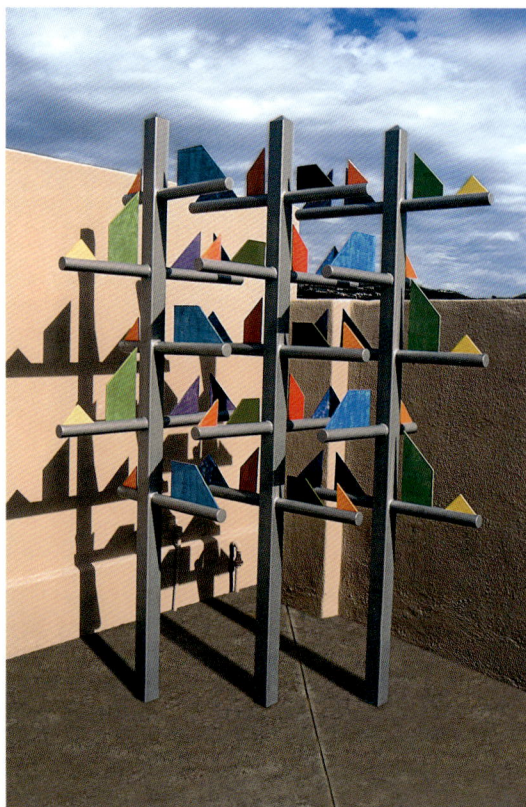

136

Left: *Kaleidosculpture* (front view), private residence, San Juan Capistrano, steel and ceramic, 3' × 8'. Top right: *Kaleidosculpture*, private residence, Corona Del Mar, steel and ceramic, 5' × 8'. Bottom right: *Kaleidosculpture* (side view), private residence, Corona Del Mar, steel and ceramic, 5' × 8'. Photographs: Bill Reiff.

SALLY HEPLER

PO BOX 2607 ■ SANTA FE, NM 87504 ■ TEL 505-471-7611 ■ FAX 505-983-1118
E-MAIL HEPLER3@EARTHLINK.NET ■ WWW.SALLYHEPLER.COM

Top left: *Full Circle*, 2000©, private collection, Dallas, TX, hand-fabricated stainless steel, 20" x 20" x 13".
Bottom left: *Rendezvous*, 1999©, private collection, Palo Alto, CA, hand-fabricated bronze, 23" x 19" x 19".
Right: *Déjà vu*, 2001©, private collection, Santa Fe, NM, hand-fabricated stainless steel, 37" x 39" x 26". Photographs: Mark Nohl.

Custom Design: Public Art

When you look at the colorful *Wave Gate* outside the Utah Park Pool in Aurora, Colorado, the winter solstice may not be the first thing that pops into your mind. But it certainly influenced artists Andy Dufford and Christian Muller when they created this kinetic piece. "The sculpture gets a lot of southern exposure, which casts very strong shadows on the ground behind the piece," Dufford says. "The shadow cast by the tallest point on the sculpture touches the entrance to the pool on the winter solstice. It's our way of reminding the swimmers that winter will not last forever and that summer is on its way." ■ The sculpture's role outside of this public facility is also important to Dufford. "We pride ourselves on making a place, not just a piece of artwork," he notes. "The great thing about the *Wave Gate* is that it's a significant marker—its presence creates a foyer for gathering outside the pool." One of the first major commissions for the City of Aurora, the *Wave Gate* reflects the spirit of play and celebration that typifies this active family center. ■ The completed project was just as meaningful to the pool's patrons as it was to Dufford and Muller. The artists were on hand for the unveiling, signing beach balls for members of the community who came so show their support and gratitude. Now the pool buzzes with bright energy outside, just as it does within.

ARTIST
Andy Dufford and Christian Muller,
Denver, Colorado

PROJECT
Wave Gate, 1998, aluminum and steel

COMMISSIONED FOR
Utah Park Pool, City of Aurora, Colorado
(Art in Public Places Program)

TIMELINE
1 year

DIMENSIONS
23' x 20' x 3'

LUIS TORRUELLA

COND. TENERIFE, APARTMENT 1201 ■ ASHFORD AVENUE 1507 ■ SAN JUAN, PR 00911 ■ TEL/FAX 787-722-8728 (STUDIO)
TEL 787-268-4977 (HOME) ■ E-MAIL LUISTORRUELLA@AOL.COM ■ WWW.LUISTORRUELLA.COM

139

Top left: *Baileteo*, 2001, Museo de Puerto Rico, painted aluminum, 8' × 7' × 6'.
Right: *Ascenso*, 2003, aluminum and cement with fused and cast glass, 8' × 2' × 8'. Bottom left: *Fogoso*, 2002, painted aluminum, 6' × 8' × 5'.

MALDONADO CERAMICS ■ 2331 HOLGATE SQUARE ■ LOS ANGELES, CA 90031
TEL 323-225-2668 ■ FAX 323-441-8456 ■ E-MAIL RAM5553@AOL.COM ■ WWW.RICKYMALDONADO.COM

Top: *Terra Madre*, ceramic, 2002, 19"H × 17"D × 27"W. Bottom: *Tribeca*, 2002, ceramic, 15"H × 19"D × 19"W. Photographs: Image-Ination.

DANIEL OBERTI

DANIEL OBERTI CERAMIC DESIGN ■ 3796 TWIG AVENUE ■ SEBASTOPOL, CA 95472
TEL 707-829-0584 ■ FAX 707-829-2136 ■ E-MAIL DANIEL@DANIELOBERTI.COM ■ WWW. DANIELOBERTI.COM

Top: *Three Spheres*, 2002, Vineyard Creek Hotel and Conference Center, Santa Rosa, CA, ferrocement, 6.6' × 20'. Bottom left: *Patrick's Dream*, 2000, private residence, Graton, CA, stoneware and bronze, 4' × 1.5'. Photograph: Hap Sakwa. Bottom right: *Pedulum and Spheres*, 2003, stoneware, 8" to 24". Photograph: Bob Stender.

JOHN RAIMONDI

JOHN RAIMONDI, SCULPTOR, INC. ■ 1120 GATOR TRAIL ■ WEST PALM BEACH, FL 33409
TEL 561-687-1585 ■ FAX 561-687-3854 ■ E-MAIL JRSCULPTOR@AOL.COM ■ WWW.JRSCULPTOR.COM

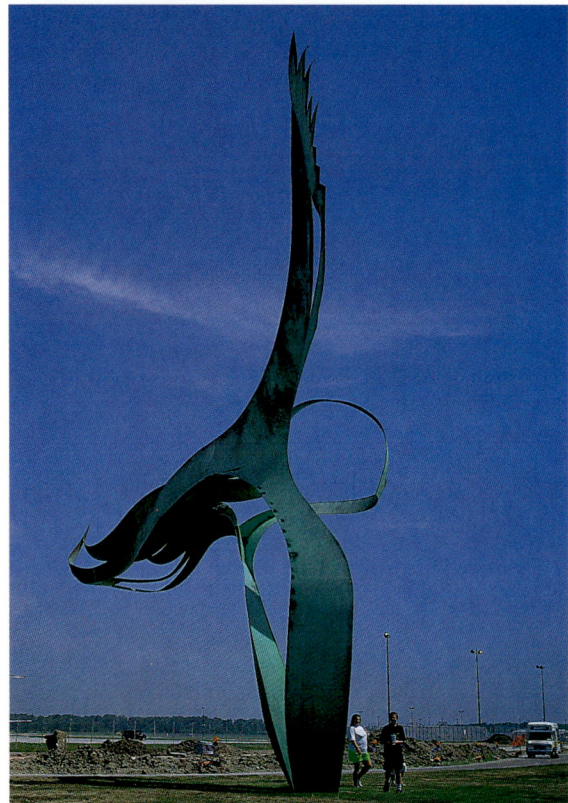

142

Top left: *Bessie*, 2003, private collection, Palm Beach, FL, bronze, 52"H. Top right: *Coyote*, 2002, private collection, East Hampton, NY, silvered bronze, 50"H.
Bottom left: *Grace*, 1990/2002, private collection, Snowmass, CO, stainless steel, 34'H. Bottom right: *Dance of the Cranes*, 1988, Collection of Omaha Airport Authority, NE, 60'H.

KEIKO NELSON

KEIKO NELSON ART & DESIGN ■ 9 ARLINGTON LANE ■ KENSINGTON, CA 94707
TEL 510-653-8849/510-524-4393 ■ FAX 510-527-4822 ■ E-MAIL KEIKO@KEIKONELSON.COM ■ WWW.KEIKONELSON.COM

Top: *Arches of Energy*, 2002. Bottom: *Water Columns*, 2002. Photographs: Kim Harrington.

NORMA LEWIS

NORMA LEWIS STUDIOS ■ 30500 AURORA DEL MAR ■ CARMEL, CA 93923
TEL 831-625-1046 ■ FAX 831-625-9733 ■ E-MAIL NORMA@DLEWIS.COM

144

Top left: *Volare*, bronze, 15.5"H. Right: *Mother Earth*, bronze, 21"H. Bottom left: *Lyric*, bronze, 44"H. Photographs: Rick Pharouh.

ANNIE PASIKOV

360 LONE STAR ROAD ■ LYONS, CO 80540 ■ TEL 303-823-6757 ■ FAX 303-823-8033
E-MAIL PASIKOV@EMAIL.COM ■ WWW.STONESCULPTURES.NET

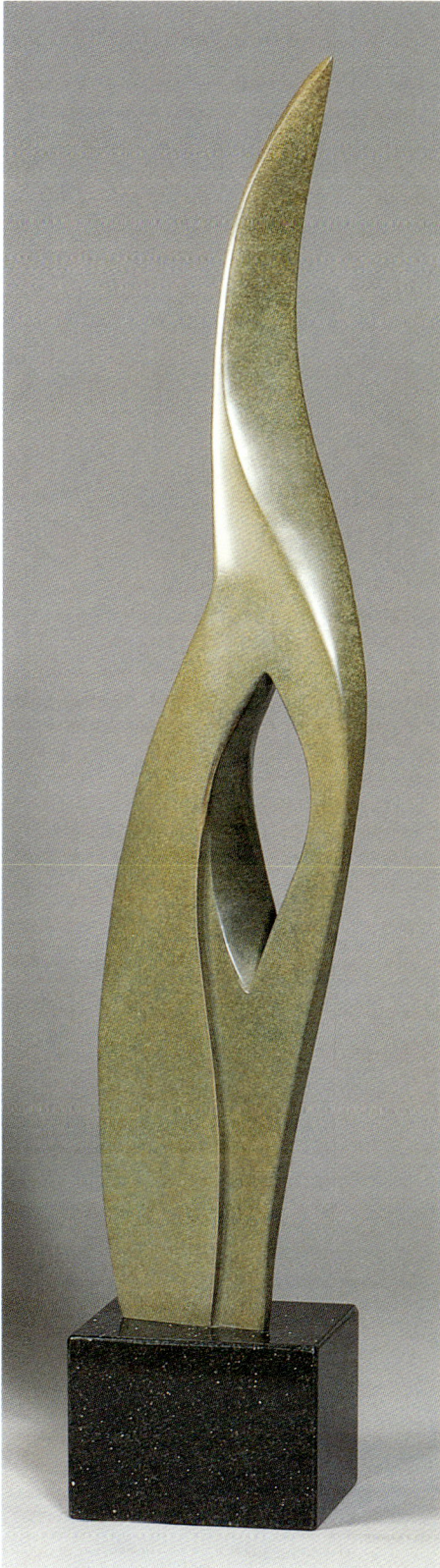

145

Left: *Awaiting the Dawn*, 2001, bronze cast from marble sculpture, 47". Photograph: Marie Commiskey.
Top right: *Sacred Fire*, 2003, calcite, 26" x 28". Photograph: Norman L. Koren. Bottom right: *Fly With Me*, 2001, alabaster, 21" x 8" x 6". Photograph: Norman L. Koren.

146

Fibonacci Fountain, 2002, Bowie, MD, granite, 18' × 20' × 6', weight: 45 tons. Photographs: Jonathan Ferguson.

BARTON RUBENSTEIN

RUBENSTEIN STUDIOS ■ 4819 DORSET AVENUE ■ CHEVY CHASE, MD 20815
TEL 301-654-5406 ■ FAX 301-654-5496 ■ E-MAIL BARTSHER@AOL.COM ■ WWW.RUBENSTEINSTUDIOS.COM

147

Top left: *Crossroads*, 2000, Jewish Community Center, Washington, DC, stainless steel with water, 6'H x 10'W x 5'D. Top right: *Manna from the Sky*, 2001, Bridgerland Applied Technology College, Logan, UT, stainless steel, 14'H x 10'Dia. Bottom: *Millennium*, 2002, Millennium Building, Washington, DC, bronze and colored/bubbled glass, 8'H x 45'W x 6'D.

JAMES THOMAS RUSSELL

JAMES RUSSELL SCULPTURE ■ 1930 LOMITA BOULEVARD ■ LOMITA, CA 90717
TEL 310-326-0785 ■ FAX 310-326-1470 ■ E-MAIL JAMES@RUSSELLSCULPTURE.COM ■ WWW.RUSSELLSCULPTURE.COM

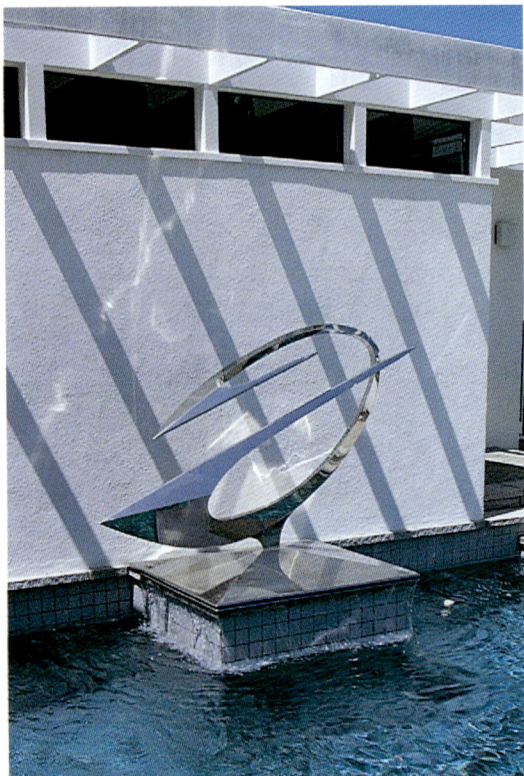

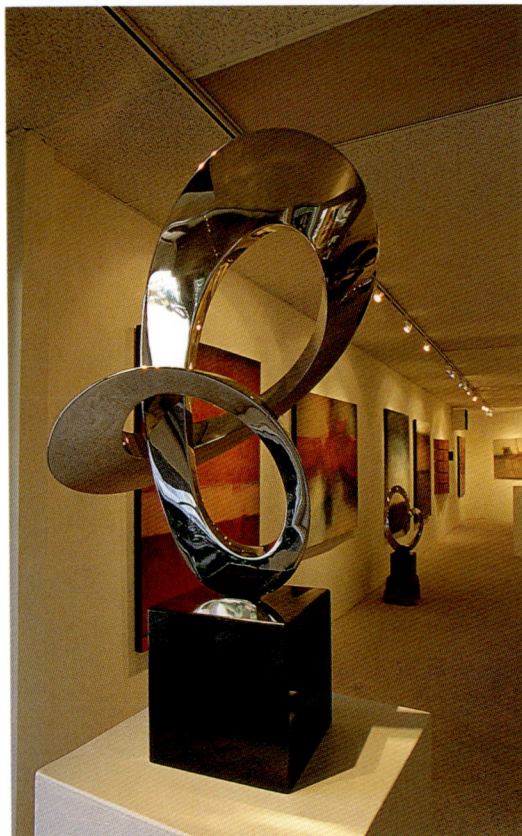

148

Top left: *Watersculpture*, ©1986, private residence, stainless steel, Newport Beach, CA, 7.5'W.
Right: *Angelic Duet*, ©1979, Los Angeles State Building, CA, stainless steel, 40'H. Bottom left: *Eternity*, ©2002, stainless steel, 42" × 24" × 18", limited edition.

JAMES THOMAS RUSSELL

JAMES RUSSELL SCULPTURE ■ 1930 LOMITA BOULEVARD ■ LOMITA, CA 90717
TEL 310-326-0785 ■ FAX 310-326-1470 ■ E-MAIL JAMES@RUSSELLSCULPTURE.COM ■ WWW.RUSSELLSCULPTURE.COM

149

Quest for Excellence, ©2002, AstraZeneca Pharmaceuticals, LP, Wilmington, DE, stainless steel, 18'H on a 3' base.

MARY ROLEY

PO BOX 3230 ■ MADISON, WI 53704
TEL 608-219-3647 ■ E-MAIL MABROLEY@HOTMAIL.COM

150

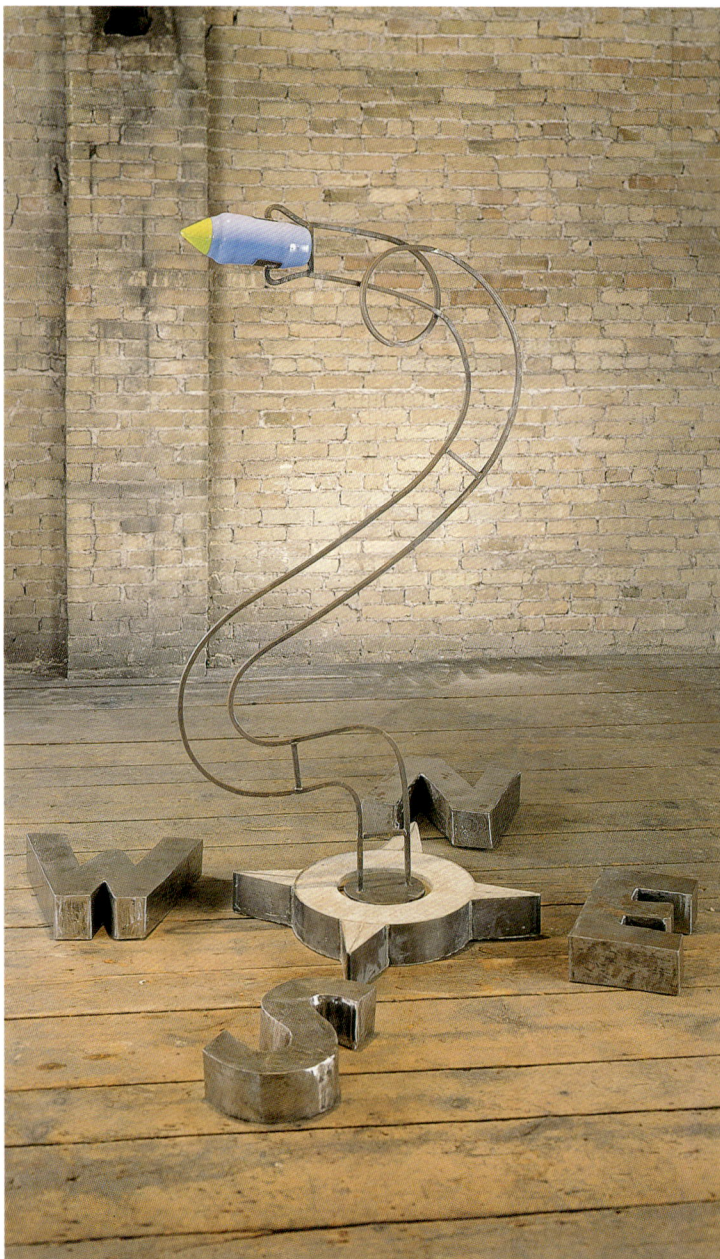

Left: *City in the Sun*, 1999, glass, steel and concrete, 9' × 4' × 2'. Right: *Indecisive Wanderer*, 1999, glass and steel, 3' × 5' × 1'. Photographs: Bill Lemke.

BRIAN F. RUSSELL

BRIAN F. RUSSELL STUDIO ■ 10385 LONG ROAD ■ ARLINGTON, TN 38002
TEL 901-867-7300 ■ FAX 901-867-7843 ■ E-MAIL INFO@BRIANRUSSELLDESIGNS.COM ■ WWW.BRIANRUSSELLDESIGNS.COM

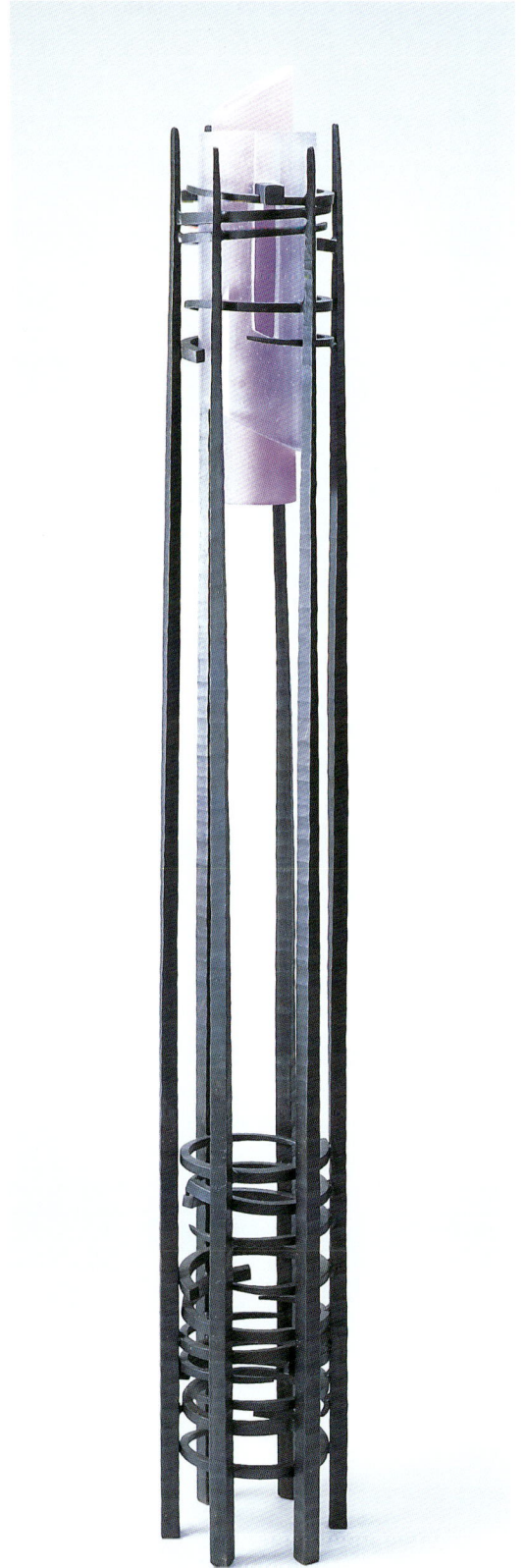

151

Top left: *Hemisphere 8 Basalt*, 2002, cast glass and forged steel, 20" × 9" × 9".
Right: *Spire*, 2002, cast glass and forged steel, 73" × 10" × 10". Bottom left: *Hemisphere 18 Twist*, 2002, cast glass and forged steel, 12" × 11" × 9".

KEVIN ROBB

KEVIN ROBB STUDIOS ▪ 7001 WEST 35TH AVENUE ▪ WHEAT RIDGE, CO 80033-6373
TEL 303-431-4758 ▪ FAX 303-425-8802 ▪ E-MAIL 3D@KEVINROBB.COM ▪ WWW.KEVINROBB.COM

152

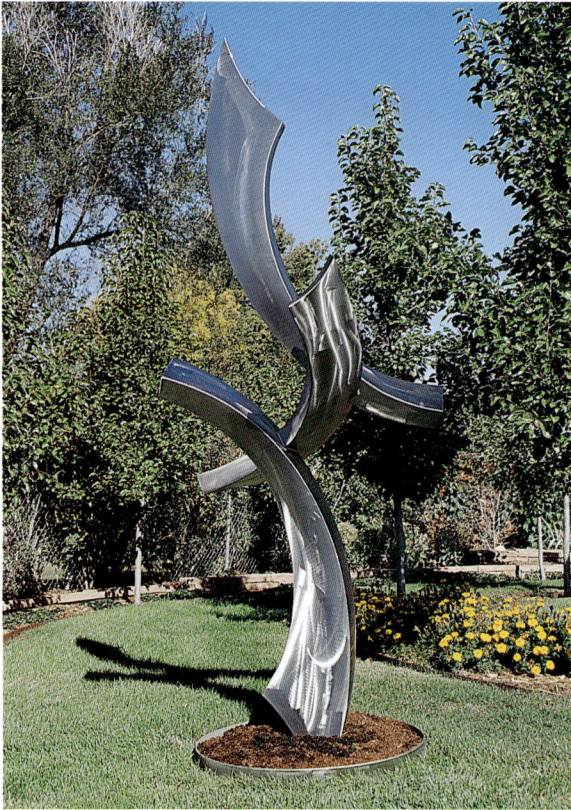

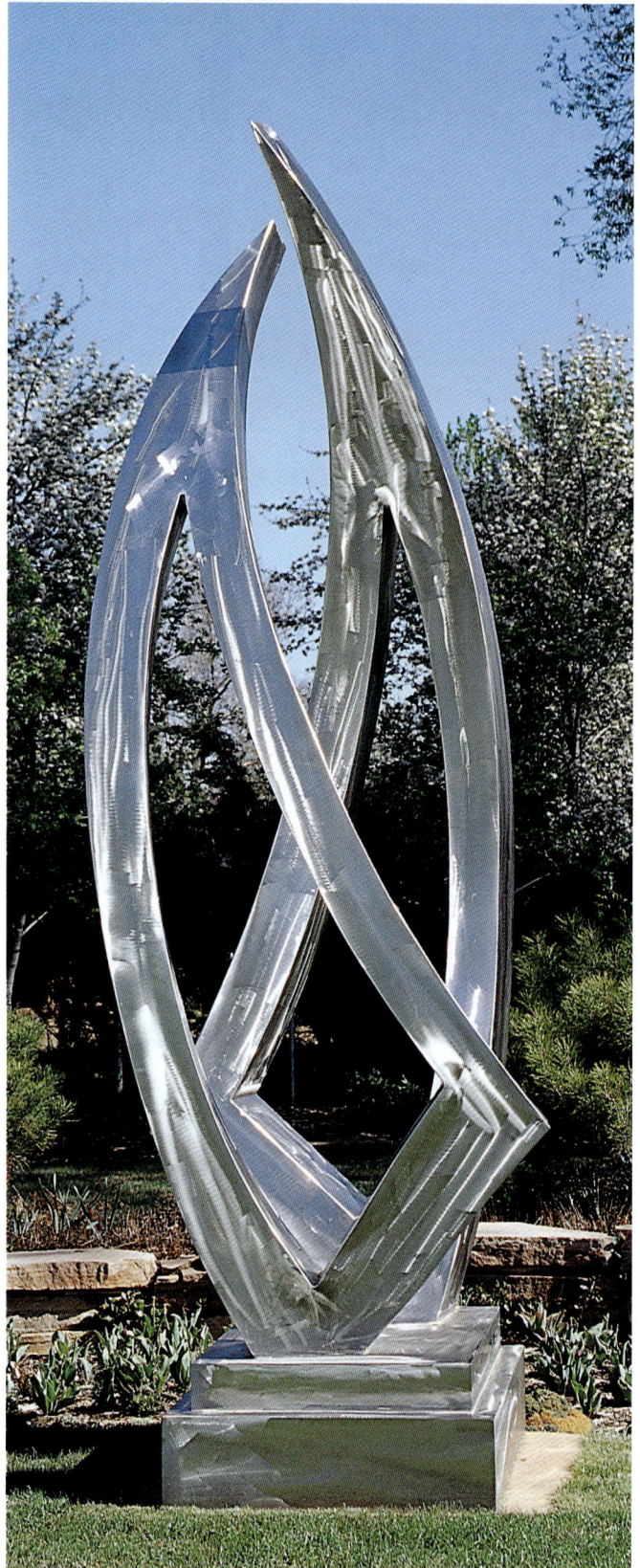

Top left: *Flute Dance*, 2002, stainless steel, 100" × 47" × 42". Bottom left: *Flying Paper*, 2002, stainless steel, 36" × 24" × 28".
Right: *Dancing Triangles*, 2002, stainless steel, 117" × 47" × 44" on 12" base.

CHU TAT-SHING

NEUBERG INTERNATIONAL LIMITED ■ UNIT 1612, CHINA MERCHANTS TOWER ■ 168 CONNAUGHT ROAD CENTRAL ■ HONG KONG
TEL 852-2540-6323 ■ FAX 852-2802-8229 ■ E-MAIL NEUBERG@SCULPTURE.COM.HK ■ WWW.SCULPTURE.COM.HK

153

Top left: *Tai Chi Dance* (maquette), 2001, Housing Authority Project, Hong Kong, bronze, 5'H.
Right: *Ancient Poet Toasted to the Moon*, 1994, private collection, Hong Kong, bronze, 2.5'H. Bottom left: *Fish Verde*, 2002, Housing Authority Project, Hong Kong, bronze, 5'H.

MATTHEW RYAN

STUDIO M ■ 4340 EAST KENTUCKY AVENUE #23 5 ■ DENVER, CO 80246
TEL 303-632-3800 ■ E-MAIL MRYANART@EARTHLINK.NET ■ WWW.ARTOFRYAN.COM

Left: *Duet*, 2002, bronze, 15"H x 8"W x 8"D. Right: *Celebration*, 2002, bronze, 20.5"H x 11"W x 11"D.

ROB STERN

ROB STERN ART GLASS ■ 1510 BARACOA AVENUE ■ CORAL GABLES, FL 33146
TEL 305-903-8566 ■ FAX 305-661-1109 ■ E-MAIL RASGLASS@AOL.COM ■ WWW.ROBSTERNARTGLASS.COM

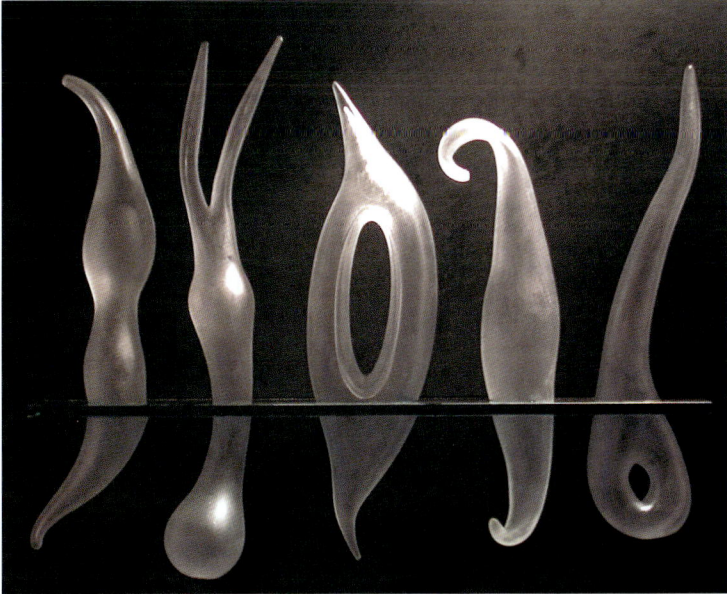

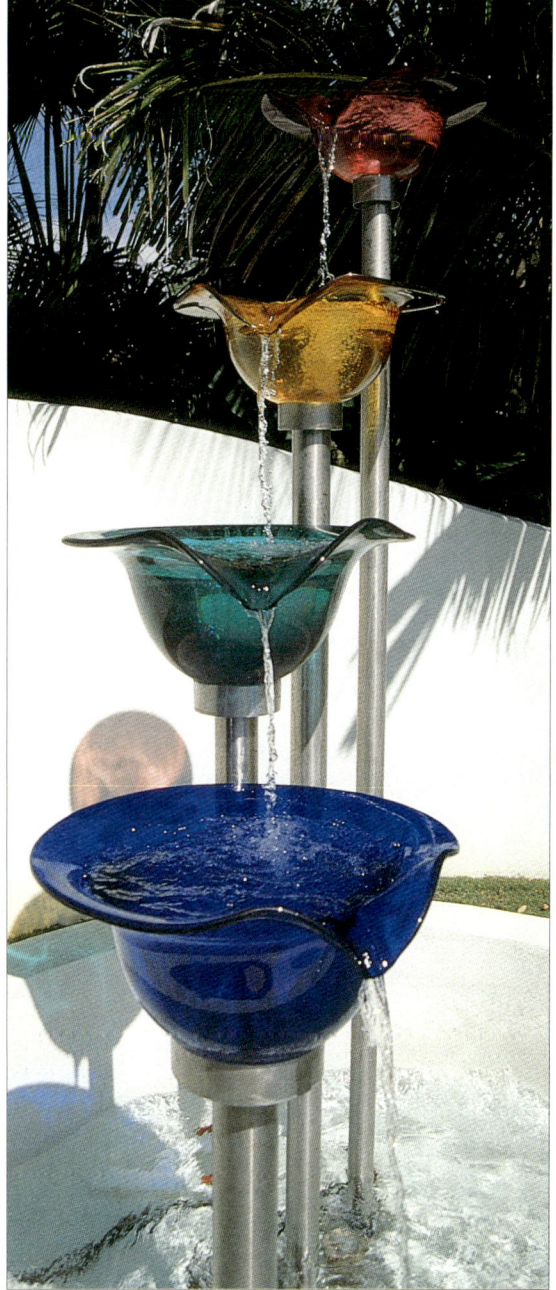

Top left: *Shelf Life I*, 2002, glass, wood and steel, 36" x 48" x 14".
Right: *Fountain*, 2001, glass, water, steel and cement, Miami, FL, 10' x 10'. Bottom left: *Shelf Life II*, 2002, glass, wood and steel, 36" x 48" x 14".

Public Art

BAD RIVER ARTWORKS

SHERRI TREEBY ■ LEE LEUNING ■ 120 NORTH MAIN STREET ■ ABERDEEN, SD 57401
TEL 605-226-3795/605-380-0550 ■ E-MAIL BADRIVER@NVC.NET ■ WWW.BADRIVERART.COM

158

World War II memorial, 2001, Pierre, SD, bronze, life-size. Photographs: Chad Coppess, South Dakota Department of Tourism.

ROBERT W. ELLISON

ELLISON STUDIO ■ 6480 EAGLE RIDGE ROAD ■ PENNGROVE, CA 94951
TEL 707-795-9775 ■ FAX 707-795-4370 ■ E-MAIL RELLISON@SONIC.NET ■ WWW.ROBERTELLISON.COM

159

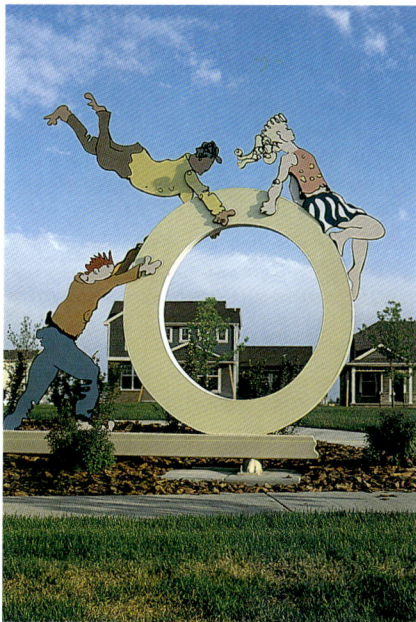

Top: *Mr. Zebra and His Friends*, 1999, Oakland, CA, steel and urethane, 14.5' × 56' × 4". Photograph: Brian Moran. Center left: *Roll Play*, 2001, Fort Collins, CO, steel and urethane, 12' × 15' × 8". Center, center right: *Mr. Zebra and His Friends* (details). Bottom: *Spin*, 2002, San Francisco Embarcadero BART, steel and urethane, 8' × 50' × 3". Photograph: Ira Schrank

ROB FISHER

ROB FISHER SCULPTURE LLC ■ 228 NORTH ALLEGHENY STREET ■ BELLEFONTE, PA 16823
TEL 814-355-1458 ■ FAX 814-353-9060 ■ E-MAIL GLENUNION@AOL.COM ■ WWW.SCULPTURE.ORG/PORTFOLIO/FISHER

160

Dihedrals, 2002, Gateway Exchange, Columbia, MD, powder-coated aluminum and stainless steel, 25' × 40' × 35'. Top photograph: Ed Stawick.

DOUGLAS OLMSTED FREEMAN

DOUG FREEMAN SCULPTURE STUDIO ■ 310 NORTH 2ND STREET ■ MINNEAPOLIS, MN 55401
TEL 612-339-7150 ■ FAX 612-339-5201 ■ E-MAIL DFREE@INFI.NET ■ WWW.FREEMANSTUDIO.COM

161

The Fountain of the Wind (details), Duluth, MN. Photographs: Jerry Mathiason.

FRANK GREGORY

FRANK GREGORY STUDIOS ■ TWO MEAD STREET, SUITE 3 ■ GREENFIELD, MA 01301
TEL 413-772-0088 ■ E-MAIL ARTIST@FRANKGREGORY.COM ■ WWW.FRANKGREGORY.COM

162

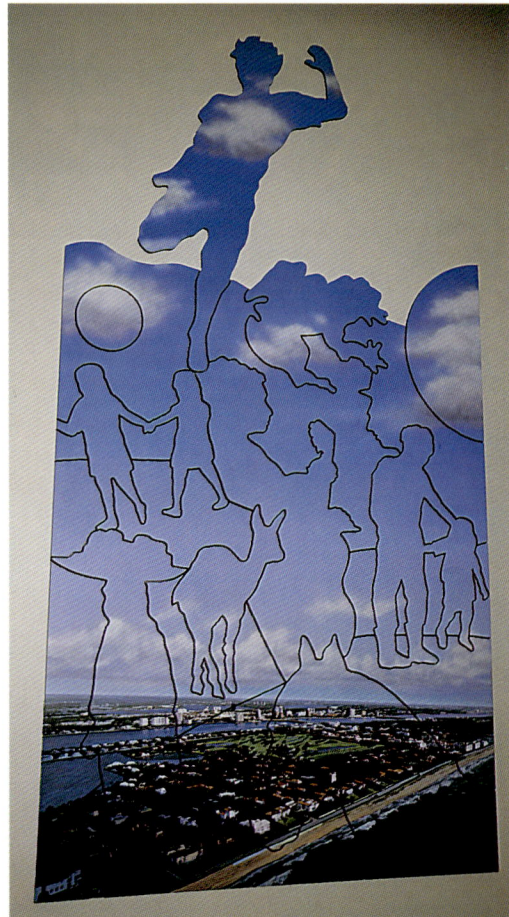

Palm Beach Puzzle, 2002, Palm Beach County Health Department, acrylic on cut and routed medium-density fiberboard.
Beach Puzzle, 2002, (detail, bottom left) and *Skyline Puzzle* (detail, bottom right), each 8' x 15'. Photographs: Perry Davis.

RENEÉ HEADINGS

PO BOX 73 ■ SKYTOP, PA 18357 ■ TEL 570-992-1754 ■ FAX 570-402-1921
E-MAIL RENEEHEADINGS@YAHOO.COM ■ WWW.SCULPTURESGALLERY.COM

163

Top left: *Soul of Africa*, permanent collection, Hiram Blauvelt Art Museum, Oradell, NJ, bronze. Top right: *Returning on the Wings of Peace*, Riviera Beach, FL, bronze, 16'H.
Bottom: *First Lesson*, Greenwich, CT, bronze, life size.

MICHAEL HAYDEN AND KRISTINA LUCAS

THINKING LIGHTLY, INC. ■ 5076 HALL ROAD ■ SANTA ROSA, CA 95401-5511
TEL 707-546-0664 ■ FAX 707-546-0661 ■ E-MAIL THINKLT@SONIC.NET ■ WWW.THINKINGLIGHTLY.COM

164

Top left: *Arpeggio*, 2001, Nashville Metropolitan Airport, TN, cast acrylic light pipe, light-emitting diodes, 126'L; transparent canopy, 3,000' sq. Top center: *Umbrella Tree*, 2001, Santa Rosa Junior College, CA, welded, painted with color-shifting ChromaFlair® pigments, 14'H x 6'Dia. Top right: *Skyword*, 2000, Des Plaines Public Library, IL, holographic diffraction grating film, 40'H x 20'W x 30'L. Bottom: *Zag*, 2002, Vineyard Creek Inn, Santa Rosa, CA, side-emitting fiber optics, 163'L.

ARCHIE HELD

ARCHIE HELD STUDIO ■ 5-18TH STREET ■ RICHMOND, CA 94801
TEL 510-235-8700 ■ FAX 510-234-4828 ■ E-MAIL ARCHIEHELDSTUDIO@ATTBI.COM

165

Top left: *Community*, 2002, Sunnyvale, CA, bronze, stainless steel and water, 10' × 10' × 20'H. Top right: *Dance*, 2002, Sunnyvale, CA, bronze, 5' × 4' × 16'H.
Bottom: *Millennium Bowl*, 2001, Bishop Ranch, San Ramon, CA, stainless steel and water, 14'Dia × 8'H.

RUSSELL JACQUES

RUSSELL JACQUES STUDIO ■ 2621 CRESTVIEW DRIVE ■ NEWPORT BEACH, CA 92663
TEL/FAX 949-645-8206 OR TEL/FAX 760-674-0470 ■ E-MAIL TREARTGALLERY@AOL.COM

166

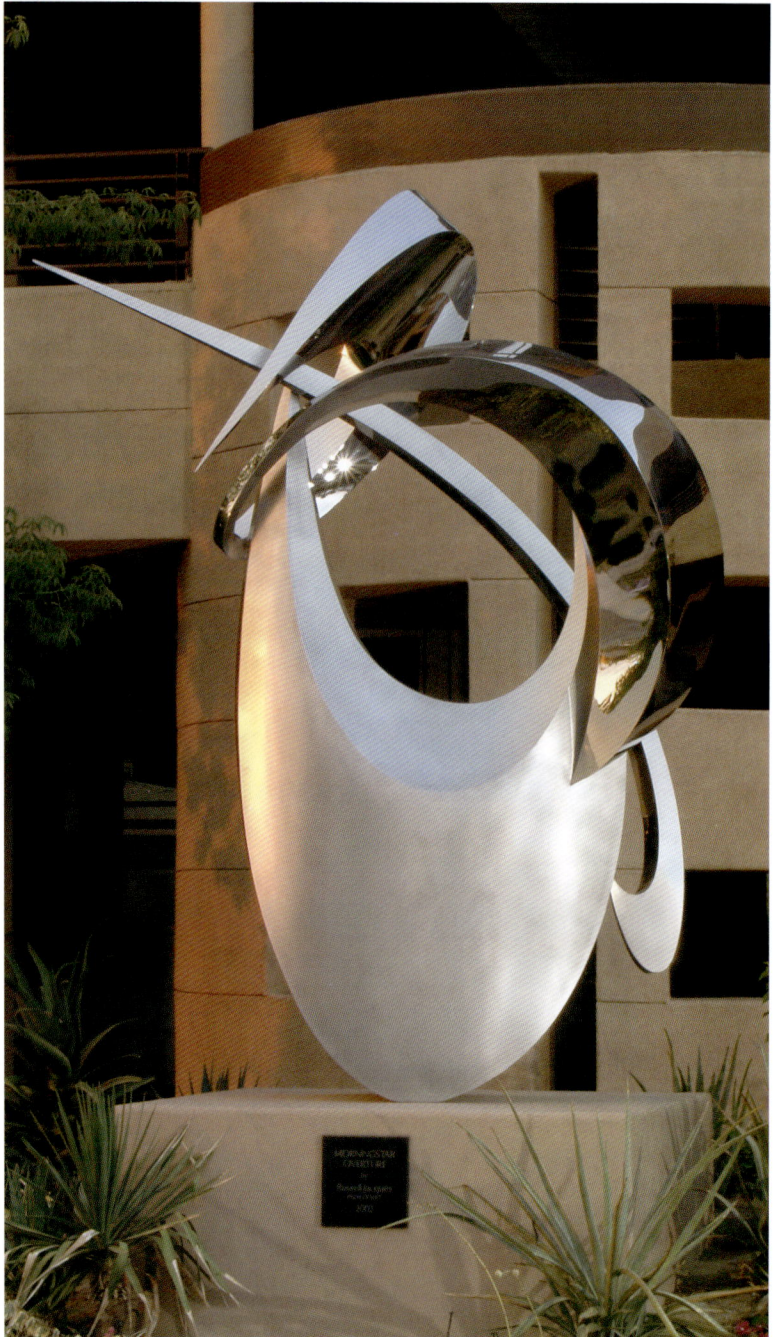

Top left: *Trè*, 2003, City of Palm Desert, CA, stainless steel, 10'H. Right: *Morningstar Overture*, 2002, Art in Public Places, Palm Desert, CA.
Bottom left: *Homage to Bernstein*, 2002, stainless steel, 4'H x 4'W x 6"D. Photograph: Sherri Breyer.

LISA KASLOW

LISA KASLOW, LLC ■ PO BOX 381 ■ HIBERNIA, NJ 07842 ■ TEL 877-276-3810 ■ FAX 973-586-4393
E-MAIL LISA@KASLOWPUBLICART.COM ■ WWW.KASLOWPUBLICART.COM

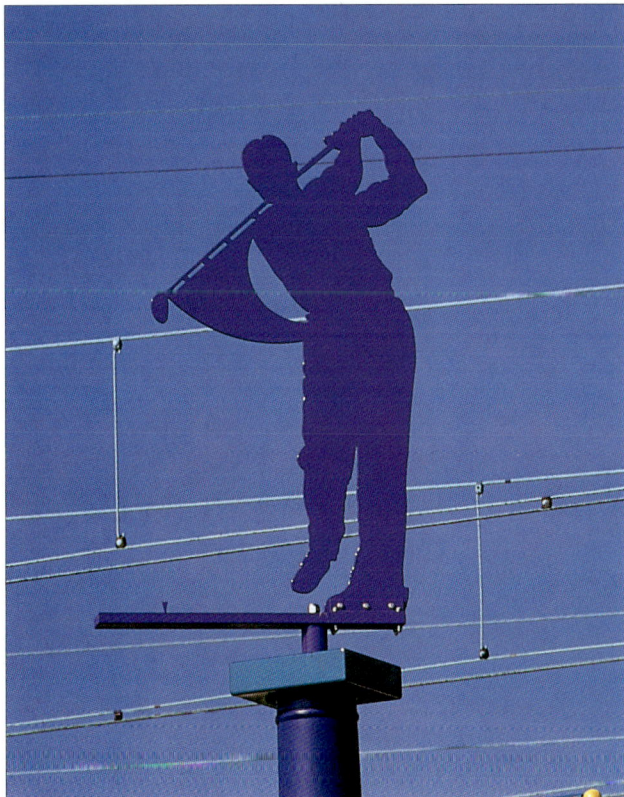

167

Re creation (three views), 1999, Hamilton Transit Center, NJ, ten kinetic sculptures along rail platform, aluminum, fiberglass and vinyl, 14'H, client: New Jersey Transit Authority. Photographs: Jay Rosenblatt.

BRUCE A. NIEMI

NIEMI SCULPTURE GALLERY ■ 13300 116TH STREET ■ KENOSHA, WI 53142
TEL 262-857-3456 ■ FAX 262-857-4567 ■ E-MAIL SCULPTURE@BRUCENIEMI.COM

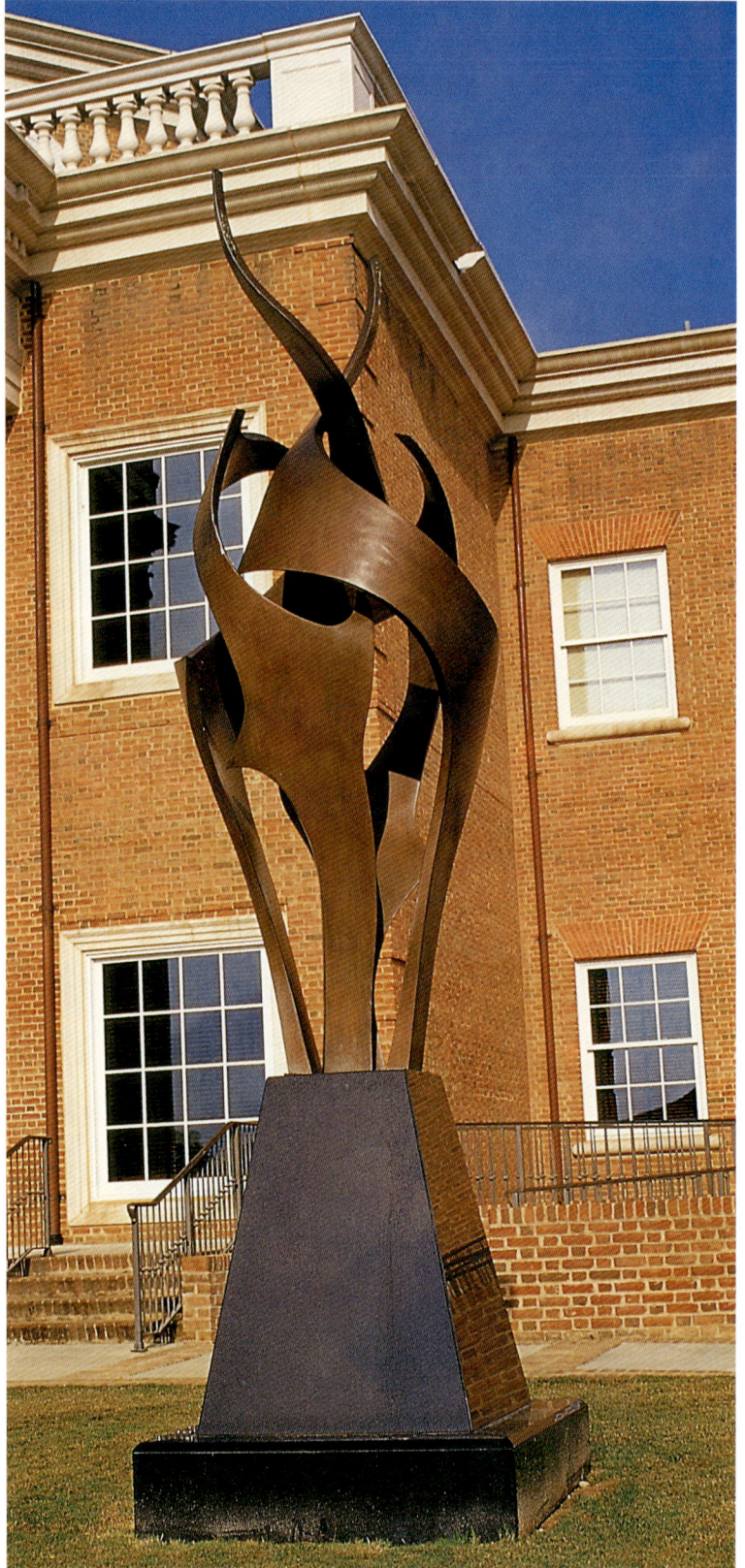

168

Top left: *Samurai*, 2002, private residence, Indianapolis, IN, bronze, 168" × 52" × 40". Photograph: Pawel Pfludzinski.
Bottom left: *Eye to the Soul*, 2002, Niemi Sculpture Gallery, Kenosha, WI, stainless steel, 10' × 9.4' × 5'. Right: *Torch*, 2000, Cary Academy, NC, bronze, 15' × 4' × 4'.

MARSHA LEGA STUDIO, INC.

MARSHA LEGA ■ 28 WEST CROWLEY AVENUE ■ JOLIET, IL 60432
TEL 815-727-5255 ■ FAX 815-727-5424 ■ E-MAIL MARSHALEGA@CS.COM ■ WWW.MARSHALEGA.COM

169

Top: *The Bicyclist*, Canal Corridor Association Wayfinding Project, 2001, Joliet, IL, Cor ten® steel, life size figure.
Bottom: *The Portals of Buell Avenue*, 2002, Joliet, IL, welded steel sculpture with automotive paint, 16' x 10'.

MARSH SCOTT

3275 LAGUNA CANYON ROAD, STUDIO M1 ■ LAGUNA BEACH, CA 92651
TEL 949-494-8672 ■ FAX 949-494-8671 ■ E-MAIL MARSH@MARSHSCOTT.COM ■ WWW.MARSHSCOTT.COM

170

Top: *Steps in the Sand*, Laguna Beach, CA, 63" × 174" × 12". Photograph: Infinity Art Photography.
Bottom left: *Wave Dance*, Laguna Beach, CA, 68" × 48" × 16". Bottom right: *Portals*, Brea, CA, 90" × 60" × 40".

BEV PRECIOUS

PRECIOUS DESIGN STUDIOS, INC. ■ 950 NORTH ALABAMA STREET ■ INDIANAPOLIS, IN 46202
TEL/FAX 317-631-6560 ■ E-MAIL BBPREC@AOL.COM

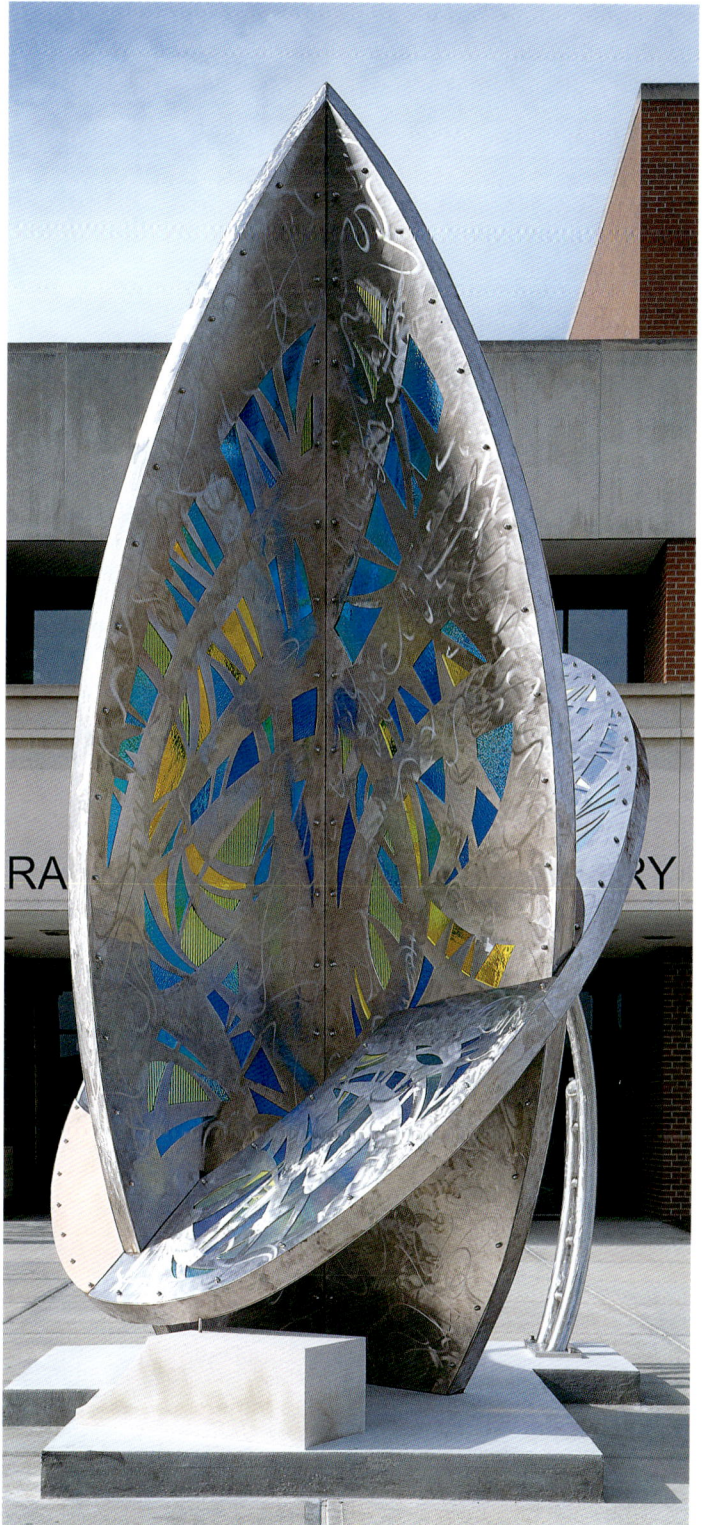

171

Universal Continuum, 2002, University of Indianapolis, IN, stainless steel, dichroic glass, bronze and limestone, 16' x 8' x 12'. Photographs: Greg Murphey.

STEVE TEETERS

ST. ELIGIUS STUDIO ■ 719 BUDDY HOLLY AVENUE ■ LUBBOCK, TX 79401
TEL 806-741-1590 ■ FAX 806-744-8507 ■ E-MAIL STEVE@STELIGIUS-STUDIO.COM

172

Seasons of the Llano Estacado, 2002, Texas Tech University, forged and welded steel, bronze and stainless steel, 6' x 800'. Photographs: Hershel Womock.

ELLEN KOCHANSKY

EKO ■ 1237 MILE CREEK ROAD ■ PICKENS, SC 29671
TEL 864-868-9749 ■ FAX 864-868-4250 ■ EKOCHANSKY@AOL.COM

Mill Memory, 2003, Spartanburg Art Center, commissioned by Hub City Writers Project, mementos contributed from textile mills, each square: 18", total size: 4' x 14'.
Bottom: *Mill Memory* (detail), transportation, recreation, tools, products, plans and machinery. Photographs: Mark Olencki, Spartanburg, SC.

Liturgical Art

ASCALON STUDIOS, INC.

DAVID ASCALON ■ 115 ATLANTIC AVENUE ■ BERLIN, NJ 08009-9300 ■ TEL 888-280-5656 (TOLL FREE)
TEL 856-768-3779 ■ FAX 856-768-3902 ■ E-MAIL ASCALONART@AOL.COM ■ WWW.ASCALONART.COM

Top left: *Holocaust Memorial for the Commonwealth of Pennsylvania*, Harrisburg, PA, Cor-ten steel, stainless steel and granite.
Top right: *The Life Cycles*, Temple Shalom, Succasunna, NJ, stained glass windows. Bottom: *Creation*, Congregation B'nai Israel, Tustin, CA, glass mosaic with bronze and oak.

HETLAND LTD.

DAVID J. HETLAND ■ 1704 MAIN AVENUE, SUITE 3 ■ FARGO, ND 58103
TEL 701-293-3066 ■ FAX 701-293-0780 ■ E-MAIL DJHETLAND@AOL.COM ■ WWW.HETLAND.COM

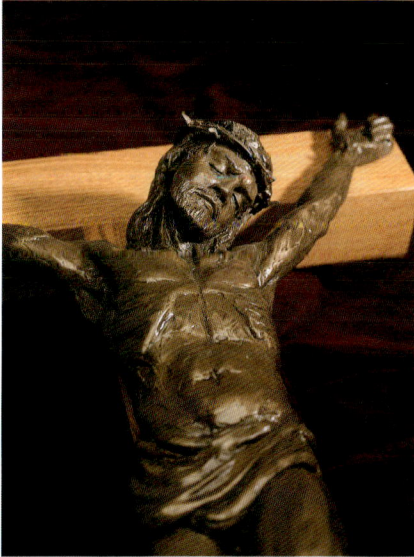

177

Top left: *Processional Cross*, 2001, Transfiguration Catholic Church, Oakdale, MN, bronze and oak, 18"H. Photograph: Mark Anthony. Top center: *Light of the World*, 2002, Cormorant Lutheran Church, Lake Park, MN, stained glass, 32" x 49". Photograph: Mark Anthony. Top right: *Tree of Life*, 2002, Olivet Lutheran Church, Fargo, ND, copper and olive wood, 17' x 20'. Photograph: Mark Anthony. Bottom: *Ezekiel 47*, 2001, Christ Lutheran Church, San Diego, CA, Mexican smalti and clear glass bevels, 20' x 15'. Photograph: Pablo Mason.

Custom Design: Liturgical Art

Tom Van Eynde

ARTIST
Laurie Wohl,
New York, NY

PROJECT
Psalms pulpit parament, 2001,
unwoven canvas and mixed media

COMMISSIONED FOR
Fourth Presbyterian Church,
Chicago, Illinois

TIMELINE
1 year (for 3 pieces)

DIMENSIONS
2'W x 5'L

Laurie Wohl's *Psalms* pulpit parament is meant to inspire congregants of the Fourth Presbyterian Church during Ordinary Time, the non-holy days of the religious calendar. "Most churches are decorated only for holy days," Wohl notes. "Sanctuaries are typically pretty bare the other days of the year." Since creating the parament, Wohl has received many e-mails from members of the congregation who appreciate the meditative quality of her work. ■ Fourth Presbyterian loves its artwork: the church has its own gallery, arts administrator and exhibits. It was at one such exhibition, *Threads That Bind,* that Wohl was discovered. The *Psalms* parament— and accompanying wall hangings—comprise just the first of 11 commissions Wohl will complete for the church. ■ "It's the most extensive commission I've ever done," Wohl reports. And a thoughtful commission, as well. The parament blends Hebrew and English calligraphy to represent the Old Testament roots behind modern-day faith. Psalm 133 appears on the piece, encouraging "brothers to be together." The message is particularly appropriate since the church is used by the Chicago Sinai Congregation during High Holy Days. Creating an interfaith dialog is important to Wohl, though much of her work is designed simply to inspire prayer or meditation. ■ Wohl has created many pieces for private homes, as well as for what she describes as "institutions of health and prayer." "For me," she muses, "these seem like the right places for my work."

PANTE STUDIO

MICHAEL DEMETZ ■ MINERT 7 ■ ORTISEI, ITALY 39046
TEL 011-39-0471-796514 ■ FAX 011-39-0471-789854 ■ E-MAIL INFO@PANTESTUDIO.IT ■ WWW.PANTESTUDIO.IT

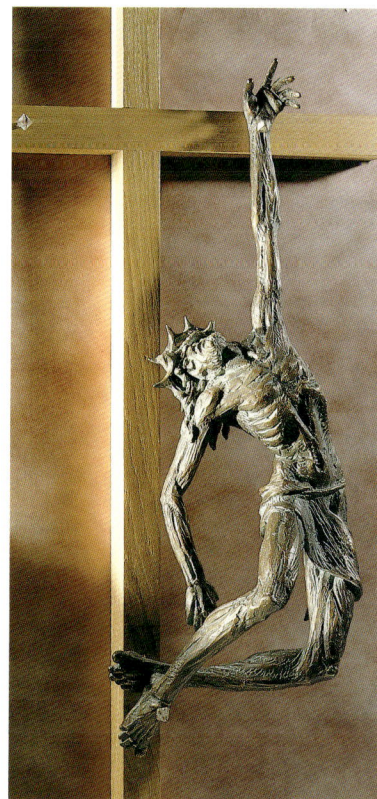

179

Left: *Crucifix*, 1985, Resurrection Catholic Church, Destin, FL, cast bronze, 5'H.
Top right: *Crucifix*, 1988, Pastor's office, Destin, FL, cast bronze, 24"H. Bottom right: *Mary and Child*, 2001, Meridian, ID, oil-colored linden wood, 6'H.

JOHN LEWIS GLASS STUDIO

10229 PEARMAIN STREET ■ OAKLAND, CA 94603 ■ TEL 510-635-4607 ■ FAX 510-569-5604
E-MAIL INFO@JOHNLEWISGLASS.COM ■ WWW.JOHNLEWISGLASS.COM

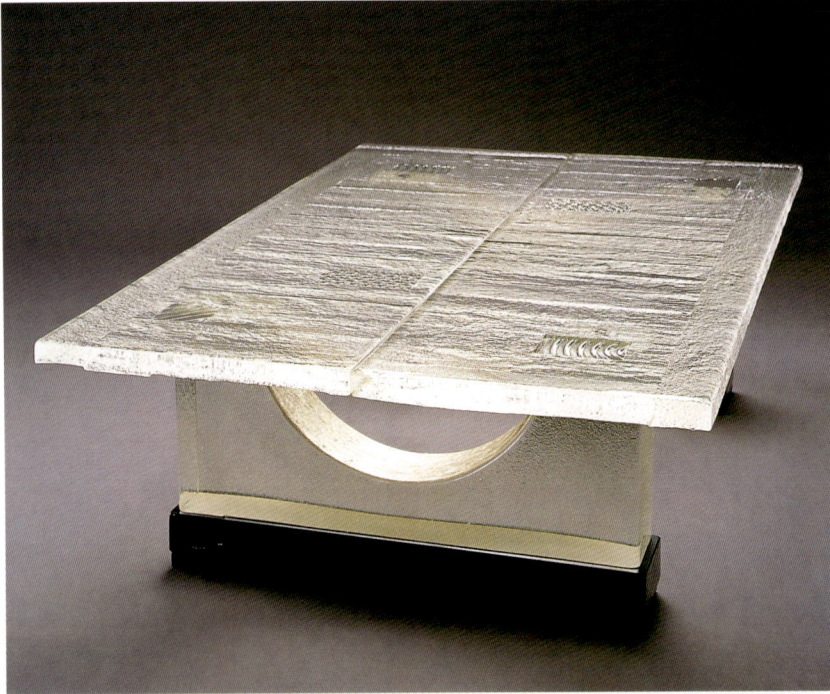

Top left: *Glacier Coffee Table*, 2002, cast glass with white gold leaf, 18"H x 60"W x 40"D. Top right: *Ovo Pedestal*, 2002, cast glass with tinted epoxy, 37"H x 23"Dia.
Bottom: *Ell Coffee Table*, 2002, cast glass, 19"H x 59"W x 36"D. Photographs: Charlie Frizzell.

RAY ZOVAR

SILK PURSE ENTERPRISES, INC. ■ 2499 KEENAN ROAD ■ McFARLAND, WI 53558
TEL 608-345-2991 ■ TEL/FAX 608-838-6617 ■ E-MAIL RAY@ZOVAR.COM ■ WWW.ZOVAR.COM

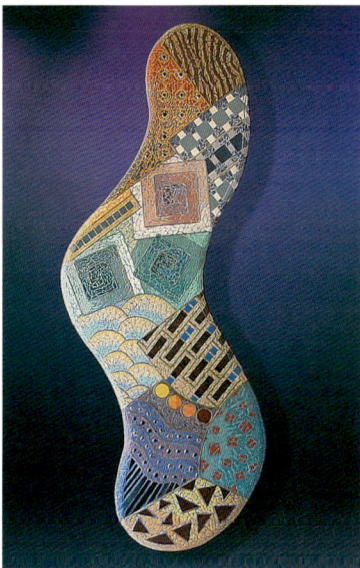

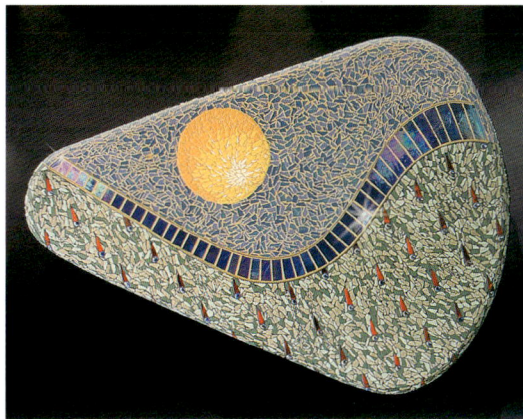

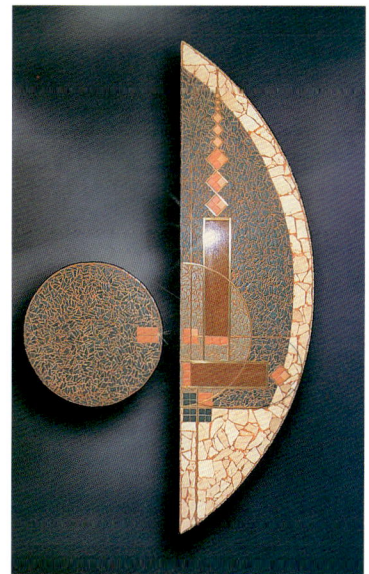

Top: *Leaf Table*, 2002, porcelain, brass and glass beads, 36" x 55" x 19"H.
Bottom left: *Pieces*, 2002, porcelain with inlays of stained glass, brass and exotic woods, 28" x 68". Bottom center: *Neutrinos*, 2002, porcelain, brass and stained glass, 35" x 49".
Bottom right: *Frankish*, 2002, porcelain, lacewood, brass and tumbled marble, 18" x 63" with 18"Dia. side piece.

EILEEN JAGER

LIGHTHUNTER ■ ONE COTTAGE STREET ■ EASTHAMPTON, MA 01027 ■ TEL/FAX 413-527-2090
E-MAIL EJAGER@EARTHLINK.NET ■ WWW.EILEENJAGER.COM

184

Top left: *Fleur D'Ange*, 2001, glass mosaic table-fountain, 45" x 16". Top right: *Verde Bench*, 2002, glass mosaic bench, 70" x 18" x 19".
Bottom: *FloWing*, 2002, glass mosaic table-fountain, 54" x 32" x 16". Photographs: Tommy O. Elder.

BINH PHO

WONDERS OF WOOD ■ 48W175 PINE TREE DRIVE ■ MAPLE PARK, IL 60151
TEL 630-365-5462 ■ FAX 630-365-5837 ■ E-MAIL TORIALE@MSN.COM ■ WWW.WONDERSOFWOOD.NET

185

Top: 18-seat dining room set, 2002, Goldmeier estate, St. Louis, MO, bird's-eye maple and lacewood, 29"H × 14.1'L × 40"W.
Bottom left: Captain chair, fiddleback maple and lacewood, 42"H × 24" × 20". Bottom right: Chair, fiddleback maple and lacewood, 40"H × 20" × 20".

MARTIN STURMAN

MARTIN STURMAN SCULPTURES ■ 3201 BAYSHORE DRIVE ■ WESTLAKE VILLAGE, CA 91361
TEL 818-707-8087 ■ FAX 818-707-3079 ■ E-MAIL MLSTURMAN@AOL.COM ■ WWW.STEELSCULPTURES.COM

186

Top left: *Tropical Bedside Table*, 2002, acrylic and steel, 29"H x 19"W x 19"D. Right: *Art Deco Bedside Table*, 2002, acrylic and steel, 29"H x 19"W x 19"D.
Bottom left: *Floral Cocktail Table*, 2002, acrylic and steel, 19"H x 23"W x 21"D. Photographs: Barry Michlin.

CHRISTOPHER P. VESPERMANN

VESPEX, LLC ■ 10 SCOTLAND ROAD ■ KINGSTON, NH 03848
TEL 603-642-3384 ■ FAX 603-642-6601 ■ E-MAIL VESPERMANN@VESPEX.COM ■ WWW.VESPEX.COM

187

Top left: Cast trestle table, cast plate glass, plate glass and steel, 60" x 36" x 18".
Top right: *Garden*, cast glass, 36" x 12" x 3". Bottom: Dining table, cast/bent glass, cast crystal, bronze and painted steel, 72" x 45" x 30". Photograph: Bill Truslow.

NANCY GRAY

GRAY STUDIO ■ 508 EAST FOURTH STREET ■ LAMPASAS, TX 76550
TEL 512-525-1963/512-556-6997 ■ FAX 512-556-3608 ■ E-MAIL NANCY@GRAYSTUDIO.NET ■ WWW.GRAYSTUDIO.NET

Hillside in the Fall, screen/room divider, 2002, oil on birch with tiger-stripe maple frame, 71.5" x 77", reverse side upholstered with suede. Photograph: Vernon Gaston.

SLEDD/WINGER GLASSWORKS

NANCY SLEDD ■ MARY LU WINGER ■ 1912 EAST MAIN STREET ■ RICHMOND, VA 23223
TEL 804-644-2837 ■ FAX 804-644-6821 ■ E-MAIL SLEDDWINGER@AOL.COM

Antoinette room divider, 1996, stained, beveled and etched glass, crystals and jewels, 70" x 66". Photograph: Tony Sylvestro.

Lighting

PAM MORRIS DESIGNS EXCITING LIGHTING

PAM MORRIS ■ 14 EAST SIR FRANCIS DRAKE BOULEVARD, STUDIO D ■ LARKSPUR, CA 94939
TEL 415-925-0840 ■ FAX 415-925-1305 ■ E-MAIL LIGHTING@SONIC.NET

192

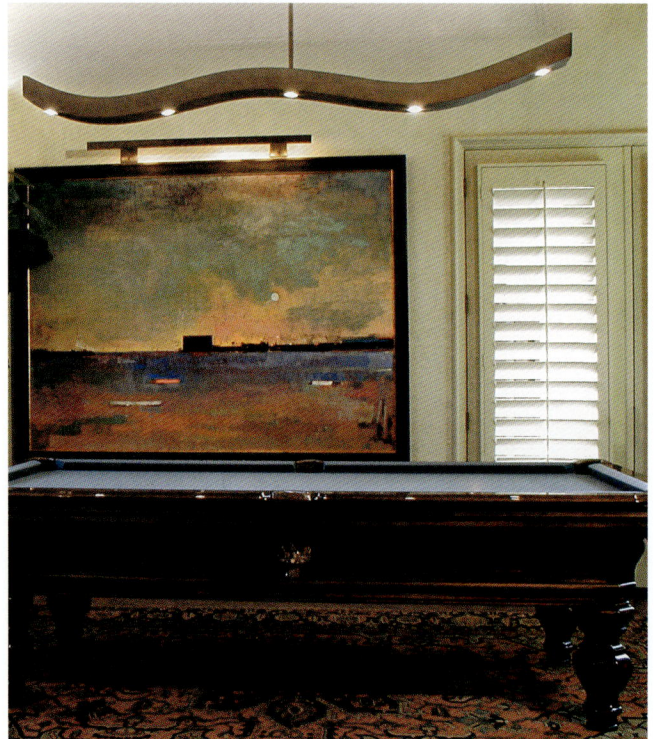

Left: Glass fireplace façade, kiln-formed glass, fiber optic. 14'H. Top right: *Zen Zero*, mixed media, 42"H. Bottom right: *Pool Table Wave Light*, steel, 72"l.

PAM MORRIS DESIGNS EXCITING LIGHTING

PAM MORRIS ■ 14 EAST SIR FRANCIS DRAKE BOULEVARD, STUDIO D ■ LARKSPUR, CA 94939
TEL 415-925-0840 ■ FAX 415-925-1305 ■ E-MAIL LIGHTING@SONIC.NET

193

Zen Zero chandelier, mixed media, 42"H.

TRIO DESIGN GLASSWARE

RENATO FOTI ■ 253 QUEEN STREET SOUTH ■ KITCHENER, ON N2G1W4 ■ TEL 519-749-2814 ■ FAX 519-749-6319
E-MAIL RENATOFOTI@ROGERS.COM ■ WWW.TRIODESIGNGLASSWARE.COM

194

Top: Ceiling lamp, 2002, fused glass with stainless steel fixture, 24" x 24". Bottom left: *Retro-Mesh* wall sculpture, 2003, fused glass, 28" x 18".
Bottom right: *Geo-Square Style* glass sink and panels, 2002, 32" x 20", cabinet by McKaskell-Haindl Design Build. Photographs: JPB Photography.

ROCK COTTAGE GLASSWORKS, INC.

DIERK VAN KEPPEL ■ 6801 FARLEY ■ MERRIAM, KS 66203
TEL 913-262-1763 ■ FAX 913-262-0430 ■ E-MAIL RCGLASS@GRAPEVINE.NET ■ WWW.VANKEPPELARTGLASS.COM

195

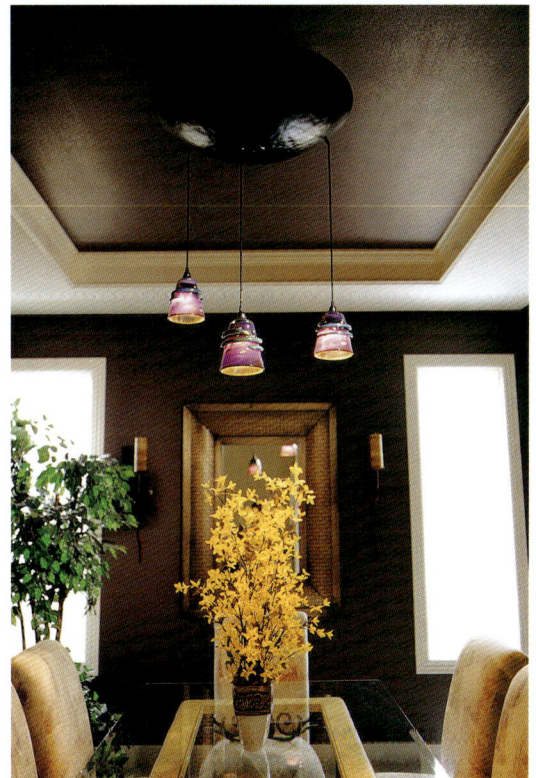

Top left: lester pendants, 2002, Gilman residence, blown glass, each: 8". Photograph: Tim Pott. Top right: Pendant sconces, 2001,
Daugherty residence, blown glass and iron, 12" x 5". Photograph: Tim Pott. Bottom left: *Fogo de Chao*, Chicago, cast glass and iron, 48"Dia. Photograph: Charlie Mayer.
Bottom right: Pendant cluster, 2002, Crabtree residence, blown glass, each: 7". Photograph: Tim Pott.

JOHN B. MAY

THREE60 STUDIO ■ 141 NORTON ROAD ■ KITTERY, ME 03904
TEL 207-439-8267 ■ E-MAIL THREE60STUDIO@ATTBI.COM ■ WWW.THREE60STUDIO.COM

196

Left: *Blue Fin Table Lamp*, cherry and linen, 30"H × 14"Dia.
Top right: *Mademoiselle Table Lamp*, maple and Thai rice paper, 24"H × 20"Dia. Bottom right: *Irving Table Lamp*, mahogany and sagebrush, 27"H × 16"Dia. Photographs: Bill Truslow.

NIKOLAS WEINSTEIN

NIKOLAS WEINSTEIN STUDIOS ■ 1649 VALENCIA STREET ■ SAN FRANCISCO, CA 94110
TEL 415-643-5418 ■ FAX 415-643-3723 ■ E-MAIL INFO@NIKOLAS.NET ■ WWW.NIKOLAS.NET

197

Chandelier, 2002, blown glass with satin-etched exteriors, 30" x 36", suspended height adjustable, limited edition.

Murals & Trompe L'Oeil

200

Top: *Estuary, Griswold Point*, 2001, acrylic on canvas, 32' × 10'. Bottom: *Estuary, Grasses* (detail), 2001, acrylic on canvas, 32' × 10'. Photographs: Lewis Becker.

ANDRE N. KOUZNETSOV

BUON FRESCO WALL ARTISTRY ■ 6442 OVERLOOK DRIVE ■ ALEXANDRIA, VA 22312
TEL 888-637-3726 ■ FAX 703-914-5605 ■ E-MAIL WALLART@BFRESCO.COM ■ WWW.BFRESCO.COM

201

Top: *Placido Domingo* (detail), 2000, Café Milano, Georgetown, DC, mixed media on canvas, 15' × 8'. Photograph: Joe Weber Photography.
Bottom: *Baroque Cupola*, 1999, private residence, acrylic and gold leaf trompe l'oeil, 16' × 24'. Photograph: Robert McComas Photography.

BARBARA MASLEN

MASLEN STUDIO ■ 55 BAYVIEW AVENUE ■ SAG HARBOR, NY 11963
TEL 631-725-3121 ■ FAX 631-725-4608 ■ E-MAIL MASLEN@OPTONLINE.NET ■ WWW.BARBARAMASLEN.COM

202

Top: Entrance foyer, private residence, East Hampton, NY, 25'H × 20'W. Photograph: Jeff Heatley Photography.
Bottom left: Café signage, Bath & Tennis Hotel, Westhampton Beach, NY, 3'H × 25'W.
Bottom right: Fresco on wood panels, Thai restaurant, Sag Harbor, NY, 6' × 6'. Photograph: ©2003 Liz Steger Photography/*New York Magazine*.

TRENA McNABB

McNABB STUDIO, INC. ■ PO BOX 327 ■ BETHANIA, NC 27010
TEL 336-924-6053 ■ FAX 336-924-4854 ■ E-MAIL TRENA@TMCNABB.COM ■ WWW.TMCNABB.COM

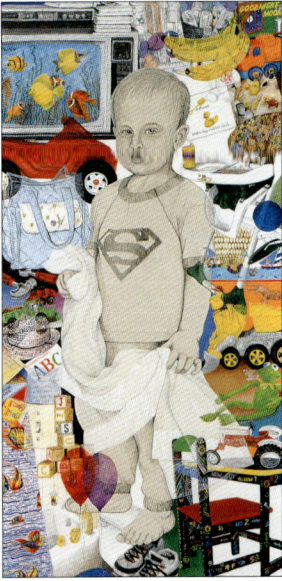

203

Top left: *Toddler (18 months)*, 48" x 24". Bottom left: *Art Collector*, 72" x 24".
Center: *First Grade Schoolteacher*, 72" x 24". Right: *Third-Generation Blacksmith*, 72" x 24". All works shown: acrylic and graphite on canvas. Photographs: Tommy McNabb.

MIRO ART INC.

ROMAN KUJAWA ■ 704A LOCUST STREET ■ MOUNT VERNON, NY 10552
TEL 914-663-8350/914-237-6306 ■ FAX 914-663-8360 ■ E-MAIL MROMANK@EARTHLINK.NET

204

Pool House. Photograph: Richard Trabka.

KATHRYN PALMER

K.P. MURALS ■ 19748 LEITERSBURG PIKE ■ HAGERSTOWN, MD 21742
TEL 866-576-8725 (TOLL FREE) ■ WWW.D2MEDIA.COM/KP

205

Top: *Interpretation of Sebastiano Ricci's Punishment of Cupid*, ceiling mural, 2001, Old Library Building, Hagerstown, MD, 12' x 12'. Bottom left: *Interpretation of Monet's Woman with a Parasol*, wall mural, 2000, Hagerstown, MD, acrylic, 6' x 8'. Bottom right: *Peacocks*, fireplace screen, 2001, Hagerstown, MD, 3' x 3.5'.

Custom Design: Collage

ARTIST
Cheryl Holz,
Aurora, Illinois

PROJECT
Serenity, 1999, mixed media

COMMISSIONED FOR
Private residence, Illinois

TIMELINE
3 months

DIMENSIONS
22" x 70" x 2"

When Cheryl Holz creates a custom design, she makes it a truly personal reflection of her client. *Serenity,* which was one of her earliest commissions, is no exception. Commissioned by a husband and wife for their new home, it represents a marriage of individuals and the things they value and enjoy. The left panel reflects the husband's interests, including cigar labels, tax accounting sheets and academic references. The right side highlights interests of the wife: the first piece of sheet music she learned to play and a piece of her grandmother's lace. The center panel represents those interests that are common to both, while the "Serenity Prayer" runs across the entire piece. ■ Though Holz met with the couple beforehand, the resulting artwork was a true surprise; neither husband nor wife saw any drawings or samples beforehand. Needless to say, Holz was relieved when the couple loved their new piece: "She was really moved," Holz reports of the wife. "She loved it." ■ It is this sense of creating something truly meaningful that is most gratifying for Holz. "Commissions can be really difficult—like working with someone standing over your shoulder. But it's gratifying to know that my clients were truly involved in the creation of the collage when I incorporate things they value."

CITY ARTS/G. BYRON PECK

PECK STUDIOS ■ 1857 LAMONT STREET NW ■ WASHINGTON, DC 20010
TEL/FAX 202-331-1966 ■ E-MAIL BYRONPECK@EARTHLINK.NET ■ WWW.PECKSTUDIOS.COM ■ WWW.CITYARTSDC.ORG

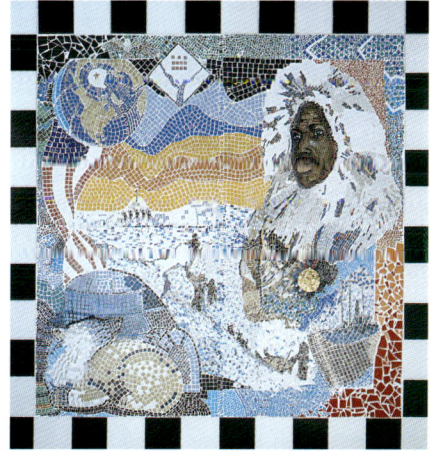

207

Top left: *General Wallace* mural, Ottawa II, 2002, Keim® paint, 30' x 60'. Top right: *Matthew Henson* mosaic, 2002, 8' x 8' Photograph: Greg Staley.
Center and bottom: *George Washington* murals, 2002, Mt. Vernon Estate, VA, acrylic, 8' x 20'. Photographs: Greg Staley.

JOHN PUGH

PO BOX 1332 ■ LOS GATOS, CA 95031 ■ TEL 408-353-3370 ■ FAX 408-353-1223
E-MAIL JOHN@ARTOFJOHNPUGH.COM ■ WWW.ARTOFJOHNPUGH.COM

208

Top: *Light Walk* (left half of mural), Palo Alto Medical Foundation, CA, 6' x 26'. Center left: *Light Walk* (trompe l'oeil detail). Center right: *Gates of Opa Locka II* (partial view), state building, Miami, FL, 10' x 18'. Bottom: *Path Around Son*, mural in main lobby, El Camino Hospital, Mountain View, CA, 10' x 32'. Photographs: Brian Brumley.

MILLENNIUM MURALS / MILLING AROUND

ZALUCHA STUDIO, LLC ■ 119 SOUTH SECOND STREET ■ MOUNT HOREB, WI 53572
TEL 866-881-8509 (TOLL FREE) / 608-437-7880 ■ FAX 608-437-2250 ■ E-MAIL INFO@EMILL.COM ■ WWW.EMILL.COM

209

Top: *Leaf-Bordered Sky*, 2003, Burn Center, University of Wisconsin Hospital and Clinics, vinyl on tile, 46' x 32', available for installation in other venues.
Bottom: *Madison Scenes*, 2002, Lakeside Cafeteria, University of Wisconsin Hospital and Clinics, hand-painted acrylic on vinyl panels, 50' wall. Photograph: Joe De Maio.

Paintings, Prints & Drawings

BOB BROWN STUDIO ■ 2725 TERRY LAKE ROAD ■ FORT COLLINS, CO 80524
TEL/FAX 970-224-5473 ■ E-MAIL BOBBROWN-ARTIST@ATT.NET

#61 Yolavivia, 2002, acrylic, 30" x 38".

BRIDGET BUSUTIL

BUSUTIL IMPRESSIONS, LLC ■ 1130 PIEDMONT AVENUE ■ ATLANTA, GA 30309
TEL 404-234-9375 ■ FAX 404-875-9155 ■ E-MAIL BUSUTILART@BELLSOUTH.NET ■ WWW.BRIDGETBUSUTIL.COM

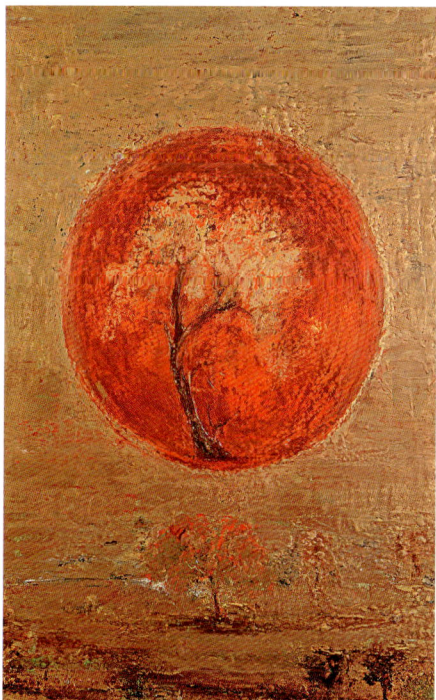

Top left: *Moon Tree*, 2001, encaustics on board, 26" x 40". Top right: *Rivers & Tides*, 2001, encaustics on wood, 40" x 30".
Bottom: *Blistering Heat*, 2001, encaustics on canvas, 40" x 36".

MARGARET-ANN CLEMENTE

ART FOR THE PLANET ■ 519 SPINDRIFT WAY ■ HALF MOON BAY, CA, 94019
TEL/FAX 650-712-0572 ■ E-MAIL MACLEMENTE@USEMAIL.COM ■ WWW.ART4THEPLANET.COM

214

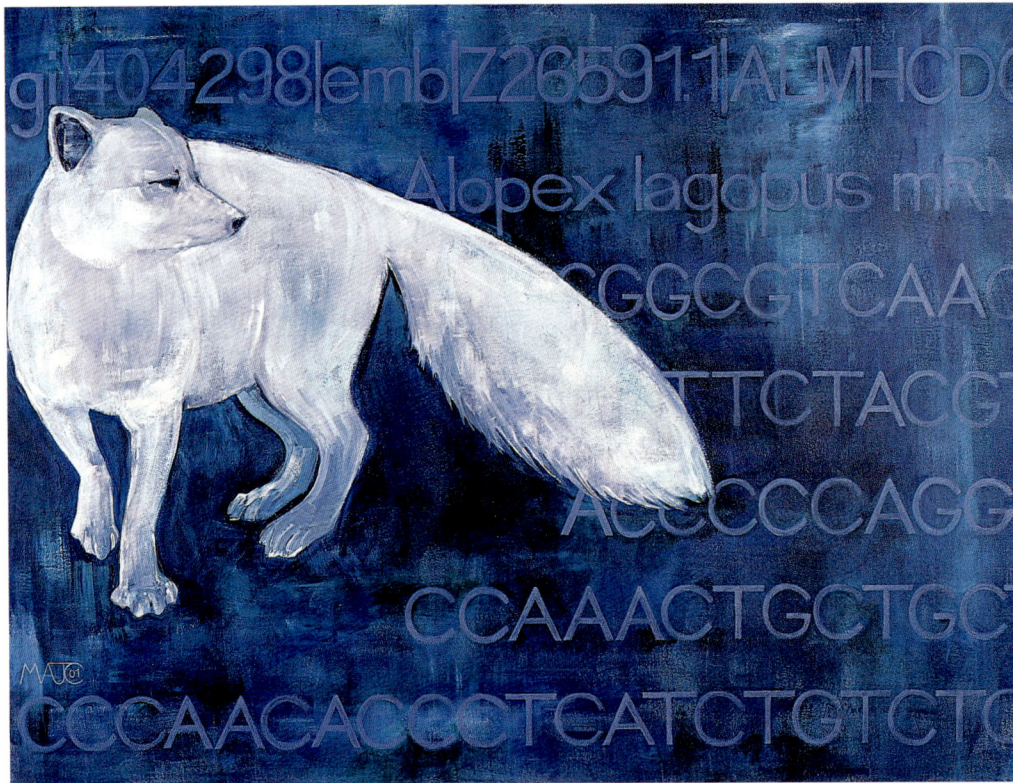

Top: *Alopex Lagopus* (arctic fox), *with Genetic Code*, 2001, Damasco & Associates, acrylic on wrap-around canvas, 30" x 40" x 1.5".
Bottom: *Absolution #16*, 2002, acrylic and pastel on wrap-around canvas, 8" x 10" x 1.5". Photographs: Michael Wong.

PAMELA COSPER

4439 ROLLING PINE DRIVE ■ WEST BLOOMFIELD, MI 48323
TEL 248-366-9569 ■ E-MAIL PAMELACOSPER@HOTMAIL.COM ■ WWW.GO.TO/PCOSPER

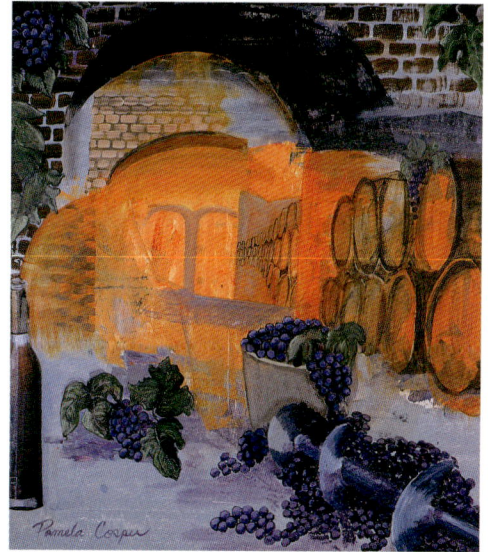

215

Top: *Chinese Columns*, acrylic, 59" x 32". Bottom left: *Wine Cellar*, acrylic, 30" x 20".
Bottom right: *Wine Heaven*, acrylic, 32" x 35". Photographs: Tomiko Gumbleton.

KATHRYN JACOBI

654 COPELAND COURT ■ SANTA MONICA, CA 90405 ■ TEL 310-399-8423 ■ FAX 310-399-5350
E-MAIL KATHRYNJACOBI@ADELPHIA.NET ■ WWW.KATHRYNJACOBI.COM

216

Portrait of Anna #1, 2002, oil on panel, 36" x 24". Photograph: H. van Pelt.

KEN ELLIOTT

250 LEAD KING DRIVE ■ CASTLE ROCK, CO 80108
TEL/FAX 303-814-1122 ■ E-MAIL ELLIOTTKC@EARTHLINK.NET ■ WWW.KENELLIOTT.COM

217

Top: *Yellow Trees*, oil on linen, 24" x 36".
Bottom: *Evening Glow*, giclee print, limited edition of 195, 11" x 11", 17" x 17" or 28" x 28", plus 3-inch white borders.

Custom Design: Tapestry

Barney Taxel

ARTIST
Martha Roediger,
Portland, Maine

PROJECT
Sinusoidal Rhythm, 2001, fiber

COMMISSIONED FOR
Agnar Pytte Center for
Science Education and Research,
Case Western Reserve University,
Cleveland, Ohio

TIMELINE
4 months

DIMENSIONS
3' × 12' × 3"

Martha Roediger did not expect her 1999 solo exhibition in Cleveland, Ohio, to lead to her first public art commission. But an anonymous donor to Case Western Reserve University (and a former graduate of the school) saw Roediger's work at the exhibition and knew immediately that it would be perfect for the university's new science center. ■ The artist admits that although she had completed commissions in the past for private residences and corporations, there was something a little bit formidable about such a large project for a public setting. "I knew I would have to do this kind of piece sometime, but there were definitely moments of trepidation," she notes. The final piece, Sinusoidal Rhythm, was based on a design she had already conceptualized, but it took two trips to Cleveland with color samples and models in tow before she could really get down to work. ■ Her moments of trepidation paid off when she saw her piece installed at the dedication ceremony. More than relief, Roediger says she felt truly happy when she saw her piece in its new space. "It was enormously satisfying to see the way my work enriched the space and complemented the architecture. And the donor and the university officials were pleased too." Now Roediger is eager to do her next public commission—and this time, she thinks, with a little extra confidence.

JOHN PETER GLOVER

JP GLOVER FINE ART ■ 108 LAKELAND DRIVE ■ MARS, PA 16046
TEL/FAX 724-538-8879 ■ E-MAIL JOHN@JPGLOVERART.COM ■ WWW.JPGLOVERART.COM

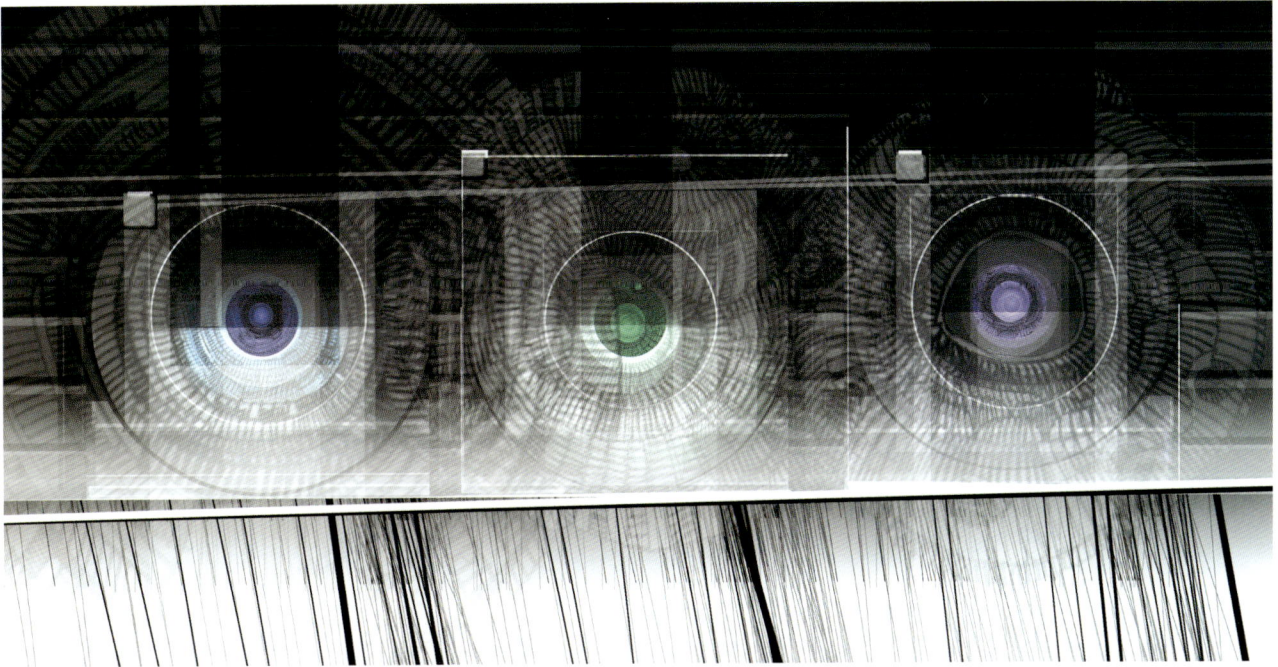

219

Top: *Triple Ion Module*, 2001, pigmented digital output, 40" × 25", limited edition of 100. Bottom: *Aurora with Spheres*, 2001, pigmented digital output, 46" × 36", limited edition of 100.

LISA KESLER FINE ART

LISA KESLER ■ 12015 THIRD AVENUE NW ■ SEATTLE, WA 98177
TEL 206-782-3730 ■ FAX 206-784-3304 ■ E-MAIL LISA@LKESLER.COM ■ WWW.LKESLER.COM

220

Top: *Structural Rhythm 3*, 2003, mixed media on paper, 24" x 36". Bottom left: *Opening Night*, 2002, hand-painted linoleum block print, 24" x 18". Bottom right: *Tropical 2*, 2002, hand-painted linoleum block print, 19" x 15". Photographs: Art & Soul Photography.

ALEXANDER KUBAISKI

ALEXANDER KUBAISKI STUDIO ■ 3646 FREDONIA DRIVE ■ HOLLYWOOD, CA 90068
TEL/FAX 323-876-8828 ■ E-MAIL KUBAISKI@SBCGLOBAL.NET ■ WWW.KUBAISKI.COM

221

Top left: *26/Cat 4*, signed giclee on canvas, 32" x 20". Top right: *31/Cat 2*, signed giclee on canvas, 29" x 44".
Bottom: *Echo Sound*, 19" x 38", signed and numbered serigraph, edition of 285.

SILJA TALIKKA LAHTINEN

SILJA'S FINE ART STUDIO ■ 5220 SUNSET TRAIL ■ MARIETTA, GA 30068 ■ TEL 770-993-3409 ■ FAX 770-992-0350
E-MAIL PENTEC02@BELLSOUTH.NET ■ WWW.WARDNASSE.ORG/3000P.HTM

222

Top: *Medicine Woman's Hide*, 2002, Nuutti Galleria, Virrat, Finland, acrylic on canvas, 32" × 32".
Bottom: *Pale Moon*, 2002, artist's collection, acrylic on canvas, 32" × 32".

MICHELLE LINDBLOM

MICKART STUDIO ■ 3316 HACKBERRY STREET ■ BISMARCK, ND 58503 ■ TEL/FAX 701-258-2992
E-MAIL MICKART@BIS.MIDCO.NET ■ WWW.MICK-ART.COM

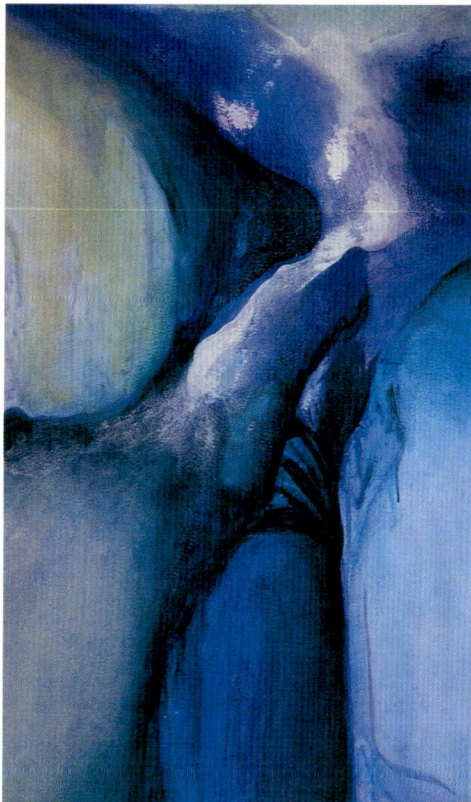

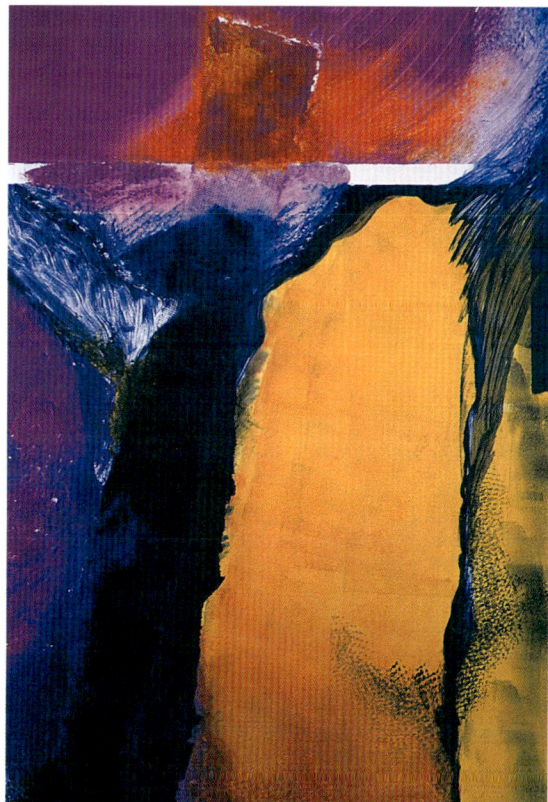

223

Top left: *Thrust*, 2001, monotype, 24" x 15". Top right: *Evolving Essence*, 2000, acrylic on canvas, 50" x 40".
Bottom right: *Resurrection from Pain*, 1999, monotype, 24" x 15". Bottom left: *Spiritual Revelation*, 2000, acrylic on paper, 30" x 22".

224

Portrait commission, 2002, Vence, France, oil on canvas, 24" x 20". Photograph: Daniel Portnoy.

AMOS MILLER

5741 SW 84 STREET ■ MIAMI, FL 33143
TEL 305-668-3536 ■ E-MAIL AMILLER1307@EARTHLINK.NET

225

Portrait commission, 2002, Vence, France, oil on canvas, 24" x 20". Photograph: Daniel Portnoy.

DAVID MILTON

4750 DEGOVIA AVENUE ■ WOODLAND HILLS, CA 91364
TEL 818-224-2164 ■ FAX 818-224-2163 ■ E-MAIL DAVID@DAVIDMILTON.COM ■ WWW.DAVIDMILTON.COM

226

Top: *Transparent Scream*, mixed media on canvas, 102" x 67".
Bottom left: *Cosmic Flora*, oil on paper, 30" x 22". Bottom right: *Shooting Star*, oil pastel on paper, 16" x 14".

JAMES C. NAGLE

JAMES C. NAGLE FINE ART ■ 1136 EAST COMMONWEALTH PLACE ■ CHANDLER, AZ 85225-5716
TEL 480-963-8195 ■ FAX 480-857-3188 (CALL FIRST) ■ E-MAIL EXTRAICE@MSN.COM ■ WWW.JCNAGLEFINEART.COM

227

Spectres, 2000, acrylic on canvas, 68" x 60". Photograph: Craig Smith.

MICHAEL-BRIAN NORRIS

PO BOX 160 ■ GRIMSLEY, TN 38565 ■ TEL 888-510-3758 (TOLL FREE)
MBNORRIS@MBNORRIS.COM ■ ■ WWW.MBNORRIS.COM

Top: *The Misadventures of the California Blue Rhino,* 2002, private residence, San Francisco, CA, mixed media on canvas, 48" × 36".
Bottom: *Even Alligators Get the Measles,* 2001, private residence, Tokyo, Japan, mixed media on wood, 12" × 24".

MURIEL VAUGHN

MOOD MOMENTS ■ 6745 EAST SUPERSTITION SPRINGS ■ MESA, AZ 85206
TEL 602-403-2213 ■ E-MAIL JZTIME@COX.NET

229

Top: *Swirling Tree*, 2000, acrylic on canvas, 24" x 16". Bottom: *Out There*, 1997, acrylic on canvas, 24" x 48". Photographs: Finer Image Editions.

RHONA LK SCHONWALD

HISTORIC SAVAGE MILL ■ 8600 FOUNDRY STREET ■ CARDING BUILDING #205 ■ SAVAGE, MD 20763
TEL 410-880-4118 ■ WWW.RHONALKSCHONWALD.COM

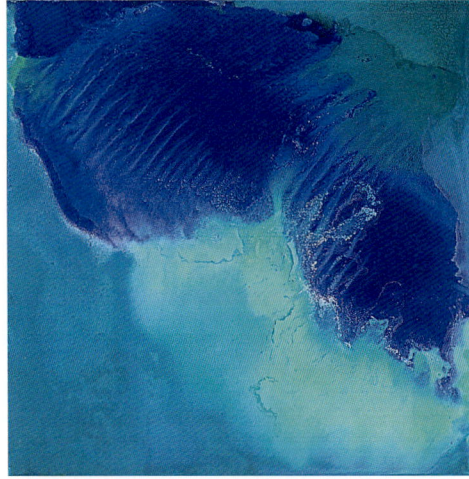

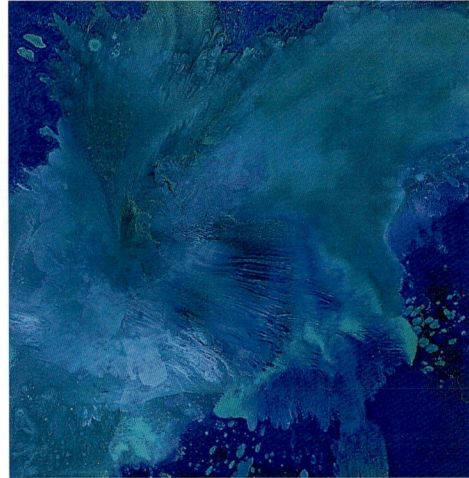

230

Color Poems: Blue (installation piece), 2003, each painting: 24" x 24". Photographs: Straight Shots, Ellicott City, MD.

231

Top: *The Sky Beyond*, 2002, oil stick on paper, 28" x 39". Bottom left: *Apricot Trees*, 2001, oil stick on canvas, 32" x 34".
Bottom right: *In the Hothouse*, 1998, oil stick on canvas, 40" x 40". Photographs: Steve Perry.

ROSENFELD

16 EAST 96TH STREET #4B ■ NEW YORK, NY 10128 ■ TEL 212-996-5013 ■ FAX 212-360-1774
E-MAIL INFO@ROSENFELDART.COM ■ WWW.ROSENFELDART.COM

232

Top: *Pink Sand, Blue Water*, acrylic on linen, 26" x 38". Bottom: *Town Beach*, acrylic on linen, 34" x 50". Photographs: Ed Watkins.

CASSIE TONDRO

1348 GRANT STREET ■ SANTA MONICA, CA 90405
TEL 310-452-2964 ■ E-MAIL CASSIE@CASSIETONDRO.COM ■ WWW.CASSIETONDRO.COM

Top left: *Sun Dance*, 2002, acrylic on canvas, 36" x 36". Right: *Red Sky at Night*, 2003, acrylic on canvas, 48" x 24".
Bottom left: *Blue Moon*, 2002, acrylic on canvas, 36" x 36".

PAM PRINCE WALKER

C/O IMAGE SPIRIT ■ 137 RIDGEWOOD PLACE ■ MARION, VA 24354
TEL 276-783-2887 ■ E-MAIL IMAGES@IMAGESPIRIT.COM ■ WWW.IMAGESPIRIT.COM

San Francisco Chinatown, acrylic collage on paper, 25.5" x 19.5". Photograph: Michael Harrington.

Printed in China © 2003 GUILD LLC: The Sourcebook of Architectural & Interior Art

PAM PRINCE WALKER

C/O IMAGE SPIRIT ■ 137 RIDGEWOOD PLACE ■ MARION, VA 24354
TEL 276-783-2887 ■ E-MAIL IMAGES@IMAGESPIRIT.COM ■ WWW.IMAGESPIRIT.COM

235

Top: *Jazz Combo New Orleans*, acrylic on canvas, 28" × 22". Bottom left: *Study in Brown, Opus II (Guitar)*, acrylic on canvas, 40" × 28".
Bottom right: *The Popcorn Wagon*, acrylic collage on canvas, 40" × 30". Photographs: Michael Harrington.

SUSAN WEINBERG

1605-1/2 OCEAN FRONT WALK ■ SANTA MONICA, CA 90401 ■ TEL/FAX 310-392-5042
E-MAIL INFINITYSTUDIO@AOL.COM ■ WWW.GLASSUMBRELLA.COM

Top: *Columbia River Gorge*, oil on canvas giclee, 24" x 36".
Bottom: *The Georgian*, watercolor giclee, 22" x 29".

Printed in China © 2003 GUILD.LLC · *The Sourcebook of Architectural & Interior Art*

YOSHI HAYASHI

255 KANSAS STREET, SUITE 330 ■ SAN FRANCISCO, CA 94103 ■ TEL 415-552-0755/415-924-9224 ■ FAX 415-552-0755
E-MAIL YOSHIHAYASHI@ATT.NET ■ WWW.YOSHIHAYASHI.COM

237

Top: *Silver Moon*, 2001, silver, copper leaf and oil paint, 48" × 72". Bottom: *Waterfall*, 1998, silver leaf and oil paint, 48" × 96". Photographs: Ira D. Schrank.

Fine Art Photography

JIM DeLUTES

JIM DeLUTES PHOTOGRAPHY ■ PO BOX 1634 ■ BOULDER, CO 80306
TEL/FAX 303-678-9089 ■ E-MAIL JDPHOTOS@EARTHLINK.NET ■ WWW.JDLPHOTOS.COM

240

Top: *Calla Bouquet*, 1999, various sizes available. Bottom: *Gold Rush*, 2002, various sizes available.

FRANK DIENST

FRANK DIENST PHOTOGRAPHY ■ 3940 PINETOP BOULEVARD ■ TITUSVILLE, FL 32796
TEL 321-268-0386 ■ FAX 321-268-3719 ■ E-MAIL MD1@BREVARD.NET ■ WWW.FRANKDIENST.COM

241

Top left: *Untitled,*© 2000, bromoil, sizes up to 16" × 20". Top right: *Untitled,*© 2001, platinum, sizes up to 16" × 20".
Bottom left: *Untitled,*© 1999, gelatin silver (gold tone), sizes up to 28" × 28". Bottom right: *Untitled,*© 2002, gum dichromate, sizes up to 16" × 20".

CALI GOREVIC

377 LANE GATE ROAD ■ COLD SPRING, NY 10516
TEL 845-265-4625 ■ FAX 845-265-4620 ■ CALIG@MINDSPRING.COM ■ WWW.CALIGOREVIC.COM

Top left: *Twig Tunnel 2*. Top right: *Dinner Bells 3*. Bottom: *On My Way Home*. All photographs available as silver or giclee prints.

DAR HORN

UNION ART WORKS ■ 402 WEST 5TH STREET ■ SAN PEDRO, CA 90731
TEL 310-833-1282 ■ FAX 310-833-1592 ■ E-MAIL DAR@DARHORN.COM ■ WWW.DARHORN.COM

243

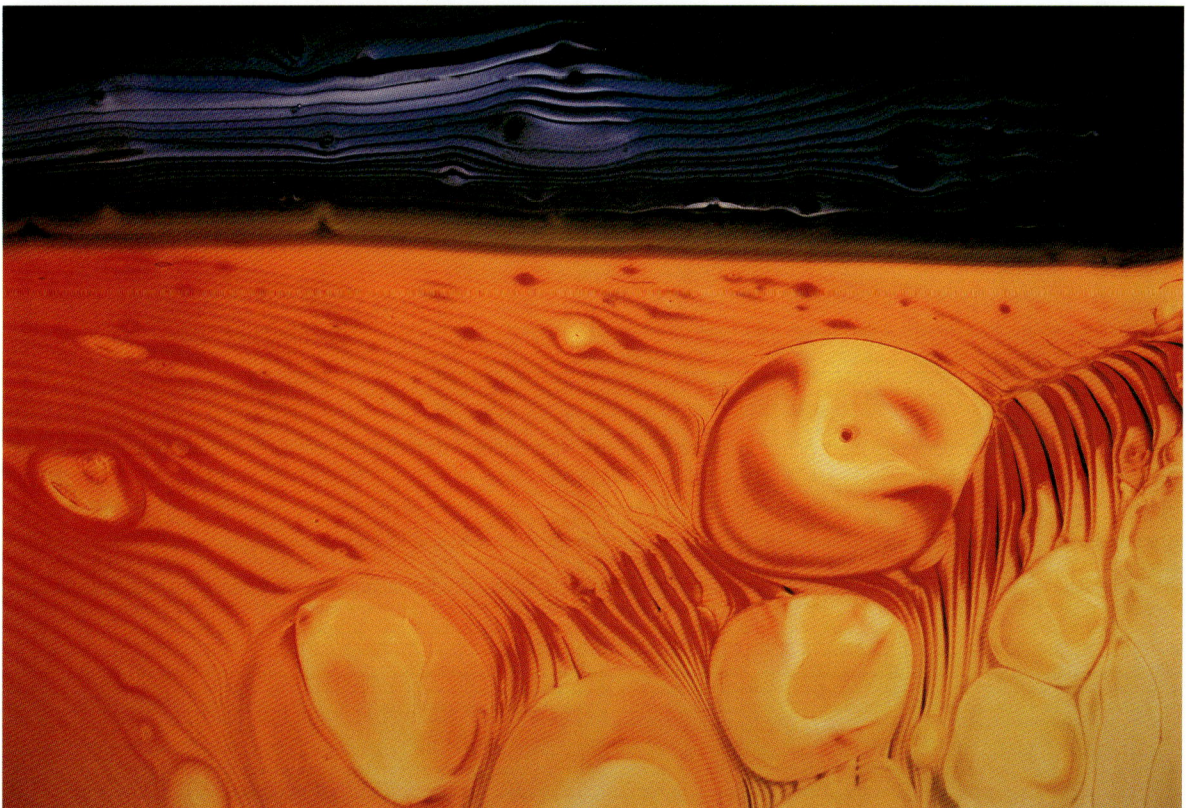

Top: *Stardust*, 2002, Ilfochrome™ print on aluminum panel, 20" x 30". Bottom: *Fire Fall*, 2002, Ilfochrome™ print on aluminum panel, 20" x 30".

TALLI ROSNER-KOZUCH

PHO-TAL INC. ■ 15 NORTH SUMMIT STREET ■ TENAFLY, NJ 07670
TEL 201-569-3199 ■ FAX 201-569-3392 ■ E-MAIL TAL@PHOTAL.COM ■ WWW.PHOTAL.COM

Top left: *Tulip Male*, 1997. Top right: Head of *Amaryllis*, 1997. Bottom: *Agav*, 1997.

JD MARSTON

JD MARSTON PHOTOGRAPHY ■ 13 BACA GRANT WAY ■ PO BOX 294 ■ CRESTONE, CO 81131
TEL/FAX 719-256-4162/800-253-4701 ■ E-MAIL JD@JDMARSTON.COM ■ WWW.JDMARSTON.COM

Top left: *Wheeler Geologic Site*, 1989, silver gelatin photographic print, 8" × 10" to 20" × 24". Top right: *Cedar Woman*, 1990, silver gelatin photographic print, 8" × 10" to 20" × 24".
Bottom: *Snake River and Mt. Moran*, 1989, silver gelatin photographic print, 8" × 10" to 20" × 24".

DANA MONTLACK

STUDIO MONTLACK ■ 1204 EMERALD STREET ■ SAN DIEGO, CA 92109 ■ TEL 858-342-5889
E-MAIL DANA@STUDIOMONTLACK.COM ■ WWW.STUDIOMONTLACK.COM

246

Top left: *1-13*, iris print, 37" × 29". Top right: *1-15*, iris print, 37" × 29". Bottom left: *1-2*, iris print, 37" × 29". Bottom right: *1-3*, iris print, 37" × 29".

LEN MORRIS

LEONARD MORRIS ■ TEL 917-992-3313 ■ FAX 718-636-6021
E-MAIL LENMORRIS@EARTHLINK.NET ■ WWW.LENMORRIS.NET

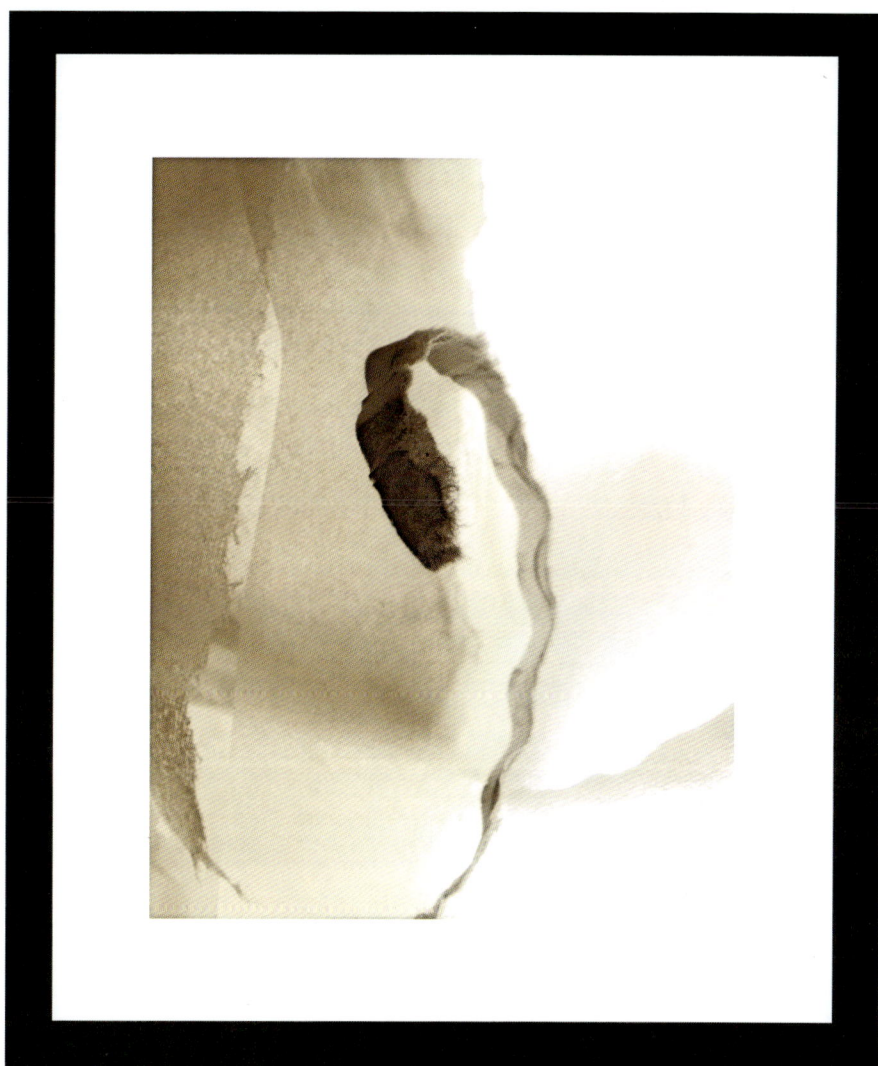

Beginnings, from the *Paper Plate* series, photograph of a paper plate fragment on paper background, 16" x 20", limited edition of 125.

CHRISTOPHER PETRICH

COOLPHOTO ■ 3741 NORTH 29TH STREET ■ TACOMA, WA 98407
TEL 253-752-4664 ■ FAX 253-276-0116 ■ E-MAIL CPETRICH@COOLPHOTO.COM ■ WWW.COOLPHOTO.COM

Top left: *Old Glory Through the Crab Apple Tree at Stadium High School*, 2001, Tacoma, WA, gelatin silver, 24" x 20".
Top right: *Old Woman Crabbing*, 2002, Tacoma, WA, gelatin silver, 8" x 10". Bottom: *Entering, Child's Hand on the Door*, 1990, Bridal Veil, OR, gelatin silver, 8" x 10".

MARV POULSON

IMAGEDANCER ■ 3631 SOUTH CAROLYN STREET ■ SALT LAKE CITY, UT 84106 ■ TEL 801-558-0875
E-MAIL MARV@IMAGEDANCER.NET ■ WWW.IMAGEDANCER.NET

Top left: *Sunset Tree*, 1979, Mt. Moriah, giclee print, 30" × 20". Top center: *Double Arch*, 2002, giclee print, 20" × 30".
Top right: *Desert Ice*, 1982, Canyon Lands, giclee print, 30" × 20". Bottom: *Dream Leaves*, 1985, Pine Creek, giclee print, 20" × 30".

VICKI REED

VICKI REED PHOTOGRAPHY ■ N66 W5594 COLUMBIA ROAD ■ CEDARBURG, WI 53012
TEL 262-377-1197 ■ FAX 262-377-9273 ■ E-MAIL TINTER8X10@AOL.COM ■ WWW.VICKIREED.COM

250

Top left: *Table*, hand-colored photograph, 13" x 9". Top right: *Dancing Light*, hand-colored photograph, 13" x 9". Bottom: *Maine Chairs*, hand-colored photograph, 9" x 13".

WOODLAND STUDIOS

GARY WALKER ■ CINDY LOU HOESLY ■ 4378 JORDAN DRIVE #4 ■ McFARLAND, WI 53558
TEL 608-576-6868 ■ FAX 608-835-8006 ■ E-MAIL GWALKER@WOODLAND-STUDIOS.COM ■ WWW.WOODLAND-STUDIOS.COM

Top left: *Spirit of the Forest*, mixed media on giclee print. Top right: *Hotel California*, mixed media on giclee print. Bottom: *Fall Calm Lake*, mixed media on giclee print.

Custom Design: Architectural Glass

Joan Baron

ARTIST
Harriet Hyams,
Palisades, New York

PROJECT
The Joshua Window (detail) and *The David Window*, 1996-1998,
stained glass with sandblasted and painted Hebrew lettering
glass fabrication by Wilmark Studios

COMMISSIONED FOR
Jewish Cadet Chapel at West Point Military Academy,
West Point, New York

TIMELINE
2 years

DIMENSIONS
32'H

The west windows of the Jewish Cadet Chapel at West Point were a long time coming for artist Harriet Hyams. The commission was awarded to her in 1996 as a result of a project she had completed in 1995. The architect for the earlier project loved Hyams' design and knew her work would be perfect for the chapel. ■ Representatives for the chapel were not initially sure what they wanted in terms of design. The three-story windows flanked the pipes of the chapel's organ, so Hyams proposed a musical theme depicting David's lyre and the trumpets of Joshua's Jericho. These stories feature two of the most famous Jewish generals of biblical history—subjects, all agreed, pertinent for a chapel at West Point. Cascading down the background of each window is the Torah, which, Hyams says, represents the stories being told from above. ■ Hyams visited the chapel many times to gauge the light, and experimented with various pieces of glass in her own home. "I put pieces of glass up in the west windows of my bedroom to see how the light would come through. I wanted to block out the hills behind the chapel's west windows, so I used the Palisades behind my own home as an opacity test for the glass." The experimentation was worth it when she saw the windows installed. "The windows looked beautiful—I wouldn't miss this installation for all the world."

EDDIE SOLOWAY

EDDIE SOLOWAY PHOTOGRAPHY ■ PO BOX 6745 ■ SANTA FE, NM 87502
TEL/FAX 505-466-6030 ■ E-MAIL SOLOWAY@ANATURALEYE.COM ■ WWW.ANATURALEYE.COM

253

Top: *Dawn*, from the *Gentle Edges* series.   Bottom: *Last Light, Winter Aspens*, from the *Forest Abstracts* series.

256

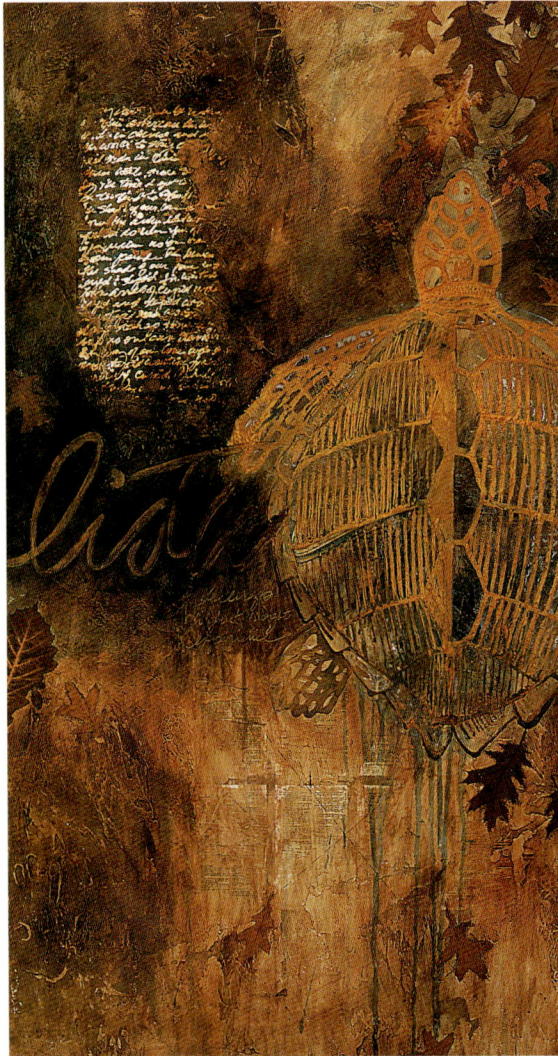

Top left: *Listen*, 2001, acrylic, plaster, copper, patina, leaves and bible pages on wood, 32" x 60". Photograph: Pete Cherwin. Top right: *Lurching Forward*, 2001, acrylic, plaster, eggshells, metal and leaves on wood, 24" x 28" x 3". Photograph: Pete Cherwin. Center: *Keeping Time*, 2001, acrylic, plaster, inks, birch bark, sheet music and graphite on wood, 24" x 36". Photograph: Pete Cherwin. Bottom: *Planet Groans*, 2001, acrylic, plaster, grasses and pine needles on wood, 60" x 32" x 2". Photograph: Dan Grych.

DEBORAH T. COLTER

PO BOX 1517 ■ EDGARTOWN, MA 02539
TEL 508-627-3829 ■ E-MAIL DTC@DEBORAHCOLTER.COM ■ WWW.DEBORAHCOLTER.COM

257

Top left: *Timely Arrival,* 2002, mixed media on paper, 30" × 22". Top right: *Fantasy Diversion,* 2002, mixed media on paper, 30" × 22".
Bottom left: *Atmospheric Marl,* 2002, mixed media on paper, 30" × 22". Bottom right: *Outlook Aligned,* 2002, mixed media on paper, 30" × 22". Photographs: Betsy Corsiglia.

TREMAIN SMITH

4520 LOCUST STREET ■ PHILADELPHIA, PA 19139
TEL 215-387-1869 ■ FAX 215-387-6337 ■ E-MAIL LOOK@TREMAINSMITH.COM ■ WWW.TREMAINSMITH.COM

258

Top: *Layers of My Ancestors*, 2003, oil, wax and collage on panel, 33" x 48". Bottom left: *Points of Power*, 2002, oil, wax and collage on panel, 22" x 26".
Bottom right: *At the Crossroads*, 2002, oil, wax and collage on panel, 40" x 48". Photographs: Joseph Painter.

259

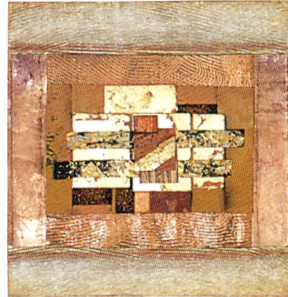

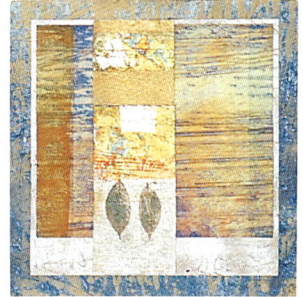

Top left: *Garden of Delight*, mixed media, 20" x 20". Top right: *Myths Suite*, mixed media, each: 20" x 20".
Bottom: *Narrative XX3*, mixed media, 30" x 40". Photographs: Adam Fulmer.

CHRISTINA ROE

FANTAN STUDIO ■ 2716 NORTH ADOLINE AVENUE ■ FRESNO, CA 93705
TEL 559-226-1533 ■ FAX 559-226-7490 ■ E-MAIL FANTANSTUDIO@YAHOO.COM

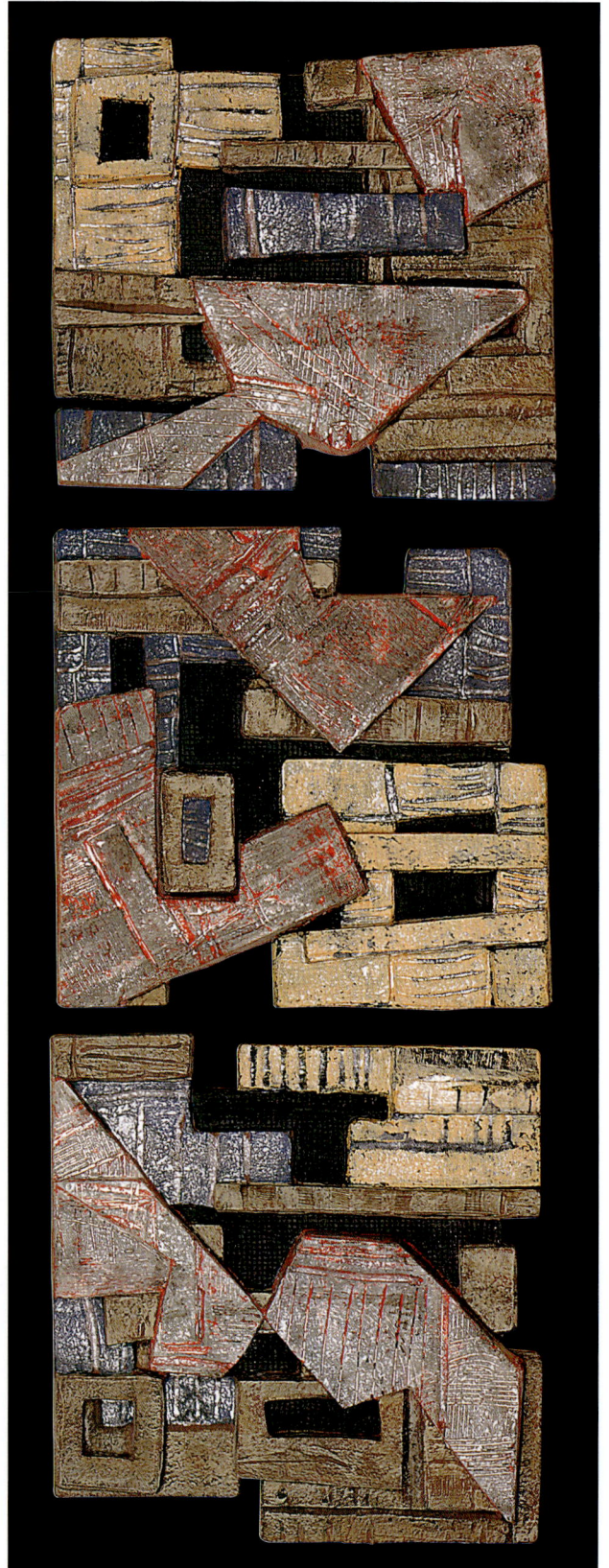

Top left: *Zig-Zag,* 2002, cast-paper relief, 28" x 49.5". Bottom left: *Portal,* 2001, cast-paper relief, 26.5" x 30".
Right: *Tripartite Stela,* 2002, cast-paper relief, 23.5" x 23", 22.5" x 23.5" and 21" x 24". Photographs: E.Z. Smith.

JOAN KOPCHIK

1335 STEPHEN WAY ■ SOUTHAMPTON, PA 18966-4349
TEL 215-322-1862 ■ FAX 215-322-5031 ■ E-MAIL JKOPCHIK@VOICENET.COM

Evocation, 2002, commission for private residence, East Hampton, NY, cast handmade paper and river stones, 4'W x 8'H. Photograph: Gary J. Mamay.

NEW AGE ARTWORKS

THOMAS MATCHIE ■ 140 HUNTINGTON ROAD ■ DELAFIELD, WI 53018
TEL 262-646-2945 ■ E-MAIL NEWAGEARTWORKS@HOTMAIL.COM

262

Top: *Colors Uncoordinated*, 2003, acrylics on drywall compound, 22" × 42.75".
Bottom: *Blob on the Edge*, 2003, acrylics on drywall compound/plaster, 24.5" × 48". Photographs: Raymond Llanas.

BARBARA BROTHERTON

BARBRO DESIGNS ■ 1006 OAK VIEW DRIVE ■ IONE, CA 95640
TEL 209-274-6248 ■ FAX 209-274-6246 ■ E-MAIL BARBRO38@EARTHLINK.NET

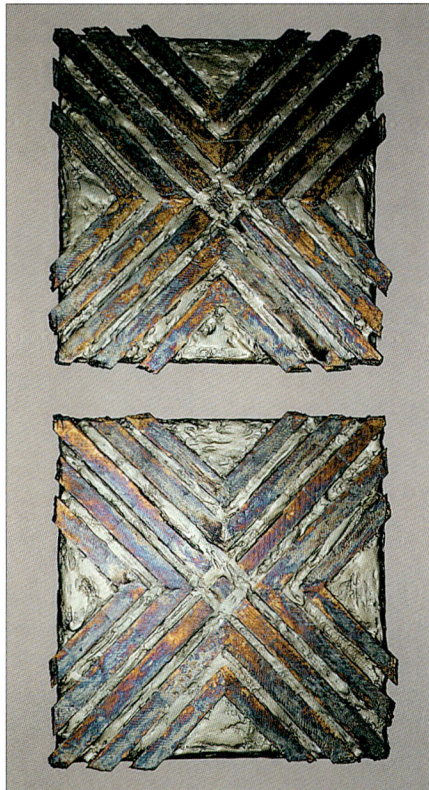

Top: *Allende Flying Wall*, 2002, wood, poured stone and silver leaf with acid patina, 21"H x 42"W.
Bottom left: *Abstract #4*, wood, poured stone and silver leaf with acid patina, 2.5' x 2.5' (each panel).
Bottom right: *Small Japanese Paths*, 2000, wood, poured stone and silver leaf with acid patina, 54"H x 18"W (each panel), personal collection of former president Bill Clinton.

SUSAN SINGLETON

AZO ■ 728 GRINDSTONE HARBOR ■ PO BOX 39 ■ ORCAS, WA 98280
TEL 360-376-5898 ■ FAX 360-376-5519 ■ E-MAIL AZO@ROCKISLAND.COM ■ WWW.AZOART.COM

Top: *Golden Excavations* (detail). Bottom: *Golden Excavations*, paper constructions, 2002,
Mitsubishi Shiodome Rotunda, Tokyo, Japan, washi paper with metallic leafing, each: 36"W x 72"H.

RED WOLF

RED WOLF FINE ART ■ PO BOX 396 ■ LAYTONVILLE, CA 95454 ■ TEL 707-984-7003 ■ FAX 707-984-9377
E-MAIL REDWOLF@REDWOLFFINEART.COM ■ WWW.REDWOLFFINEART.COM

265

Nagoya Marriott Associa Hotel, 52nd-floor Sky Lounge ceiling art, 2000, JR Towers,
Nagoya, Japan, mixed-media thermoset plastic painting on 31 sandwiched aluminum panels, 19' × 47'. Photograph: P. Mealin Photography.

LAURIE WOHL

236 WEST 27TH STREET SUITE 801 ■ NEW YORK, NY 10001
TEL 646-486-0586 ■ E-MAIL LAURIEWOHL@HOTMAIL.COM

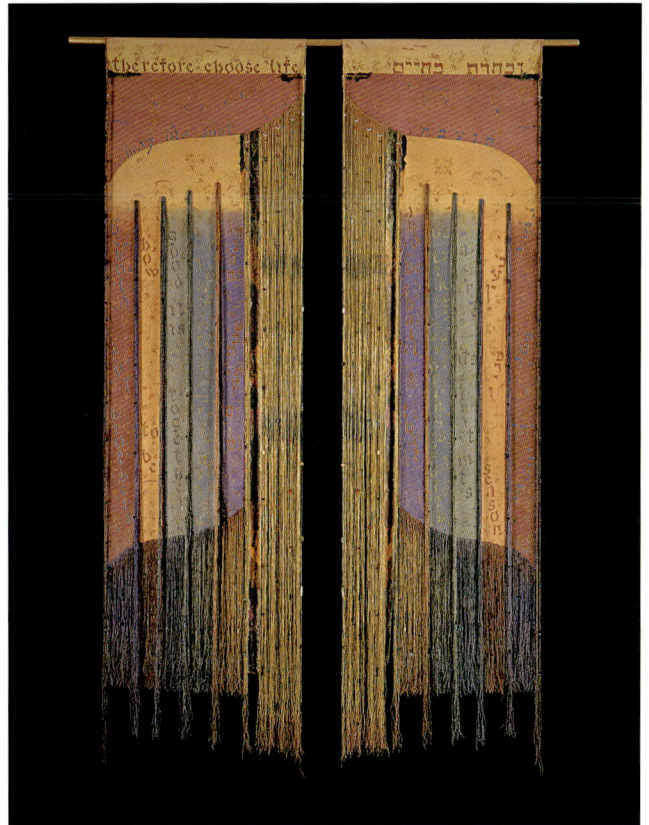

Left: *Well of Living Waters*, 2000, collection of Donald and Betsy Landis, White Plains, NY, Unweaving® with mixed media, 3'W × 1'D × 82"L. Photograph: Tom Van Eynde.
Top right: *Psalms*, 2002, Fourth Presbyterian Church, Chicago, IL, Unweaving® with mixed media, two panels, each: 9.5'L × 2'W. Photograph: Tom Van Eynde.
Bottom right: *Rainbow Wings*, 2002, Catholic Theological Union, Chicago, IL, Unweaving® with mixed media, 6'L × 4'W. Photograph: Eva Heyd.

JUNCO SATO POLLACK

11 POLO DRIVE NE ■ ATLANTA, GA 30309
TEL/FAX 404-892-2155 ■ E-MAIL JUNCO@JUNCOSATOPOLLACK.COM ■ WWW.JUNCOSATOPOLLACK.COM

268

Top left: *Locus Improvisation,* 2000, polyester and metallic silk, 6' x 10'. Photograph: Dennis Baus. Top right: *Origami #2,* 1998, dye sublimation on polyester organza, 25" x 25". Photograph: Departure. Bottom: *Locus Improvisation,* 2001, Hotel Mandarin Oriental, Miami, FL, 7' x 15'. Photograph: George Apostolidis.

KAREN URBANEK

314 BLAIR AVENUE ■ PIEDMONT, CA 94611-4004
TEL 510-654-0685 ■ FAX 510-654-2790 ■ E-MAIL KRNURBANEK@AOL.COM

269

Top: *Reaches 7*, 2002, naturally dyed silk fiber, polymer, 27" x 130", may be hung horizontally or vertically. Bottom left: *An Orb 5*, 2003, naturally dyed silk fiber, polymer, 34" x 15". Bottom right: *An Orb 3*, 2002, naturally dyed silk fiber, polymer, 53" x 40". Photographs: Don Tuttle Photography.

SUSAN McGEHEE

METALLIC STRANDS ■ 540 23RD STREET ■ MANHATTAN BEACH, CA 90266
TEL 310-545-4112 ■ FAX 310-546-7152 ■ E-MAIL SUSAN@METALSTRANDS.COM ■ WWW.METALSTRANDS.COM

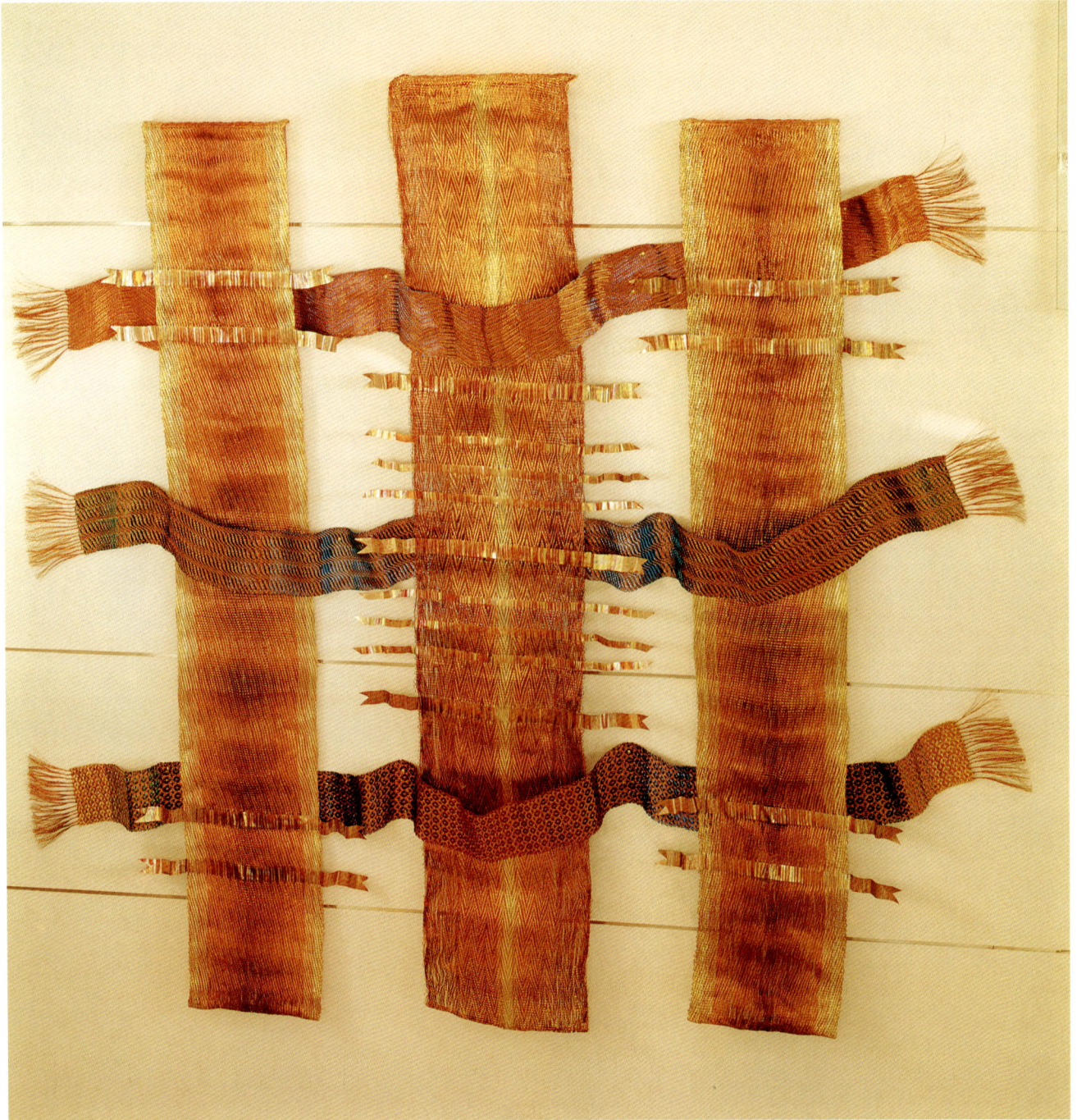

270

St. Paul Strands, 2002, Lawson Commons, St. Paul, MN, woven wire and metal, 11' x 11'. Photograph: Chris Faust.

JOHN SEARLES

SEARLESART ■ 642 SOUTH LOMBARD AVENUE ■ OAK PARK, IL 60304
TEL 708-222-8160 ■ E-MAIL JOHNSEARLES@AMERITECH.NET ■ WWW.SEARLESART.COM

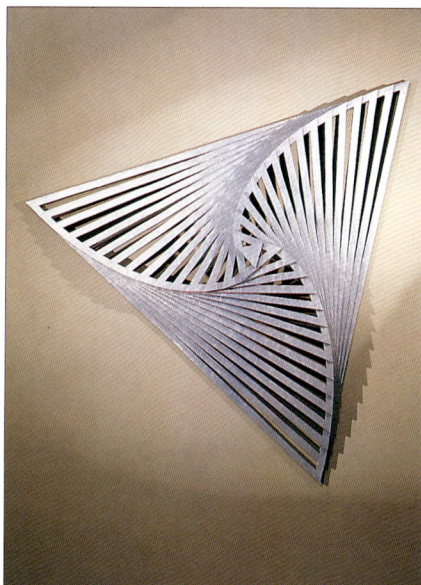

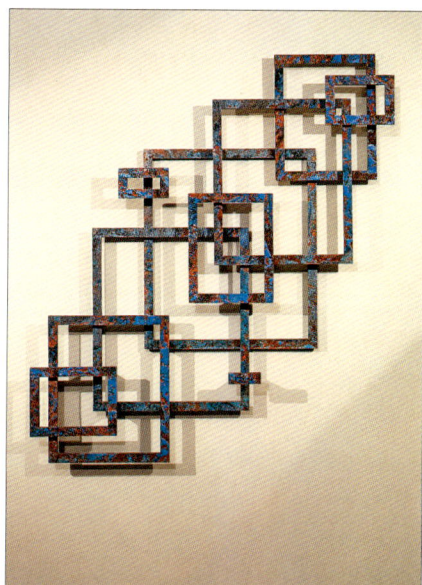

Top left: *Wavy Weaving*, 2003, copper with flame colors, 36" x 48" x 1". Top center: *Rotating Triangles*, 2003, aluminum, brushed finish, 55" x 55" x 55" x 8".
Top right: *Blue Rectangles*, 2002, copper with patina, 50" x 54" x 4". Bottom: *Thunderbird*, 2002, copper and brass with patina, 45" x 85" x 5".

SUSAN VENABLE

VENABLE STUDIO ■ 2323 FOOTHILL LANE ■ SANTA BARBARA, CA 93105 ■ TEL 805-884-4963 ■ FAX 805-884-4983
E-MAIL SUSAN@VENABLESTUDIO.COM ■ WWW.VENABLESTUDIO.COM

272

Top: *Sol Saga*, mixed media, 3' x 9'. Bottom: *Mystery Mambo*, mixed media, 4.5' x 10'. Photographs: William Nettles.

LINDA LEVITON

LINDA LEVITON SCULPTURE ■ 1011 COLONY WAY ■ COLUMBUS, OH 43235
TEL 614-433-7486 ■ E-MAIL GUILD@LINDALEVITON.COM ■ WWW.LINDALEVITON.COM

Top: *Three Red Vessels*, copper, oil and patina, each vessel: 30" × 20" × 9".
Bottom: *Circle Quilts: Winter/Spring*, copper and dye, each panel: 20" × 26" × 4". Photographs: Jerry Anthony.

NAOMI TAGINI

1902 COMSTOCK AVENUE ■ LOS ANGELES, CA 90025 ■ TEL 310-552-1877 ■ FAX 310-552-2679
E-MAIL NAOMI@NAOMITAGINI.COM ■ WWW.NAOMITAGINI.COM

274

Top: *Belize*, 2001, painted wood, 87" x 54". Bottom: *Uncut*, 2002, painted wood, 8' x 34", 72" x 72" or 72" x 36". Photographs: Claudio Tagini.

JEFF EASLEY

PO BOX 502 ■ WELLMAN, IA 52356 ■ TEL 319-646-2521 ■ FAX 319-628-4766
E-MAIL JEASLEY811@AOL.COM

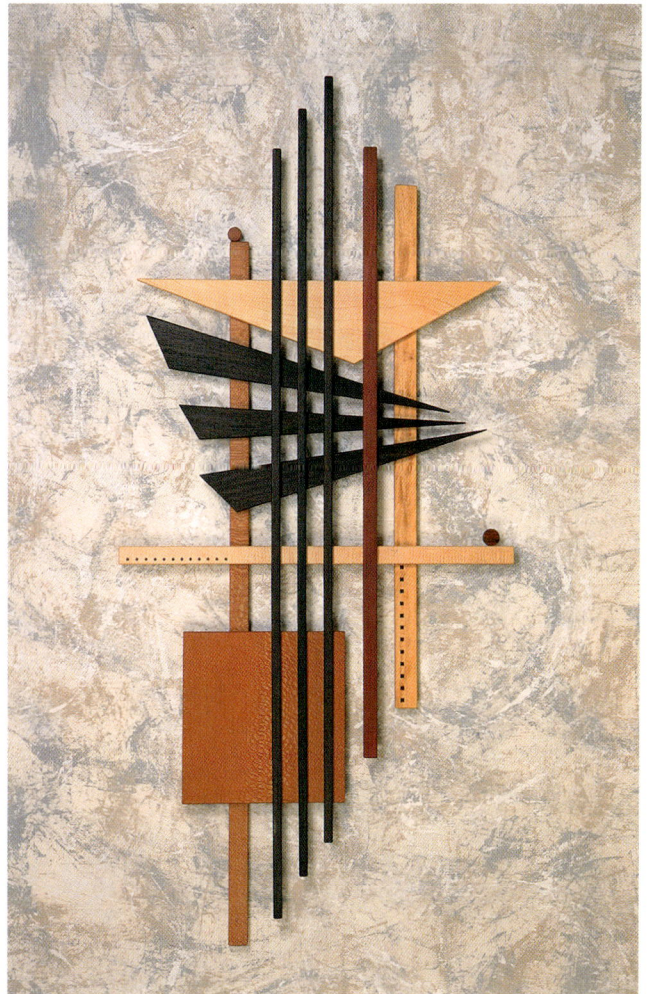

275

Top: *Music Knows No Boundaries*, 30" x 78" x 2.5". Bottom left: *The Ninth Dimension*, 60" x 48" x 2.5". Bottom right: *Available Space*, 71" x 34" x 2.5". Photographs: Jeff Batterson.

JANE B. GRIMM

1895 PACIFIC AVENUE #305 ■ SAN FRANCISCO, CA 94109
TEL 415-922-2823 ■ FAX 415-563-6926 ■ E-MAIL JBGRIMM2000@YAHOO.COM ■ WWW.JANEBGRIMM.COM

276

Top: *Vortex VI*, 1998, ceramic and wood, 27" × 27" × 3". Bottom: *Eddy I*, 2003, ceramic and wood, 8" × 8" × 1". Photographs: Donald J. Felton.

CAMEY McGILVRAY

STAIRWAY STUDIO ■ 670 RADCLIFFE AVENUE ■ PACIFIC PALISADES, CA 90272
TEL 310-459-3287 ■ FAX 310-459-0891 ■ E-MAIL SSTAIRWAY@AOL.COM ■ WWW.CAMEYMCGILVRAY.COM

277

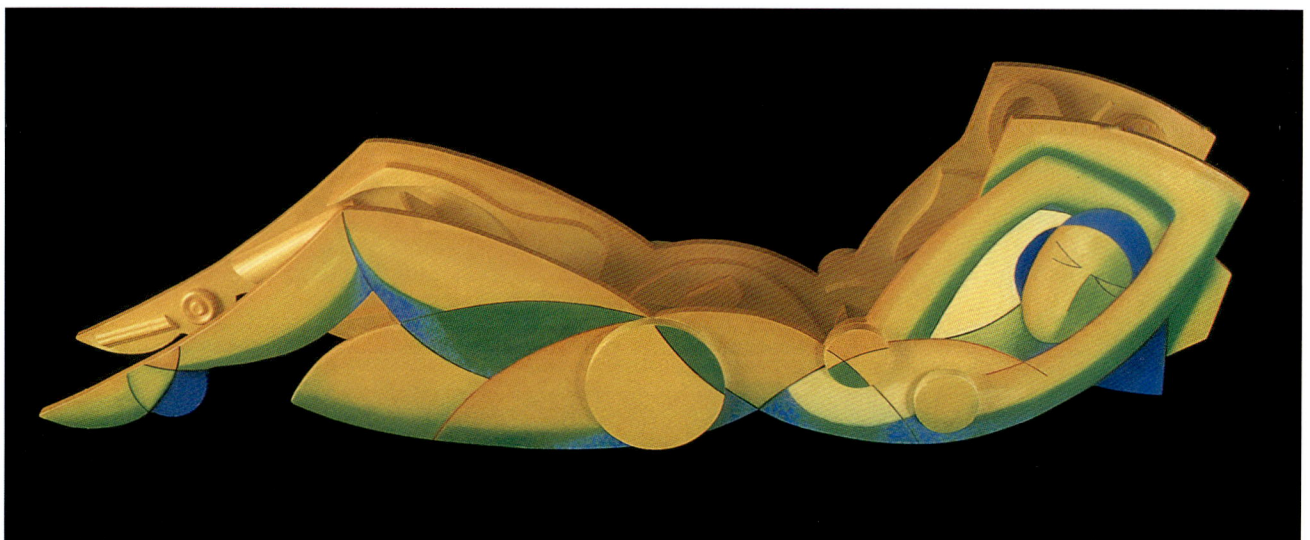

Top left: *Blue Moon,* painted wood and metal, 48" x 24" x 6". Top right: *Spin Cycle,* painted wood, 37" x 49" x 5".
Center right: *Horizontal Forms,* painted wood, 26" x 68" x 5". Bottom: *Sunbather,* painted wood, 13" x 45" x 6". Photographs: CopyTrans.

Custom Design: Three-Dimensional Painting

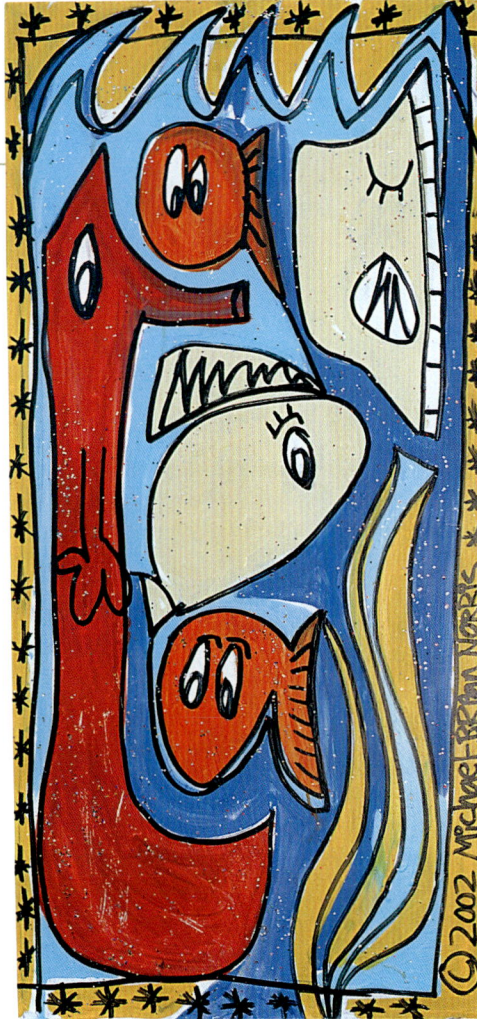

278

ARTIST
Michael-Brian Norris,
Nashville, Tennesee

PROJECT
Underwater Playtime Fish Frolics, 2002,
sand, glitter and paint,

COMMISSIONED FOR
Private residence, Atlanta, Georgia

TIMELINE
2 weeks

DIMENSIONS
24" x 12"

Michael-Brian Norris likes to think of himself as an approachable, modern-day Jean duBuffet, the French painter and sculptor best known for "art brut." It's not the style of work that the two artists share, but the nature of bridging the gap between artwork and viewer. Indeed, many of Norris' customers are first-time art collectors who, the artist says, are surprised to learn that "good art can be hip." ■ His work also provides children with a great introduction to art (and it can be viewed with 3D glasses, making it even more entertaining.) Such is the case with *Underwater Playtime Fish Frolics,* which Norris created as a play-room commission for an established collector. "I had done work for children's spaces before—bedrooms, libraries, museums—but this marked the first time I actually collaborated with the mind of an eight year old," he says. The work came out just the way the two collaborators imagined. ■ It is the way his art affects people that is most rewarding to Norris, and he makes it a point to get to know his client before he creates a commission. He asks for personal facts and photographs, and incorporates these elements into the artwork, making each collaboration a unique, personal work. He once painted a portrait of a woman's dog, working primarily from her statements about her pet. In the end, the dog was depicted as a queen, and the client had an image that reflected her sentiments exactly. Norris reports that he has never had a client who has been disappointed with a commission; with this type of collaborative effort, it's easy to understand why.

GEORGE FOSTER

SEALIGHT GALLERY ■ 151 SHERRIE LANE ■ DEL MAR, CA 92014
TEL 858-755-5421 ■ FAX 858-755-5192 ■ E-MAIL GFOSTER324@AOL.COM

Top: *Barracuda,* copper, glass and mica with low-voltage lighting, 5'L × 1'H. Center left: *Grouper,* copper, glass and paper with low-voltage lighting, 3.4'L × 18"H.
Center right: *Stingray,* copper and glass with low-voltage lighting, 2.4'L × 2'W. Bottom: *Sailfish,* copper, glass and paper, 8'L × 3'H.

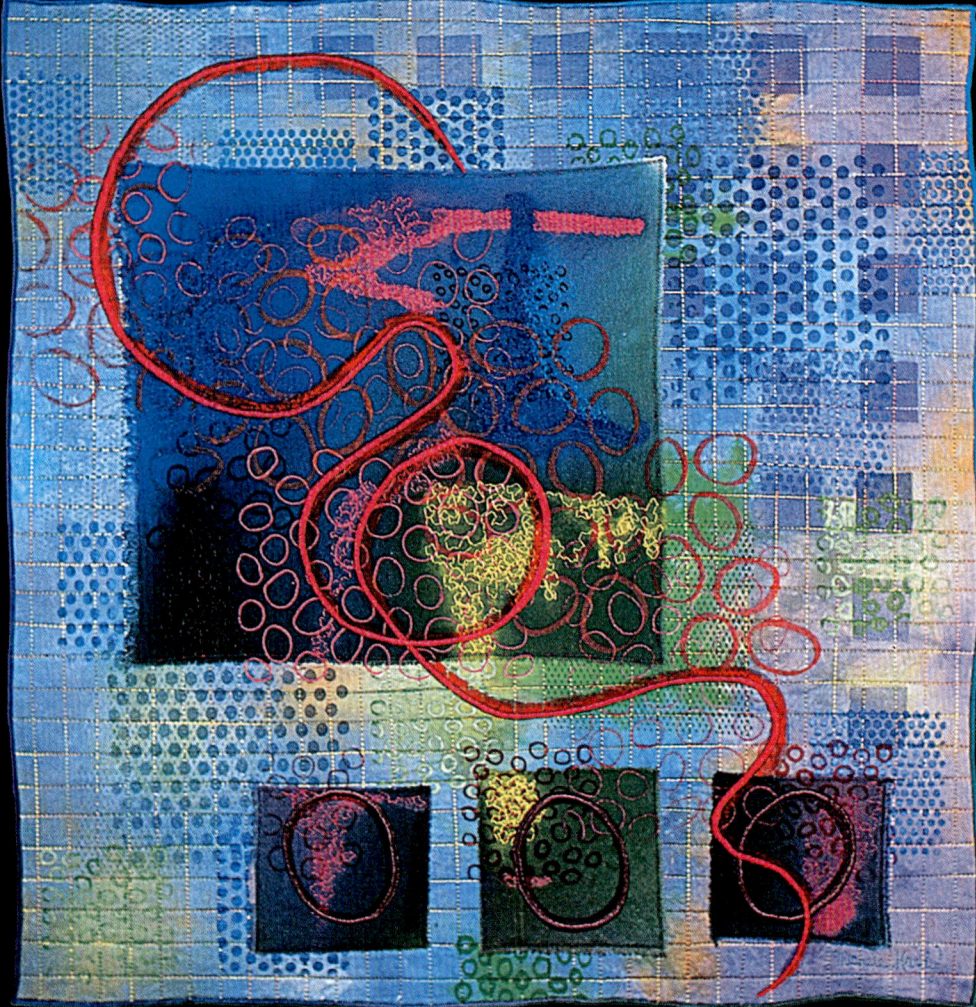

Art for the Wall | Fiber

LOUISE LEMIEUX BÉRUBÉ

1751 RICHARDSON STREET #5530 ■ MONTREAL, QC H3K1G6 ■ CANADA
TEL 514-933-3728 ■ FAX 514-933-6305 ■ E-MAIL LOUISE@LEMIEUXBERUBE.COM ■ WWW.LEMIEUXBERUBE.COM

282

Top: *Indian Summer*, 2002, woven textiles, 10'W x 7'H. Bottom: *Indian Summer* (detail). Photographs: Pierre Arpin.

GEORGE-ANN BOWERS

1199 CORNELL AVENUE ■ BERKELEY, CA 94706
TEL 510-524-3611 ■ FAX 510-559-3152 ■ E-MAIL TMSLBWRS@EARTHLINK.NET

283

Top: *Annie Creek*, 2002, woven wall sculpture, 30" x 68" x 8".
Bottom left: *Rift*, 2001, weaving, 28" x 40". Bottom right: *Aspen*, 2001, weaving, 24" x 34". Photographs: Dana Davis.

LAURA MILITZER BRYANT

PRISM ARTS ■ 2595 30TH AVENUE NORTH ■ ST. PETERSBURG, FL 33713
TEL 727-327-3100 ■ FAX 727-321-1905 ■ E-MAIL LAURA@PRISMYARN.COM

284

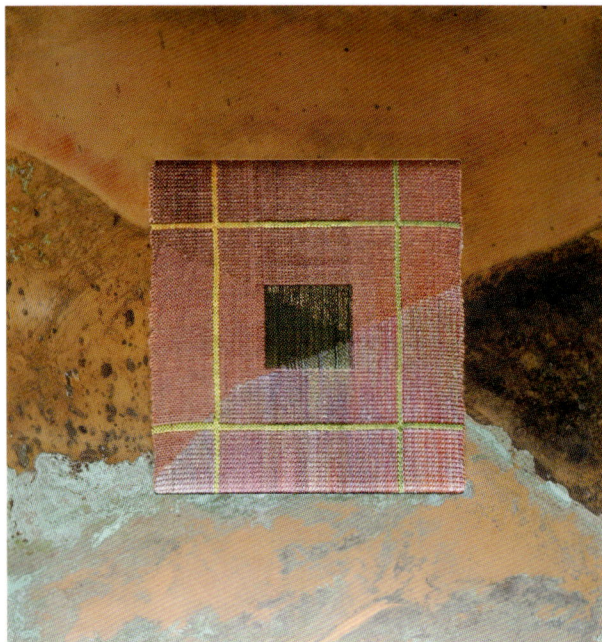

Top: *Prismawave*, 2002, Freeman residence, Tampa, FL, weaving with aluminum, 112" × 45". Photographs: Thomas Bruce.
Bottom left: *Rose: Olive*, 2002, weaving on copper, 20" × 20". Bottom right: *Periwinkle: Gold*, weaving on copper, 20" × 20".

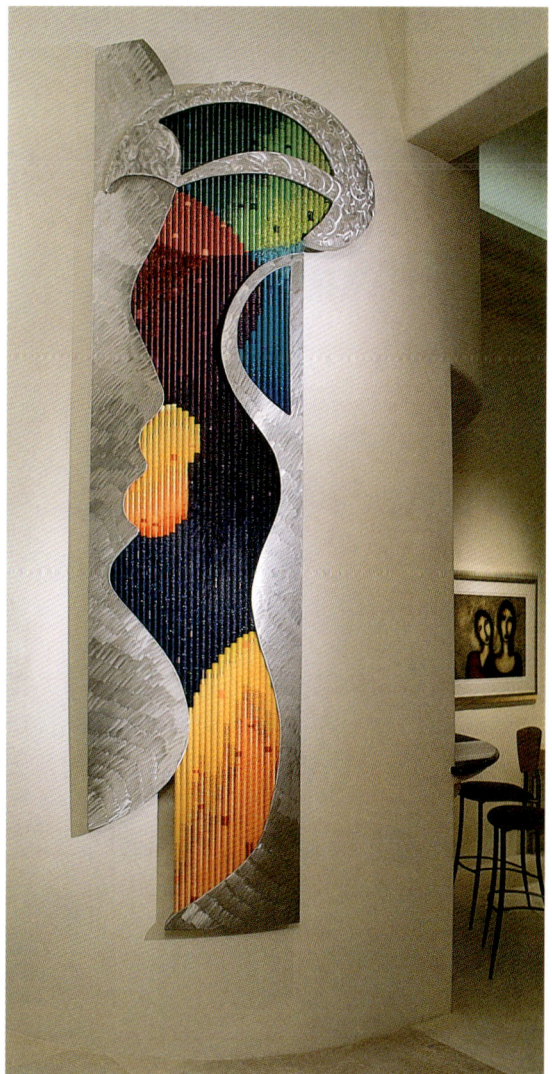

Top: *Quiet Oboes*, wrapped fiber, total size: 7.5' × 2.5'. Bottom left: *Indonesian Oboes*, wrapped fiber, total size: 7' × 8'.
Bottom right: *Jenny*, wrapped fiber and burnished aluminum, 3' × 12'. Photographs: Ron Luxemburg.

286

Kalaloch Rocks, wool with handmade felt, 40"L × 28"W × 6"D. Photograph: Cindy Momchilov.

CONTEMPORARY, COLORFUL TEXTILE ART ▪ 2451 POTOMAC STREET ▪ OAKLAND, CA 94602-3032
TEL 510-530-1134 ▪ FAX 510-482-9465 ▪ E-MAIL ART@ROBINCOWLEY.COM ▪ WWW.ROBINCOWLEY.COM

Hiroshige Reflections, 2002, layered fabric construction, 60"H × 47"W. Photograph: Don Tuttle Photography.

RANDY FROST

11 SUNSET AVENUE ▨ BRONXVILLE, NY 10708 ▨ TEL 914-337-7122 ▨ FAX 914-337-2701
E-MAIL FIBERARCH@EARTHLINK.NET

288

Top: *Bugged System*, 2001, quilt, Museum of Arts & Design, commercial and hand-dyed cottons, 36" x 36".
Bottom: *Almost Perfect Timing*, 2000, quilt, commercial and hand-dyed cottons, 36" x 36". Photographs: James Dee.

MICHELE HARDY

147 ACADIAN LANE ■ MANDEVILLE, LA 70471 ■ TEL 985-845-0792
E-MAIL MHARDY@MICHELEHARDY.COM ■ WWW.MICHELEHARDY.COM

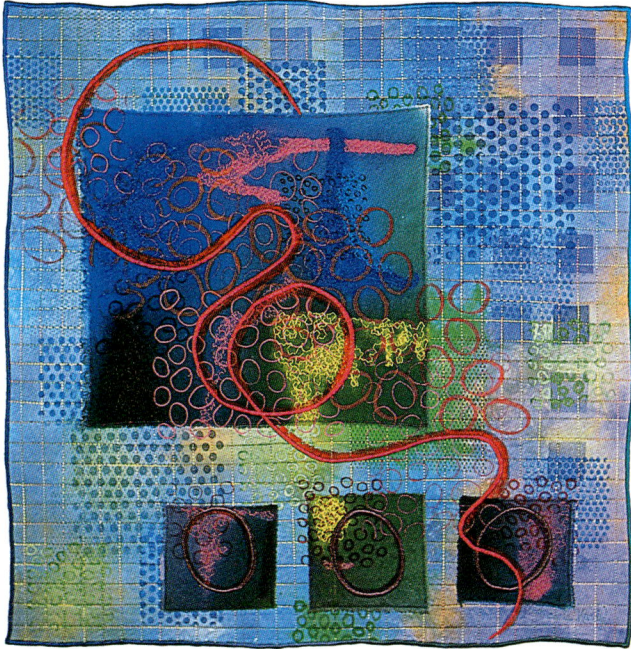

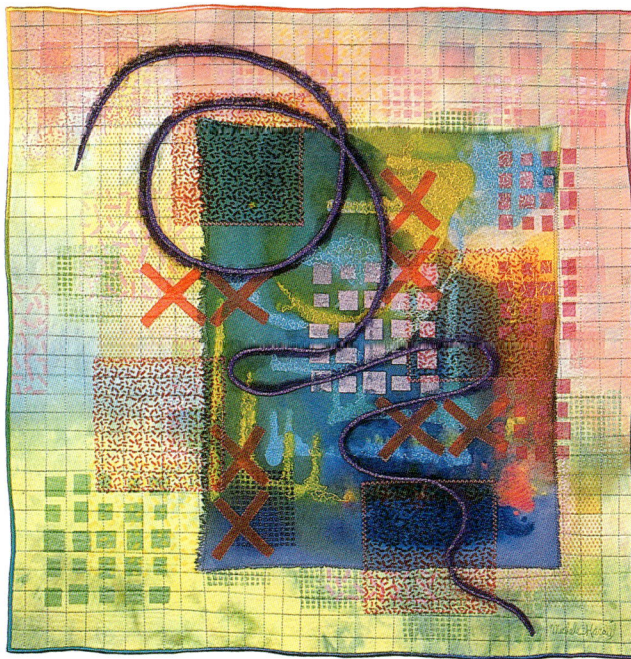

Top left: *Directions #1*, 2003, fiber, 32" × 32". Right: *Directions #4*, 2003, fiber, 24" × 48". Bottom left: *Directions #2*, 2003, fiber, 32" × 32".

JOYCE P. LOPEZ

JOYCE LOPEZ STUDIO ▨ 1147 WEST OHIO STREET #304 ▨ CHICAGO, IL 60622
TEL 312-243-5033 ▨ FAX 312-243-7566 ▨ E-MAIL JOYCEPLOPEZ@SBCGLOBAL.NET ▨ WWW.JOYCELOPEZ.COM

290

Top: Sculpture commission, 2002, private residence, French thread and chromed steel, 5.5' × 9' × 2.5".
Bottom: *Brocaded Dreams,* North Pier Tower, Chicago, IL, French thread and chromed steel, two pieces, each: 53" × 10' × 3". Photograph: Mark Belter.

LIBBY AND JIM MIJANOVICH

MIJA ■ 651 LONG BRANCH ROAD ■ MARSHALL, NC 28753
TEL 828-649-0200 ■ E-MAIL CONTACT@MIJAARTQUILTS.COM ■ WWW.MIJAARTQUILTS.COM

291

Top: *Daybreak*, 2002, pieced and quilted vintage cotton clothing, metallic thread, 31" x 51".
Bottom: *Technicolor Yin Yang* (diptych), 2001, pieced and quilted vintage cotton clothing, 46" x 74". Photographs: Tim Barnwell.

MARTHA ROEDIGER

66 PEARL STREET ■ PORTLAND, ME 04101 ■ TEL 207-828-8771 ■ FAX 207-828-8772
E-MAIL MARTHAR@IME.NET ■ WWW.MARTHAROEDIGER.COM

292

Top: *Reflections/Summer Rainbow,* woven and constructed wool, rayon and metallic fibers, 24" x 82" x 2". Bottom left: *Coastal Waves,* woven and constructed wool, rayon and metallic fibers, 62" x 22" x 3". Bottom right: *Down into Deep Water,* woven and constructed wool, cotton, rayon and metallic fibers, 88" x 27" x 3". Photographs: Jeffrey Stevensen.

JOY SAVILLE

244 DODDS LANE ■ PRINCETON, NJ 08540
TEL/FAX 609-924-6824 ■ E-MAIL JSAVILLE@PATMEDIA.NET ■ WWW.JOYSAVILLE.COM

293

Top: *Summer's End*, Bristol-Myers Squibb, Pennington, NJ, pieced cotton, linen and silk, 48" × 67" × 1".
Bottom: *Turbulent Rhythm*, GoodSmith, Gregg & Unruh, Chicago, IL, pieced cotton, linen, silk and wool, 48" × 63" × 1". Photographs: William Taylor.

Silja

Artist Information

ARTIST LISTINGS

The pages that follow provide important information on the artists featured in *The Sourcebook of Architectural & Interior Art 18*. ■ Listings in the Artist Information section are arranged in alphabetical order according to the heading on each artist's page. These listings include the artist's contact information, as well as details about materials and techniques, commissions, collections and more. References to past GUILD sourcebooks are also included so that you can further explore the breadth of a particular artist's work. The heading at the top of each listing includes a page reference to the artist's display within the book. ■ As you explore *The Sourcebook of Architectural & Interior Art 18*, use the Artist Information section to enrich your experience. If something intrigues you while perusing the sourcebook — a shape, a form, an exotic use of the commonplace — please give the artist a call. Serendipity often leads to a wonderful creation.

ARTIST LISTINGS

MARY LOU ALBERETTI
Page 22

Alberetti Studios
16 Possum Drive
New Fairfield, CT 06812
Tel 203-746-1321
E-mail mlalb@aol.com
www.southernct.edu/~alberett/

Mary Lou Alberetti creates contemporary ceramic reliefs inspired by the ancient ruins of Italy, Turkey and Spain. Layered with texture and color, and incorporating architectural details, these carved reliefs can be displayed individually or in groups. Completed pieces are available, and commissions are welcomed.

COLLECTIONS: Mint Museum of Art, Charlotte, NC; Ancell School of Business; Western Connecticut State University, Danbury; General Electric world headquarters, Fairfield, CT

EXHIBITIONS: HBO corporate gallery, 2002, New York, NY

AWARDS: Master craftsperson, honorary lifetime member, Society of Connecticut Crafts

PUBLICATIONS: *Sculptural Clay*, 1992; *Architectural Ceramics*, 1999

GUILD SOURCEBOOKS: *Architect's 14, 15; Architectural & Interior Art 16, Artful Home 1*

ANAHATA ARTS
Page 124

Eric David Laxman
478 Mountainview Avenue
Valley Cottage, NY 10989
Tel 845-353-8521
Fax 845-348-3687
E-mail eric@anahata.com
www.anahata.com

Eric David Laxman is an accomplished sculptor and furniture designer who works in a wide range of materials, including steel, bronze, stainless steel, wood, marble and granite. Laxman explores the abstract and the realistic by assembling stone fragments and welded metal into intricate compositions. He finds his inspiration from both Eastern and Western art traditions, and uses themes that express transformation, balance and movement. With Anahata Arts, Laxman has extended his unique sculptural sensibility to the realm of metal furniture and functional art. Laxman customizes his unique designs for particular tastes and environments by working closely with clients. Recent commissions include numerous decorative metal elements for Ashford and Simpson's Sugar Bar Restaurant, New York, NY, and a bronze fountain for an estate in New Canaan, CT.

ARCHITECTURAL GLASS ART, INC.
Pages 46-47

Kenneth F. vonRoenn, Jr.
815 West Market Street
Louisville, KY 40202
Tel 502-585-5421
Fax 502-585-2808
E-mail info@againc.com
www.againc.com

Architectural Glass Art, Inc. uses a broad range of new techniques to expand the roles of glass in architecture. These techniques have been developed and refined from new and emerging technologies, creating dynamic opportunities for architectural applications. Architectural Glass Art provides a complete range of services, from design to fabrication to installation. Kenneth vonRoenn's work is noted for its sympathetic integration with architecture and for its innovative application to new technologies.

RECENT PROJECTS: Conference room entry doors, U.S. Voice and Data, sandblasted and laminated beveled glass; suspended sculpture, Jewish Hospital Medical Center East, 30'H × 18W, dichroic glass, acrylic with holographic film, steel rings, stainless steel cables and internal low-voltage lighting; Gill residence windows, 6' × 10', laminated beveled glass and 3D blown glass gesture elements

297

ART GLASS ENSEMBLES
Page 48

Christie A. Wood
208 West Oak Street
Denton, TX 76201
Tel 940-591-3002
Fax 940-591-7853
E-mail ensembles@compuserve.com

Art Glass Ensembles has been creating custom stained glass and mosaic glass artwork for a variety of clients since 1995. They specialize in creating stained glass artwork for private homes, working as the primary artist, as the fabricating studio for other artists, or in collaboration with furniture makers, cabinetmakers, interior designers and clients. Art Glass Ensembles welcomes inquiries regarding projects, whether one of a kind or limited editions.

COMMISSIONS: Children's Hospital of Philadelphia PA, Oncology Unit, collaboration with artist Stefania Luciani, 1999

PUBLICATIONS: *International Guild of Glass Artists* magazine, 1999

ASCALON STUDIOS, INC.
Page 176

David Ascalon
115 Atlantic Avenue
Berlin, NJ 08009-9300
Tel 888-280-5656 (toll free)
Tel 856-768-3779
Fax 856-768-3902
E-mail ascalonart@aol.com
www.ascalonart.com

For three generations, the artwork of Ascalon Studios has adorned places of worship and public spaces throughout North America. Today, the studio, under the direction of David Ascalon (whose background includes architecture and interior design), works closely with architects, art committees and liturgical leadership to design and fabricate site-specific works and design elements. Projects range from monumental sculpture, bas reliefs and sculptural memorials in a variety of media, to stained glass windows, carved glass, mosaics and donor recognition projects. Please see website for a list of commissions.

AWARDS: American Institute of Architects Interfaith Forum on Religion, Art & Architecture award

BAD RIVER ARTWORKS
Page 158

Sherri Treeby and Lee Leuning
120 North Main Street
Aberdeen, SD 57401
Tel 605-226-3795/605-380-0550
E-mail badriver@nvc.net
www.badriverart.com

Monumental bronze sculpture. Public art and private commissions. Human figures and animals. Emotion in bronze, cold cast bronze and cast marble. Partners Lee Leuning (a game warden) and Sherri Treeby (an art and art history teacher) team up to bring you some of the finest representational art available.

RECENT PROJECTS: World War II memorial, 2001, Pierre, SD; *City of Presidents*, Rapid City, SD

COMMISSIONS: James Madison University, 2002, Harrisonburg, VA; Central High School, 2003, Aberdeen, SD; University of South Dakota, Vermillion

EXHIBITIONS: Dakota Prairie Museum, 1998, Aberdeen, SD; Dakota State University, Madison, SD

GUILD SOURCEBOOKS: *Architectural & Interior Art 17*

ARTIST LISTINGS

LOUISE LEMIEUX BÉRUBÉ
Page 282

1751 Richardson Street #5530
Montreal, QC H3K1G6
Canada
Tel 514-933-3728
Fax 514-933-6305
E-mail louise@lemieuxberube.com
www.lemieuxberube.com

The creation of Bérubé's woven works starts with the scanning of different photos. The digital images are then modified, combined with other images or drawings, and resized. The colors of the final image are ultimately replaced by different weaving textures. When the image is all transferred, it is woven on an electronic Jacquard handloom. Trees have been present in Bérubé's artwork since the beginning of her career; their texture, stability, strength and silent presence have always inspired her.

COMMISSIONS: Temple Manuel Beth Shalom, 2000, Montreal, Canada

COLLECTIONS: Sodec, Ministry of Culture, Quebec Government, Canada; Deutsches Technikmuseum, Berlin, Germany

EXHIBITIONS: Shelburne Craft School Gallery, 2002, VT; Sambikiya Gallery, 2002, Tokyo, Japan; Sculpture, Objects and Functional Art, 1999-2002, New York, NY

BIGBIRD-STUDIOS
Page 97

Pat Payne
2121 Alameda Avenue
Alameda, CA 94501
Tel 510-521-9308
E-mail ppbigbird@aol.com
www.bigbird-studios.com

Pat Payne has created one-of-a-kind, large steel sculpture for the public and private sectors for over 25 years. She quotes: "I love the strength and immediacy of the material; nothing is more immediate than working in steel." The majority of her sculpture is suitable for indoor or outdoor placement.

COLLECTIONS: Robin Williams; Gary Larson; Cypress Gardens; Broadway Plaza

EXHIBITIONS: Los Angeles Natural History Museum, CA; El Paseo Sculpture, Palm Desert, CA; One Bush, San Francisco, CA

PATRICK MICHAEL BIRGE
Page 107

Reunion Studios
1614 Manchester Lane NW
Washington, DC 20011
Tel 202 352-4853
Fax 202 882-9487
E-mail pbirge@gwu.edu

Patrick Birge creates figurative sculptures that express universal themes in contemporary ways. He works masterfully in bronze, gold leaf, terra cotta, resins, cast gold and silver, mosaic, wood and Lucite. He finds that art has lasting significance when it is born out of a sincere exploration of conflict. This conflict invites the artist to explore the ways in which harmony is discovered, thereby transcending the discord.

COMMISSIONS: University of Maryland, 2000, College Park

EXHIBITIONS: *The New Humanity*, 2000, Georgetown University, Washington, DC

AWARDS: The Alfred Steck Memorial Prize for Art, 2001, George Washington University, Washington, DC

PUBLICATIONS: *Environment and Art Letter*, "Discoveries of Her Face," 1998

GEORGE-ANN BOWERS
Page 283

1199 Cornell Avenue
Berkeley, CA 94706
Tel 510-524-3611
Fax 510-559-3152
E-mail tmslbwrs@earthlink.net

George-Ann Bowers works with a variety of yarns to create lush impressions of nature—both contemplative and dynamic—for residential and commercial interiors. Richly colored and textured, Bowers' multi-layered weavings capture the drama and subtlety of her natural subject matter, whether in two-dimensional format or sculptural form. Visuals and pricing available upon request.

COMMISSIONS: Private residence, Princeton, NJ, 1999; Home News Enterprises, Columbus, IN, 1998

EXHIBITIONS: Solo exhibition, North State University, Aberdeen, SD, 2003; solo exhibition, Maturango Museum, Ridgecrest, CA, 2002; Crater Lake artist-in-residence exhibition, Schneider Museum, Ashland, OR, 2002

PUBLICATIONS: *Craft of Northern California*, 2002

GUILD SOURCEBOOKS: *Designer's 11, 13, 14, 15*

KATHY BRADFORD
Page 49

North Star Art Glass, Inc.
142 Wichita
Lyons, CO 80540
Tel/Fax 303-823-6511
E-mail kathybradford@webtv.net
www.kathybradford.com

Visitors arriving at the Marriott Hotel in Anaheim, CA, are greeted by a lovely image of a glass bamboo forest. This 7' × 14' installation is sandblast-carved and lit from within. Many of Bradford's large glass walls use imagery from nature indigenous to the location of the commission. The walls often serve as a donor recognition piece, or they may become the signature work of a corporation. Installations may be single, double or triple layers of glass, sand-carved with many details. The element of surprise is always present in Bradford's work.

RECENT PROJECTS: Centura Health Executive Offices, Denver, CO; Longmont Historical Museum, Longmont, CO; Hotel Caribe, Orlando, FL; Marriott Hotels, Anaheim and San Mateo, CA; Russian Tea Room, New York, NY; Philadelphia Geriatric Center, PA

GUILD SOURCEBOOKS: *Architect's 14, 15; Architectural & Interior Art 16, 17*

DOUGLAS BRETT
Page 125

Modern Life Designs
668 Post Street
San Francisco, CA 94109
Tel 415-441-7118
E-mail doug@modernlifedesigns.com
www.modernlifedesigns.com

Douglas Brett creates fantastic and entertaining bronze sculptures. By using minimalist-yet-dramatic, forms, he brings environments to life. Brett is trained in early-twentieth-century modern art of the French School. A self-described Cubist, he uses soft geometric forms that combine the styles of Surrealism, Futurism, Pop and Folk. Brett's work is provocative, and there is a softness about his sculpture that begs to be touched. Whether you're looking for a small, intimate bronze for home or office, or a monumental goliath for a corporate park, he will create a truly remarkable piece of art that will be a signature of style and a destination.

ARTIST LISTINGS

BARBARA BROTHERTON
Page 263

Barbro Designs
1006 Oak View Drive
Ione, CA 95640
Tel 209-274-6248
Fax 209-274-6246
E-mail barbro38@earthlink.net

By utilizing materials such as wood, poured stone, metal leaf and patinas, mixed-media artist Barbara Brotherton creates wall pieces that reflect her deep appreciation of Mediterranean and Far Eastern design. Her layering process evokes "crusty surfaces," and can be seen as a representation of natural processes like sedimentation, erosion, entropy and the cycle of birth, death and rebirth. Brotherton's work is widely represented in private and corporate collections. Slides and pricing available upon request. Site-specific commissions are welcomed.

COMMISSIONS: Kaiser Permanente Medical, 2002, Redwood City, CA

COLLECTIONS: St. Vincent Hospital, Indianapolis, IN; Hilton Hotel, Los Angeles, CA; Ocean Park Community Center, Santa Monica, CA; former president Bill Clinton, New York, NY

GUILD SOURCEBOOKS: *Designer's 10, 12, 14; Architectural & Interior Art 16*

BOB BROWN
Page 212

Bob Brown Studio
2725 Terry Lake Road
Fort Collins, CO 80524
Tel/Fax 970-224-5473
E-mail bobbrown-artist@att.net

Bob Brown's colorful paintings highlight an area by bringing the bright outdoors to the inside. The thick texture created with durable acrylic paint and a painting knife provides an intriguing surface. Subjects are representational and mostly landscapes. Unframed paintings range from 16" x 20" to 36" x 48". Commissions considered. A brochure is available.

COLLECTIONS: McGraw Hill Companies, New York; Prince Albert, Monte Carlo, Monaco

EXHIBITIONS: Galleries and public spaces in the U.S., Monaco and France

GUILD SOURCEBOOKS: *Designer's 13, 14, 15; Architectural & Interior Art 16, 17; Artful Home 1*

GARY ALLEN BROWN
Page 126

5420 West Del Rio Street
Chandler, AZ 85226
Tel 480-705-8300
Fax 480-785-7577
E-mail baffin@cox.net
www.gabsculpture.com

Sculptor Gary Allen Brown works in wood, metal and stone, seeking a balance between organic and abstract forms. His work has a visual, tactile and structural integrity that makes it ideal for display in both private and public settings. For over 15 years, Gary owned a design firm specializing in custom architectural signage. This background gives him a unique perspective on the client-focused aspects of his art: a combination of art and engineering. Gary was chosen by *The Bulletin of Atomic Scientists* to produce the "Doomsday Clock." A portfolio is available upon request.

COLLECTIONS: Private collections nationwide.

EXHIBITIONS: Galleries and shows nationwide.

GUILD SOURCEBOOKS: *Architectural & Interior Art 17*

JOY BROWN
Page 24

463 Segar Mountain Road
South Kent, CT 06785
Tel/Fax 860-927-4946
E-mail joycbrown@mac.com
www.artwithin.net

Joy Brown has created sculpture in clay and bronze for over 30 years. Her work reflects the influence of her early life in Japan and her apprenticeship in traditional Japanese ceramics. The warm, rich colors and textures of these sculptures, wall murals and public installations have found their way into many private collections, museums and galleries in the United States, France, Thailand and Japan.

COMMISSIONS: Ceramic mural, 20' x 5', 2002, Hartford Hospital, CT

EXHIBITIONS: Bachelier-Cardonsky Gallery, 1989-2002, Kent, CT; Elena Zang Gallery, 1996-2002, Woodstock, NY

PUBLICATIONS: *The New York Times; International Herald Tribune; House and Garden; Ceramics Monthly*

LAURA MILITZER BRYANT
Page 284

Prism Arts
2595 30th Avenue North
St. Petersburg, FL 33713
Tel 727-327-3100
Fax 727-321-1905
E-mail laura@prismyarn.com

Landscape-inspired geometrics inform the weavings of Laura Bryant. Whether flat, or twisting and moving in space, her richly dyed textiles are partnered with hand-finished metals. The images speak to the ages, to things that have passed and events yet to come. Scale of works ranges from intimate to grand.

COMMISSIONS: Freman residence, 2002, Tampa, FL

COLLECTIONS: City of St. Petersburg, FL; Xerox Corporation, Rochester, NY; Eli Lilly

AWARDS: Florida State Individual Artist Fellowship, 1994-1995; National Endowment for the Arts Individual Artist Fellowship, 1990-1991

PUBLICATIONS: *American Craft* magazine, *Fiberarts* magazine

GUILD SOURCEBOOKS: *Designer's 10, 11, 12, 13, 14, 15; Architectural & Interior Art 16, 17*

MYRA BURG
Page 285

6180 West Jefferson, Suite Y
Los Angeles, CA 90016
Tel 310-399-5040
Fax 310-399-0623
www.myraburg.com

Somewhere between tapestry and jewelry, the "quiet oboes" and sculptural installations of Myra Burg adorn spaces in a free-floating, peaceful way. She combines hand-wrapped fiber and burnished metals to create inspired sculptural pieces that meet the clients' needs and wants within the requirements of the space. "The bigger the challenge, the more the fun." Collaborations are welcome.

RECENT PROJECTS: *Japonaise,* Universal, Japan; *Galactic Curve,* Universal, Japan; *Quiet Oboes,* Caribé Hilton, Puerto Rico; Travelocity, Dallas, TX

EXHIBITIONS: SOFA, Chicago; LA County Museum of Art, CA; Howard Hughes Center, Los Angeles, CA; Orange County Museum of Art, CA

AWARDS: First place, 2002, *Artfest of Henderson;* first place, *Beverly Hills Affaire in the Gardens,* 2001, 1999, 1998

GUILD SOURCEBOOKS: *Designer's 10, 13, 14, 15; Architect's 14, 15; Architectural & Interior Art 16, 17; Artful Home 1*

ARTIST LISTINGS

RUTH BURINK
Page 127

Burink Sculpture Studio
1550 Woodmoor Drive
Monument, CO 80132
Tel/Fax 719-481-0513
E-mail ruth@burinksculpture.com
www.burinksculpture.com

Ruth Burink creates stone and bronze sculpture for public and personal enjoyment, exterior and interior spaces, by commission and for galleries. Burink's creative design and technical mastery have established her reputation for exceptional quality and for singular grace and elegance. Burink Sculpture Studio collaborates closely with clients, creating sculpture in complete harmony with the space for which it is designed.

COLLECTIONS: Various public, liturgical and private collections nationally and abroad

EXHIBITIONS: National galleries and various shows every year

RIIS BURWEL
Page 128

Riis Burwell Studio
3815 Calistoga Road
Santa Rosa, CA 95404
Tel/Fax 707-538-2676
E-mail riisburwell@aol.com

Riis Burwell has been creating elegant abstract sculpture for 22 years, primarily in stainless steel and bronze. Whether tabletop or large scale, his sculpture is inspired by the dynamic relationships between order and chaos, and growth and decay. Burwell's exquisitely fluid sculptures are hand fabricated so that each piece is unique. His work is found in private, museum, public and corporate collections within the United States and abroad.

COMMISSIONS: Vineyard Creek Spa & Conference Center, 2002, Santa Rosa, CA; Santa Rosa Convention Center, 2002, CA; Burbank Airport Plaza, 2001, CA; Congregation Beth Ami, 2000, Santa Rosa, CA

EXHIBITIONS: *Contemporary Constructions*, Los Angeles County Museum; Olive Grove Sculpture Gallery, Rutherford, CA; Sandy Carson Gallery, Denver, CO

GUILD SOURCEBOOKS: *Architect's 13, 14, 15; Architectural & Interior Art 16, 17*

BRIDGET BUSUTIL
Page 213

Busutil Impressions, LLC
1130 Piedmont Avenue
Atlanta, GA 30309
Tel 404-234-9375
Fax 404-875-9155
E-mail busutilart@bellsouth.net
www.bridgetbusutil.com

Bridget Busutil works with oil, acrylics and encaustics on both canvas and board. Her passion for landscapes has led to her creation of enticing horizons that have magical depths and luminosity. Perhaps what makes these landscapes so attractive is the wondrous sense of escape they offer the minds of those who immerse themselves in them.

RECENT PROJECTS: Commissioned by French and German consulates to create flags of their respective countries, 2003, encaustics on board, three panels each

COMMISSIONS: The Windsor Condominiums, Atlanta, GA; the Hilton, Aruba, Caribbean; Banque National de Paris, Basel, Switzerland

EXHIBITIONS: Walter Wickiser Gallery, 2001 and 2000, New York, NY; Gallery La Maison Francaise (French Embassy), 2000, Washington, DC

GUILD SOURCEBOOKS: *Architectural & Interior Art 16, 17, Artful Home 1*

300

BARBARA CADE
Page 286

262 Hideaway Hills Drive
Hot Springs, AR 71901
Tel 501-262-4065
E-mail cade@ipa.net

Collectible rocks, luscious vegetation, textured trees and dramatic skies: two- and three-dimensional sculptural landscape elements inspired by your geographic location, maybe using your favorite photograph. Use elements together or individually. Barbara Cade continues to be inspired by themes in nature, translating her photographs into tapestries of woven and felted wool, often incorporating other fiber techniques.

COMMISSIONS: St. Luke's Hospital, 2003, The Woodlands, TX; the Kraft Center, 1997, Paramus, NJ

COLLECTIONS: Weyerhaeuser Company, Tacoma, WA; Tacoma Art Museum, Tacoma, WA

EXHIBITIONS: *Reality Check*, Ohio Craft Museum, 2001, Columbus, OH

GUILD SOURCEBOOKS: *Designer's 8, 9, 10, 11, 12, 15; Architectural & Interior Art 17; Artful Home 1*

RENO CAROLLO
Page 129

1562 South Parker Road, Suite 336
Denver, CO 80231
Tel 303-695-6396
Fax 303-695-8560
E-mail rcar173278@aol.com
www.renocarollo.com

As an artist, Reno Carollo loves the process of creating. He is constantly pursuing new designs, new combinations of materials and new ideas for the human figure. Carollo's current work combines metal and stone in abstract figurative forms. For him, creativity occurs in pushing and pulling the space of the figure, creating new possibilities while connecting the viewer with the essence of the human form. Carollo's formal education includes a B.A. from the University of Northern Colorado in Greeley with studies at the Academy of Fine Arts in Florence, Italy.

RECENT PROJECTS: Art Expo, 2002, New York, NY

COMMISSIONS: George and Barbi Benton Gradow, 2001, Aspen, CO; Michael and Sheila Martin Stone, 1996, Oakdale, CA

EXHIBITIONS: Colorado Governor's Invitational

GUILD SOURCEBOOKS: *Architectural & Interior Art 17*

MARIANNE CAROSELLI
Page 110

8511 Alydar Circle
Fair Oaks Ranch, TX 78015
Tel/Fax 830-381-4544
E-mail artist@gvtc.com
www.mcaroselli.com

Marianne Caroselli creates sculpture—from tabletop to monumental—showing many subjects and themes. Caroselli has been an artist for 30 years. All of her work is created with a feeling of warmth, never portraying violence, as the artist believes her works should be relaxing, peaceful and loving so that they may be enjoyed for a lifetime. Most of all, she enjoys bringing a smile to the faces of her clients.

COMMISSIONS: Recreation Center, Commerce City, CO; World War II Monument

COLLECTIONS: City of Edmund, OK; City of Peoria, AZ; City of Texas City, TX

ARTIST LISTINGS

WARREN CARTHER
Page 50

Carther Studio Inc.
80 George Avenue
Winnipeg, MB R3B 0K1
Canada
Tel 204-956-1615
Fax 204-942-1434
E-mail warren@cartherstudio.com
www.cartherstudio.com

Glass artist Warren Carther explores light in varied and unusual ways, manipulating the quality of light as it is filtered through the complex layers of his work. His respect and understanding of the structural capabilities of glass, combined with his interest in working sculpturally within the architectural environment, lead him to produce unique work that crosses the boundaries between art and architecture. Innovative techniques in structure, abrasive blast carving, laminations and color application distinguish his often-large-scale work. Numerous commissions and publications throughout the world have earned him an international reputation.

COMMISSIONS: Canadian Embassy, Tokyo, Japan; Swire Group, Hong Kong; Charles de Gaulle Airport, Paris, France; Anchorage International Airport, AK

CASTLE SCULPTURE, LLC
Page 130

Joseph L. Castle III
331 Bay Horse Road
Bellevue, ID 83313
Tel 208-788-1305
Fax 208-788-2519
joscastle@aol.com

Through his work in bronze, Joseph Castle explores inner spaces and the relationships in which they are defined. The *Relationship* series, which began as a forum for testing shape and interconnectedness, continues to grow as a means for pushing the contrast between dynamic energy and reflective contemplation, continuity and dichotomy.

RECENT PROJECTS: Finalist, City of Emeryville, CA, public art project; private commission, 2002, Chicago, IL; private commission, 2002, Hobe Sound, FL

COLLECTIONS: The Secretary and Mrs. Donald H. Rumsfeld, 2002, Washington, DC

EXHIBITIONS: Anne Reed Gallery, 2002, Ketchum, ID; New Leaf Gallery, 2002, Berkeley, CA

AWARDS: Rocky Mount Sculpture Show, 2002, NC; Fourth Annual Sculpture Walk, 2002, City of Bemidji, MN; 14th Annual Outdoor Sculpture Exhibit, 2001, Lawrence, KS

PUBLICATIONS: *Wood River Journal,* 2002

JILL CASTY
Page 80

Jill Casty Design
494 Alvarado Street, Suite D
Monterey, CA 93940
Tel 831-649-0923
Fax 831-649-0713
E-mail jillcdesign@hotmail.com
www.jillcastydesign.com

Jill Casty's exuberant, graceful art, while inventive and personal, is always sensitive to a site's spirit and spaces as well as to the vision of client and architect. Her aerial pieces—from joyful atrium mobiles to innovative, large-scale hanging art projects—and her festive abstract standing sculptures (up to 30 feet high) employ diverse materials such as Plexiglas, metals and glass.

RECENT PROJECTS: Tom Ridge Center at Presque Isle, Erie, PA; City of Montclair, CA; SuperMall of the Great Northwest, Auburn, WA; Northwest Plaza, St. Louis, MO

GUILD SOURCEBOOKS: *Architect's 10, 11, 12, 13, 14, 15; Architectural & Interior Art 16, 17*

301

CHRISTIANSEN–ARNER
Page 134

Cherie Christiansen
Franz Arner
PO Box 770
Mendocino, CA 95460
Tel 707-937-3309
www.chrisarnsculpture.com

The stone and bronze sculptures of Cherie Christiansen and Franz Arner reflect both abstract sculptural shapes and forms, and those that are reflective of nature. They create sculptures with water moving over the pieces, as well as sculptures without water. Some pieces are created with humor and whimsy, some for elegance and beauty. All forms are dictated primarily by the stone they are carved from. Commissions and collectors include the Claremont Hotel, Berkely, CA; Grace Family Vineyards, St. Helena, CA; St. Gregory's Episcopal Church, San Francisco, CA; Shozo Sato, Tea Master, Cleone, CA; the Stanford Inn, Mendocino, CA; and Matanzas Creek Winery, Santa Rosa, CA

CHU TAT-SHING
Page 153

Neuberg International Limited
Unit 1612, China Merchants Tower
168 Connaught Road Central
Hong Kong
Tel 852-2540-6323
Fax 852-2802-8229
E-mail neuberg@sculpture.com.hk
www.sculpture.com.hk

Chu Tat-Shing creates sculptures in bronze and stone. His works integrate his deep roots in Chinese culture with the enlightened free spirit of Western civilization. The ideology of harmony, the praise for natural beauty and the strengths in all forms of life come into his works.

COMMISSIONS: In Hong Kong: Scout Association of Hong Kong; Great Eagle Hotel; Princess Margaret Hospital

COLLECTIONS: In Hong Kong: the Hong Kong Academy for Performing Arts; Flagstaff House Museum of Tea Ware; Kowloon Park

AWARDS: Winner of sculpture competition for Asian Games, 2000; winner of sculpture competition for Hong Kong's Handover, 1997

PUBLICATIONS: *Twentieth-Century Chinese Urban Sculpture,* 2001

CITY ARTS/G. BYRON PECK
Page 207

Peck Studios
1857 Lamont Street NW
Washington, DC 20010
Tel/Fax 202-331-1966
E-mail byronpeck@earthlink.net
www.peckstudios.com
www.cityartsdc.org

Full service studios for the production of public art, murals and mosaics for large-scale artwork or intimate private murals. Peck studios have 25 years of experience working with architects, designers and organizations to create solutions for any environment.

RECENT PROJECTS: 1,500' mosaic on the Potomac River waterfront, Washington, DC; 100' mural for the City of Los Angeles, Cultural Affairs Department; two murals for the newly built visitors center at historic Mt. Vernon, VA; 60' mural for main subway station, Washington, DC

COLLECTIONS: The Kennedy Center for the Performing Arts; Chamber of Commerce, Washington, DC; U.S. Embassy, Santiago, Chile; U.S. Embassy, Georgetown Guyana; U.S. Nuclear Energy Commission; Marriott Corporation, Bethesda, MD

GUILD SOURCEBOOKS: *Architect's 6, 7, 8, 9, 10, 11, 12, 13, 14, 15; Architectural & Interior Art 16, 17*

ARTIST LISTINGS

MARGARET-ANN CLEMENTE
Page 214

Art for the Planet
519 Spindrift Way
Half Moon Bay, CA, 94019
Tel/Fax 650-712-0572
E-mail maclemente@usemail.com
www.art4theplanet.com

Margaret-Ann Clemente's award-winning work is executed with mixed media on canvas or paper. Her style ranges from "animal expressionism," which captures an animal's essence and energy in a simple, almost abstract vocabulary, to "internal expressionism," which brings to light emotive internal environments and emphasizes abstract texture, color and structure.

COMMISSIONS: Montara, CA; Cupertino, CA; Akron, OH

COLLECTIONS: Damasco & Associates, San Francisco, CA; El Granada, Woodside, Moss Beach, Pescadero and Palo Alto, CA; Vienna, VA; Chatel-Guyon, Massy-Palaiseau, France

PUBLICATIONS: *Noetic Sciences Review,* Summer 1997 and 2000; *Décor* magazine, March 1999

CLOWES SCULPTURE
Pages 78, 81

Jonathan and Evelyn Clowes
98 March Hill Road
Walpole, NH 03608
Tel/Fax 603-756-9505
E-Mail jon@ClowesSculpture.com
www.ClowesSculpture.com

Jonathan and Evelyn Clowes are a husband and wife team who create lyrical sculpture for public and private spaces. With 30 years of experience collaborating with clients, architects and engineers, they specialize in site-specific designs. Power and elegance distinguish the Clowes' sculptural work. Organic shapes and flowing curves speak of serene seas, soft winds and gracious gestures.

COMMISSIONS: Royal Caribbean International, Oslo, Norway; Hilton Hotel International, Tokyo, Japan; Indianapolis Museum of Art, IN; Visalia Convention Center, CA; Monadnock Paper Inc., Bennington, NH; Manchester District Courthouse, NH; Antioch New England Graduate School, Keene, NH

DEBORAH T. COLTER
Page 257

PO Box 1517
Edgartown, MA 02539
Tel 508-627-3829
E-mail dtc@deborahcolter.com
www.deborahcolter.com

"…we need to be willing to let our intuition guide us, and then be willing to follow that guidance directly and fearlessly."

Shakti Gawain

The work of Deborah T. Colter is an exciting visual balance of energy, emotion, color and texture. Colter's guiding force is her trust in inner thoughts as they reveal themselves purely through the act of creating. The subconscious interface of surfaces weaves its way through a balance of stability and uncertainty. Moments of thought are captured purely through a visual language. Colter welcomes collaboration based on existing work or site-specific commission projects. More information is available on request.

COLLECTIONS: Paramount Pictures, Los Angeles, CA; Hale & Dorr, Boston, MA; Goodwin Procter LLP, Boston, MA; Biogen Corporation, Cambridge, MA; numerous private collections

302

GWENN CONNOLLY
Pages 5, 89

PO Box 1781
Benicia, CA 94510
Tel 707-747-1822
E-mail gwennart1@aol.com
www.connolly-sculpture.com

The emotion of Gwenn Connolly's sculpture transcends the human form, speaking to the deep universal human truths of hope, strength and courage. Indoors or outdoors, in a public place or a private corner, her works resonate with the viewer's spirit. They are assertive in their movement. They are affirmative. They are celebratory, and they invite and encourage the viewer to stop, to look and to feel the affirmation and joy of life. Connolly's sculpture is suitable for a range of public and private environments, including residences, gardens, health care facilities, corporate settings and resorts.

PAMELA COSPER
Page 215

4439 Rolling Pine Drive
West Bloomfield, MI 48323
Tel 248-366-9569
E-mail pamelacosper@hotmail.com
www.go.to/pcosper

Pamela Cosper has traveled extensively, and her paintings are influenced by a wide variety of architectural, cultural, historical and natural designs. She enjoys the challenge of expressing the personality and interests of her clients through her work. She accepts commissions for projects of any size and in many different mediums. Recent commissions have included what she calls "life story portraits," in which the paintings reflect the story of an individual's or family's experiences.

RECENT PROJECTS: A series of paintings about wine, recently on display at the Orchard Lake Gallery, Orchard Lake, MI

GUILD SOURCEBOOKS: *Architectural & Interior Art 16, 17*

ROBIN COWLEY
Page 287

Contemporary, Colorful Textile Art
2451 Potomac Street
Oakland, CA 94602-3032
Tel 510-530-1134
Fax 510-482-9465
E-mail art@robincowley.com
www.robincowley.com

Robin Cowley creates colorful graphic wall pieces for residential and corporate spaces. Her textiles are constructed with layers of fabric and thread, building on a complex use of color and richness of texture. She creates vivid, upbeat, meticulously crafted artwork suitable for a variety of settings.

COLLECTIONS: U.S. Embassy, Armenia; private residence, New York, NY; Children's Center, Camp Pendleton, United States Marine Corps, Oceanside, CA; Circuit City, Richmond, VA; Summit Medical Center, Oakland, CA

EXHIBITIONS: *Contemporary Art Quilts,* 2002, South Carolina State Museum, Columbia, SC; ARC Special Events Gallery, 2001, Chicago, IL; Stanford Art Spaces, 2001, Standford University, Palo Alto, CA; Contract Design Center, 2000, San Francisco, CA; Zoller Gallery, 1999, University Park, PA

ARTIST LISTINGS

EUGENE L. DAUB
Page 116

295 West 15th Street
San Pedro, CA 90731
Tel/Fax 310-548-0817
E-mail eldaub@earthlink.net

Eugene Daub is the recipient of the highest national and international awards for excellence in figurative and bas-relief sculpture. He is also a former vice president of the American Medallic Sculpture Association and a Fellow of the National Sculpture Society. Daub has exhibited extensively and has works in numerous public collections, including the Helsinki Art Museum, Finland; the British Museum; Smithsonian Institute, Washington, DC; Rhode Island School of Design; U.S. Capitol, Department of Interior; U.S. Park Service and the UNICEF Headquarters, NY.

RECENT PROJECTS: Monument to Lewis and Clark expedition, Kansas City, MO, bronze, 18'H on 21' granite base, the largest and most historically accurate sculpture of Lewis and Clark ever commissioned

DAVID WILSON DESIGN
Page 51

202 Darby Road
South New Berlin, NY 13843-2212
Tel 607-334-3015
Fax 607-334-7065
E-mail mail@davidwilsondesign.com
www.davidwilsondesign.com

Renowned for his successful collaborations with architects on large-scale works for both public and private buildings, David Wilson pursues the goal of designing glass that adds to and enriches architecture. Emphasizing the importance of harmony in the built environment, his designs are the result of reducing forms to their simplest solution.

COMMISSIONS: St. John Baptist Catholic Church, 2003, Howell, MI; Lavan House, 2002, Townsend Inlet, NJ; Plainfield Station, 2002, Plainfield, NJ; Airtrain Monorail Station, Newark Liberty National Airport, 2002, Newark, NJ

PUBLICATIONS: *The Art of Glass*, 1998; *Architectural Glass Art*, 1997

GUILD SOURCEBOOKS: *THE GUILD 1, 2, 3, 4, 5; Architect's 6, 7, 8, 9, 11, 13, 14, 15; Architectural & Interior Art 16, 17*

JIM DELUTES
Page 240

Jim DeLutes Photography
PO Box 1634
Boulder, CO 80306
Tel/Fax 303-678-9089
E-mail jdphotos@earthlink.net
www.jdlphotos.com

Jim DeLutes creates brilliantly colored photographs using only the camera, his own lighting systems and his imagination. Even when he steps out of the studio, his unique style can be seen in his nature photographs. After 30 years of photography, it is still the experimentation and fun that drives the creative forces for DeLutes' future projects. A self-taught photographer, Jim DeLutes has developed a style that is truly his own.

RECENT PROJECTS: Nationally released DVDs: "Natural Splendors," volumes 1 and 5; poster for Denver International Airport opening ceremonies, 1995

COLLECTIONS: Hewlett Packard, Fort Collins, CO

EXHIBITIONS: 20 nationally juried shows per year; see website for schedule.

AWARDS: Website of the Month, *Shutterbug* magazine, August 2000

303

ANN DELUTY
Page 92

12 Randolph Street
Belmont, MA 02478
Tel/Fax 617-484-0069
E-mail anndel@aol.com
www.ann-deluty.ws

Ann Deluty strives to express the essence of natural objects in stone and wood. Her work ranges from abstract to extremely realistic. Her mastery of textures and carving techniques gives an air of realism to any object. A graduate of the School of the Museum of Fine Arts, she is also known for her portraits of people and pets in bronze, clay and cold-cast bronze. Deluty has numerous works in private collections, and commissions are welcome. Because of the variety of colors available in alabaster, she can carve to match any color scheme.

RECENT PROJECTS: Neon sculpture for dentist office, Lawrence, MA

GUILD SOURCEBOOKS: *Architect's 15; Designer's 15; Architectural & Interior Art 16, 17*

DEMETRIOS & EAMES
Page 132

Llisa Demetrios/Lucia Eames
PO Box 870
Petaluma, CA 94953
Tel 707-769-1777
Fax 707-769-1780

Llisa Demetrios creates sculptures for contemplative retreats set in homes, private gardens and corporate spaces. Working with bronze in abstract forms, she shapes sculpture that is universally approachable yet has an individual impact. Lucia Eames designs large and small tables, benches, gates, screens and sculptures in bronze, steel and aluminum. The pieces are used indoors and outdoors. The positive/negative patterns created provide modulated light and cast rich shadows.

GUILD SOURCEBOOKS: *Architect's 7, 8, 9, 10, 12; Artful Home 1*

JOSEPH DETWILER
Page 25

13 River Ridge Lane
Fredericksburg, VA 22406
Tel 540-752-2656
E-mail joe@josephdetwiler.com
www.josephdetwiler.com

Joseph Detwiler creates ceramic wall reliefs blending elements of painting, sculpture and architectural tile work. For over 20 years, his work has appeared regularly in galleries and museums worldwide, earning many awards in the process. Whether Detwiler's commissions are large-scale or small, public or site-specific, the complex surfaces of his pieces always provide a sensuous counterpoint to the underlying terra cotta forms.

COLLECTIONS: Renwick Gallery, Washington, DC; Shapparton Art Gallery, Victoria, Australia; World Bank, Washington, DC; Instituto Statale d'Arte per la Ceramica, Castelli, Italy; Delaware Art Museum, Wilmington; City of Frejus, France

COMMISSIONS: IBM Corporation, Raleigh, NC; Howard Hughes Medical Institute, Washington, DC; Forrestal Center, Princeton, NJ; HealthSouth, Birmingham, AL

FRANK DIENST
Page 241

Frank Dienst Photography
3940 Pinetop Boulevard
Titusville, FL 32796
Tel 321-268-0386
Fax 321-268-3719
E-mail md1@brevard.net
www.frankdienst.com

Frank Dienst is a fine art photographer who has worked in his medium for over 25 years. He self-published his award-winning book, *Wetland Voices*, in 1999. Working primarily in black and white, he produces limited-edition prints in gelatin silver, platinum or alternative processes of bromoil and gum dichromate.

COMMISSIONS: Parrish Medical Center, 2002, Titusville, FL; Florida House, 2001, Washington, DC

COLLECTIONS: Museum of Art and Science, Melbourne, FL; Lindemann Gallery and Bookstore, Germany

EXHIBITIONS: *Nature Speaks*, 2000, Orlando Sentinel, FL

PUBLICATIONS: *Peterson's Photographic magazine*, 2002; *Object Lessons*, 2001; *LensWork Quarterly*, 2000; *Natural History* magazine, 2000; *Shutterbug magazine*, 1999

ANDY DUFFORD & CHRISTIAN MULLER
Pages 133, 138

Artscapes, LLC
4441 West 30th Avenue
Denver, CO 80212
Tel 303-477-3780
Fax 303-477-0737
E-mail andy@artscapesllc.com
christian@artscapesllc.com
www.artscapesllc.com

Artscapes was formed with the express purpose of reintegrating art into the everyday environment. Andy Dufford and Christian Muller create delightful living spaces. Their work is a hybrid of sculpture and image, poetry, landscape and urban design. Artscapes has a 16-year history, with extensive experience in all phases of collaboration, design and construction. In addition, Artscapes networks with exceptional subcontractors and fabricators committed to the finest of work. Together, they form a unique community of talent that makes each project shine.

RECENT PROJECTS: McDATA Corporation, Broomfield, CO; Maroon Bells National Forest, Snowmass, CO; Pinnacol Assurance, Denver, CO

COMMISSIONS: Larimer County Justice Center, Fort Collins, CO; Connecting Point, Boulder, CO; Airlife Memorial, Denver, CO

JEROME R. DURR
Page 52

Jerome R. Durr Studio
206 Marcellus Street
Syracuse, NY 13119
Tel 315-428-1322
Fax 315-478-1767
E-mail jrdurr0art@aol.com
www.jeromedurr.com

Since 1973, Jerome Durr has been designing, fabricating and installing architectural glass artworks using the techniques of painting, etching, carving, slumping, fusing and leading.

COMMISSIONS: National Baseball Hall of Fame, Cooperstown, NY; Blair Academy, Blairstown, NJ; Lehman Brothers, New York, NY; Christian Dior, various sites; Carlisle Corporation, Syracuse, NY

AWARDS: Best of Show, Art Glass Guild, Atlanta, GA; Best of Show, Cooperstown Art Open, NY

PUBLICATIONS: *Custom Home*, 2000; *Upstate Living Magazine*

GUILD SOURCEBOOKS: *GUILD 4, 5; Architect's 6, 7, 8, 9, 10, 14, 15; Architectural & Interior Art 16*

EARTH FIRE DESIGNS
Page 23

Frederick Michael King
740 Metcalf, Suite #29
Escondido, CA 92025
Tel 760-747-3347
Fax 760-871-3348
E-mail earthfiredesign@aol.com
www.earthfiredesigns.com

Michael King combines clay, metal and glass to create works of art that uplift and inspire the romantic in all of us. He specializes in custom fireplace surrounds, sculpted murals and fine art wall-mounted sculptures. He received a B.F.A. in sculpture from the University of Wisconsin-Milwaukee in 1979. His work has been collected nationally and featured on the Discovery Channel. Studio services range from concept drawings to installation. Prices, samples and a portfolio are available on request.

GUILD SOURCEBOOKS: *Artful Home 1*

JEFF EASLEY
Page 275

PO Box 502
Wellman, IA 52356
Tel 319-646-2521
Fax 319-628-4766
E-mail jeasley811@aol.com

Award-winning designer and artisan Jeff Easley creates wall sculptures and studio furniture, combining his high standards of craftsmanship with refined designs and the natural beauty of wood. Dimension requirements, wood preferences and design options may be discussed for your projects. Other designs are available upon request. Comments from clients include: "Installation was a breeze. We have enjoyed having a piece of your art in our home and know that we will continue to enjoy it in the years ahead." "We will always value and appreciate your magnificent artwork in our home." "Thank you for such beautiful works. We are so pleased to have them enhance the comfort of our home." "I feel very fortunate to have found you and your work."

MARTIN EICHINGER
Page 115

Eichinger Sculpture Studio
1302 NW Kearney Street
Portland, OR 97209
Tel 503-223-0626
Fax 503-223-0454
E-mail studio@eichingersculpture.com
www.eichingersculpture.com

Martin Eichinger's bronzes are refreshingly unique. They are evidence of a visionary artist who has something positive and eternal to say with his talent. Eichinger's profound comprehension of human anatomy has allowed him to place his sculpture studies on the edge of possibility without losing a sense of grace. Each sculpture has a personality, a story to tell, a wink of humor, a hint of tragedy or, if we look a bit more closely, an entire philosophy.

COMMISSIONS: *Whirlwind, Gaia's Breath* and *Rapture*, near life-size cast bronze sculptures; *Ronald Reagan*, portrait bust; *10th Mountain Division*, U.S. Army, 50th-anniversary commemorative sculpture; Columbus commemorative high-relief plaque

ARTIST LISTINGS

ELLEN MANDELBAUM GLASS ART
Page 53

Ellen Mandelbaum
39-49 46th Street
Long Island City, NY 11104-1407
Tel/Fax 718-361-8154
E-mail emga@ix.netcom.com
www.emglassart.com

Since 1981, Ellen Mandelbaum has been creating extraordinary glass art that attracts professionals working in the fields of art, architecture and religion. There is a rare and unique element of spontaneity and openness that Mandelbaum manages to achieve in a medium that traditionally projects great weight and formality. The beauty of stained glass's color and light remain at the heart of her work.

AWARDS: *Ministry and Liturgy* magazine, "Bene" Best of Show; AIA-IFRAA Award of Excellence, 1997

GUILD SOURCEBOOKS: *GUILD 1, 2, 3, 5; Architect's 6, 8, 9, 10, 11, 12, 13, 14, 15; Architectural & Interior Art 16, 17*

KEN ELLIOTT
Page 217

250 Lead King Drive
Castle Rock, CO 80108
Tel/Fax 303-814-1122
E-mail elliottkc@earthlink.net
www.kenelliott.com

Ken Elliott is a landscape artist who focuses primarily on color and composition. His works are direct, showing the lessons of the Impressionist as well as Modern schools. He works primarily in oils and pastels and reproduces some of his images as editioned giclee prints. His alternative way of making giclees has attracted attention, resulting in an award for one of the "50 Best Images of 2001."

COLLECTIONS: Hewlett Packard; Kaiser-Permanente; First Data Corp; Visa; Blue Shield; Hitachi; the David and Lucile Packard Foundation

PUBLICATIONS: *Pastel Journal, New York Times on the Web, Artweek, U.S. Art*

ROBERT W. ELLISON
Page 159

Ellison Studio
6480 Eagle Ridge Road
Penngrove, CA 94951
Tel 707-795-9775
Fax 707-795-4370
E-mail robertellison@sonic.net
www.rellison.com

Ellison brings three decades of experience to public art, as well as corporate and private commissions. He creates large, whimsical pieces in rich colors using steel, concrete, neon and clockworks. His in-house fabrication facility allows for excellent value and craftsmanship; all projects have been completed on schedule and within budget. Design-team collaborations are welcomed.

RECENT PROJECTS: Dublin Public Library, Open Book Plaza, Dublin, CA; City Park Lincolnshire Shopping Center, Chicago, IL; Embarcadero Station, San Francisco, CA; Harvest Community Park, Greenwood Village, CO; Jack London Aquatic Center, Estuary Park, Oakland, CA

PUBLICATIONS: *Beautiful Things*, 2000

GUILD SOURCEBOOKS: *Architect's 13, 15*

305

FARRELL ART STUDIO
Pages 86, 117

Kathleen Farrell
350 North Raynor Avenue
Joliet, IL 60435
Tel 815-723-6430
Fax 815-722-9007
E-mail farrellartstudio@cs.com
www.fcpaonline.org

Kathleen Farrell specializes in outdoor figurative sculptures. Her work is available from existing editions or by commission. She frequently casts her life-size pieces in bonded bronze over fiberglass (a much less expensive process than lost-wax bronze). Farrell is also available for commissions in limestone. Tabletop bronzes of her life-size pieces are available. Farrell is a colleague of the National Sculpture Society.

COMMISSIONS: South Chicago Street, 2002, Joliet, IL; Broadway Park, 2002, Joliet, IL; Westside Joliet Library, 2002, Joliet, IL; Union Train Station, 2001, Joliet, IL; Louis Joliet Mall, 2001, Joliet, IL; Sanchez Park, 2000, Joliet, IL; Glenwood Park, 2000, Joliet, IL

EXHIBITIONS: *Creating Art, Building Communities: Joliet and Friends of Community Public Art*, 2003, Field Museum of Natural History, Chicago, IL

PUBLICATIONS: *Sculptures: The Great Columns of Joliet*, 2004

TOM FAUGHT
Page 26

Tom Faught Studio & Foundry
200 Kaluanui Road
Makawao, HI 96768
Tel 808-572-8904
Fax 808-572-2642
Email faught@maui.net
www.tomfaught.com

Artist and master craftsman Tom Faught creates innovative pieces to fit architectural spaces. Donning protective gear and wielding a 6,000-degree Fahrenheit torch, Faught sheathes his works with bronze and copper, creating unique, shimmering surfaces. Add artistic solutions to your clients' needs with Faught's large-scale vessels, sculptures, wooden panels and doors.

COMMISSIONS: Queen Ka'ahumanu Center, 2000, Maui; Molokai Ranch Hotel, 1997, Molokai; Joe's Bar & Grill, 1994, Wailea, Maui; Hali'imaile General Store, 1991, Maui,; Dolphin Plaza, 1985, Kihei, Maui

COLLECTIONS: Kapalua Bay Hotel, Maui; Ritz-Carlton Hotel, Kapalua, Maui; Four Seasons Hotel, Tokyo; Emperor of Japan

FERROMOBIUS
Pages 38, 41

Allen Root
David Curry
PO Box 288
San Luis Obispo, CA 93406
Tel/Fax 805-544-7960
E-mail info@ferromobius.com
www.ferromobius.com

The Ferromobius team continues to evolve, pushing the limits of its craft and exploring new directions. Marrying bronze, steel and aluminum with fabric, stone, wood and glass, their work has contributed to sites across North America with artful grace. Their diverse and satisfying projects spring from a collaborative team that typically includes the client and his or her designers. From furniture to major architectural components, Ferromobius continues to play a dynamic part of residential, commercial and corporate projects, as well as works in the public sector. All inquiries are welcome.

RECENT PROJECTS: Cornerstone Professional Center, Palm Desert, CA; Desert Willow Golf Resort, Deal residence, San Luis Obispo, CA; Brown residence, Cambria, CA

GUILD SOURCEBOOKS: *Architect's 9, 10, 13, 14; Designer's 12*

ARTIST LISTINGS

BRUCE PAUL FINK
Page 135

90 Pole Bridge Road
Woodstock, CT 06281
Tel 860-974-0130
E-mail: bpfink@artmetal.com
www.artmetal.com/bpfink

Examples of Bruce Paul Fink's 900-plus internationally collected works are illustrated on the web under the signature "bpfink." His studio/foundry works are made with cast bronze, aluminum, steel, bonded stone as well as polyester and epoxy resins. Architectural doors, walls, entries and garden sculptures are often site-commissioned and have included participatory works and community projects with special-needs children and elderly groups. The piece shown in this book was done while Fink was an artist-in-residence on Lana'i, Hawaii, where he worked with elementary school children, as well as faculty and community members.

GUILD SOURCEBOOKS: *Architect's 8, 9, 11, 12, 14, 15; Architectural & Interior Art 16, 17*

ROB FISHER
Pages 82, 160

Rob Fisher Sculpture
228 North Allegheny Street
Bellefonte, PA 16823
Tel 814-355-1458
Fax 814-353-9060
E-mail glenunion@aol.com
www.sculpture.org/portfolio

Rob Fisher creates monumental artworks for public spaces in stainless steel, aluminum, glass and light. Extensive experience working with architects and designers. Project management, engineering and installation supervision. Residential commissions are accepted.

COMMISSIONS: Arrivals Hall, 2003, Philadelphia International Airport, PA; National Education Association, 2003, Washington, DC; Harbor Branch Oceanographic Institute, 2003, Ft. Pierce, FL; AstraZeneca Pharmaceuticals, 2002, Wilmington, DE; Gateway Exchange, 2002, Columbia, MD

EXHIBITIONS: Environment Art Academy, 2002, Tokyo, Japan; Grounds for Sculpture, 2001, Hamilton, NJ

GUILD SOURCEBOOKS: *Architect's 9, 11, 12, 13, 14, 15, Architectural & Interior Art 16, 17, Artful Home 1*

STEVE FONTANINI
Page 42

Steve Fontanini Architectural
& Ornamental Blacksmithing
PO Box 2298
Jackson, WY 83001
Tel 307-733-7668
Fax 307-734-8816
E-mail sfontani@wyoming.com

The confluence of the Snake and Hoback rivers is where Steve Fontanini and company produce metalwork of all kinds. Stair railings, gates and chandeliers can be built according to the customer's design or created as new designs to fit the customer's needs. Projects are built by forging hot metal and joining the pieces with traditional methods such as rivets, collars and mortise-and-tenon joints. Fontanini's work is found throughout the United States.

AWARDS: Silver award, forged interior railings, 2002, National Ornamental and Miscellaneous Metals Association (NOMMA)

GEORGE FOSTER
Page 279

Sealight Gallery
151 Sherrie Lane
Del Mar, CA 92014
Tel 858-755-5421
Fax 858-755-5192
E-mail gfoster324@aol.com

Many artists summon motivation from their captivating muse. For artist George Foster, his inspirational goddess is the enduring breath and enchanting beauty of the ocean. Foster creates sealife sculptures, coined *Sealights*. The birth of a *Sealight* begins with a simple sheet of copper. The copper is placed into scorching flames within a shoreline fire-ring. When it begins to glow, it is submerged in shallow ocean waters for cooling. The *Sealight* is now pliable and can be shaped by hammer. Copper, mica, glass, painting, and finishing solutions all add depth. Finally, light bulbs and electrical parts are attached. *Sealights* represent the ocean's strength, fluidity and beauty, they create a captivating ambiance in any indoor or outdoor space.

RON FOSTER AND MICHAEL LINSLEY
Page 136

Kaleidosculpture
379 La Perle Place
Costa Mesa, CA 92627
Tel 949-650-0662
Fax 949-650-6890
E-mail ron@kaleidosculpture.com
E-mail michael@kaleidosculpture.com
www.kaleidosculpture.com

Kaleidosculpture™ is a new concept in art and sculpture. It fuses kaleidoscope theory—multiple, duplicated, single-plane symmetrical images placed at opposing angles—with color theory, bringing to life a three-dimensional, interactive kaleidoscope effect that uniquely mimics and complements its surroundings. Like kaleidoscopes, each sculpture changes dramatically depending on the viewing angle. Creators Ron Foster, a former Vietnam combat illustrator and successful commercial artist, and Michael Linsley, a versatile ceramist with a flair for diverse techniques and styles, combine their talents and an infinite array of materials, colors and textures to spectacularly ignite any locale through this innovative, incomparable medium.

FOX FIRE GLASS
Page 54

Laurel Fyfe
180 North Saginaw Street
Pontiac, MI 48342
Tel 248-332-2442
Fax 248-332-2424
www.foxfireglass.com

Laurel Fyfe is devoted to stretching the artistic development of glass. Bringing over 20 years of artistic glass working experience to her critically acclaimed studio, Fyfe uses self-taught techniques and problem-solving skills to fuel the evolution of Fox Fire's wide range of capabilities. From architectural glass art to original sculptures, Fyfe successfully implements a variety of techniques, including glass bending, casting, sand carving and optically clear bonding.

RECENT PROJECTS: Cathedral of the Most Blessed Sacrament, Detroit, MI; Northwest World Gateway, McNamara Terminal, Detroit, MI

PUBLICATIONS: *Interior Design* magazine (cover), December 2002; *Crain's Detroit Business*, Winter/Spring 2002

ARTIST LISTINGS

DOUGLAS OLMSTED FREEMAN
Page 161

Doug Freeman Sculpture Studio
310 North 2nd Street
Minneapolis, MN 55401
Tel 612-339-7150
Fax 612-339-5201
E-mail dfree@twincities.infi.net
www.freemanstudio.com

Doug Freeman works sensitively with individuals and communities to create public art that becomes part of a neighborhood—an enduring symbol and a place for people. His figurative sculptures are cast in bronze. The fountains' palettes may also include stainless steel, concrete, glass, stone and a touch of gold leaf.

COMMISSIONS: *The Fountain of the Wind, The Seven Lucky Gods of Japan, The Cincinnati Flying Pigs*

GUILD SOURCEBOOKS: *Architect's 10, 11, 12; Architectural & Interior Art 16*

RANDY FROST
Page 288

11 Sunset Avenue
Bronxville, NY 10708
Tel 914-337-7122
Fax 914-337-2701
E-mail fiberarch@earthlink.net

Randy Frost creates quilted constructions using cottons, silks and embellishment. Abstract imagery is inspired by landscapes, still lifes and close views of plant life. Works are created using an appliquéd collage technique and are sewn by machine, layered, machine quilted and hand embellished.

RECENT PROJECTS: Supervised students in design and construction of entrance lobby quilt for United Way of New York City

COLLECTIONS: Museum of Arts and Design, New York, NY; Fish & Neave, New York, NY; United Way, 1999, New York, NY; numerous private collections.

EXHIBITIONS: *The Quilted Surface*, Columbus Museum of Art, Columbus, OH; *Artist as Quiltmaker X*, FAVA, Oberlin, OH

AWARDS: Honorable Mention, Aullwood Audubon Center, 1997; President's Award for Excellence in Education, 1999, Concorida College, Bronxville, NY

PUBLICATIONS: *Quilting Arts*, Summer 2002; *American Style*, Fall 2000

GLASSIC ART
Page 55

Leslie Rankin
5850 South Polaris Suite 700
Las Vegas, NV 89118
Tel 702-658-7588
Fax 702-658-7342
E-mail glassicart@glassicart.com
www.glassicart.com

For over 20 years, Glassic Art has been creating innovative and intriguing works of art that are both functional and decorative. Using a combination of techniques (including painting, sandblasting, etching and fusing), types of glass (dichroic, iridescent, plate, smoked, stained and streamed) and materials from all over the world, Leslie Rankin and her talented team will create anything imaginable. Bring your vision and they'll make it a reality.

RECENT PROJECTS: MGM Grand Casino, Las Vegas, NV; Turnberry Towers penthouse residence, and Park Towers residence, Las Vegas, NV

COMMISSIONS: Golden Door Spa, 2002, Puerto Rico; Street of Dreams, 2002, Las Vegas, NV

PUBLICATIONS: *"Modern Masters,"* HGTV; *American Style* magazine, 2003

GUILD SOURCEBOOKS: *Architect's 12, 15; Architectural & Interior Art 16*

JOHN PETER GLOVER
Page 219

JP Glover Fine Art
108 Lakeland Drive
Mars, PA 16046
Tel/Fax 724-538-8879
E-mail john@jpgloverart.com
www.jpgloverart.com

John Peter Glover's digital works usually begin as graphite and ink drawings. The work is scanned into his Mac system work environment, primarily using Adobe Photoshop. He then manipulates his own drawings in one of two fundamental ways. In the first approach, the drawing gets a treatment of color. Particular attention is paid to getting maximum quality at a high resolution given the final paper size of the limited edition. In the second approach, Glover uses multiple layers of his drawings and then recomposes and stacks the images until the final effect is achieved. Out of necessity, he emphasizes that the final work is digital but not computer generated. The end result is a unique art form that often mystifies the viewer. Price range: $600-$2,000 for limited-edition prints and $4,000-$8,000 for acrylic or oil paintings.

NANCY GONG
Page 56

Gong Glass Works
42 Parkview Drive
Rochester, NY 14625
Tel 585-288-5520
Fax 585-288-2503
E-mail ngong@rochester.rr.com
www.artsrochester.org/artists/ngong.htm

With a rich personal style and an impressive command of her medium, Nancy Gong creates sensitive, responsive and enduring glass designs with quality craftsmanship for architectural installations and art collections. "The spirit and energy of living things has always intrigued me. It continues to be at the very core of my art. I constantly strive to capture grace, movement and dimension of life in a simple, yet powerful style. Facets of nature are the soul of my art. Lyrical abstractions of nature and the Orient come to life through the use of line, color, texture, balance and the silent beauty of glass and metal."

LYNN GOODPASTURE
Page 57

10753 Weyburn Avenue
Los Angeles, CA 90024
Tel 310-470-2455
Fax 310-470-4257
E-mail lgoodpast@aol.com

Lynn Goodpasture designs, fabricates and installs site-specific art (including large-scale clocks), in collaboration with architects, for integration with architecture and the landscape. Materials include stone and glass mosaic, architectural glass, and metal. Public and private commissions welcomed.

COMMISSIONS: *Explorer of the Seas*, three mosaic murals (663 sq. ft.), 2000, Royal Caribbean Cruise Line; mosaic mural (715 sq. ft.) and architectural glass window (243 sq. ft.), 2000, Mott Children's Center, Good Samaritan Hospital, Puyallup, WA; *The Children's Clock*, opalescent glass and painted metal tower clock, 2003, Center for Early Education, West Hollywood, CA; architectural glass installation, 2003, East Valley Animal Services Center, Van Nuys, CA; *Station Clock*, suspended dual-faced mosaic clock, 1999, Glendale Transportation Center, Glendale, CA

GUILD SOURCEBOOKS: *Architectural & Interior Art 17*

ARTIST LISTINGS

CALI GOREVIC
Pages 96, 242

377 Lane Gate Road
Cold Spring, NY 10516
Tel 845-265-4625
Fax 845-265-4620
E-mail calig@mindspring.com
www.caligorevic.com

Man and nature, flora and fauna: these are the predominant themes in the photography and sculpture of Cali Gorevic. She creates black-and-white silver emulsion and giclee prints. The subject matter is taken from nature and transformed in her darkroom. Both silver and giclee prints are available in sizes ranging from small to mural. Gorevic's sculptures, from tabletop to life size, are cast in bronze. Human and tree forms are woven in an organic, evocative medley. The work is finely crafted, with some pieces making the transition to functional art, specifically as oil, candle or electric lighting fixtures. Gorevic has exhibited internationally, and her work appears in many private and public collections.

GUILD SOURCEBOOKS: *Architectural & Interior Art 16*

AMY GRASSFIELD
Page 98

Peas-on-Earth
901 West San Mateo
Santa Fe, NM 87505
Tel 505-982-9411
E-mail agrassfield@yahoo.com

Grassfield's earthy and eccentric vision finds poetry in a whimsical and leguminous fantasy world of oversized peapods, tendrils and foliage, which are masterfully fashioned into functional objects such as furniture, garden fixtures, lanterns, fountains and sculpture. First trained at Tiffany's and Cartier Inc., Grassfield exploits jewelry-making techniques to fabricate large-scale objects from hand-tooled, patinaed copper and steel elements. She has created installations for retails stores, public spaces, restaurants and residences, and relishes every unique opportunity to spread "Peas-on-Earth."

COMMISSIONS: Blue Fish Inc., Taos, NM; Dandelion Green Restaurant, Bellerica, MA; Barnsider Restaurant, Albany, NY; Bernadette Peters; Dudley Moore

PUBLICATIONS: *Victoria, Home & Garden, Sunset*

NANCY GRAY
Page 188

Gray Studio
508 East Fourth Street
Lampasas, TX 76550
Tel 512-525-1963/ 512-556-6997
Fax 512-556-3608
E-mail nancy@graystudio.net
www.graystudio.net

Figurative and nonrepresentational paintings were hallmarks of Nancy Gray's art until she moved from the city to settle in rural central Texas. The area's rugged environment fueled a passion for landscape painting. Design decisions for her new country house and studio also inspired the award-winning artist to explore new applications for her work. She now paints her bold, romantic landscapes on trifold screens and designed metal gates that feature stylized representations of native flora.

RECENT PROJECTS: Set of double-entry gates to span a driveway; freestanding metal sculpture using metal techniques from Gray's own garden gates

FRANK GREGORY
Pages 162, 198, 200

Frank Gregory Studios
Two Mead Street, Suite 3
Greenfield, MA 01301
Tel 413-772-0088
E-mail artist@frankgregory.com
www.frankgregory.com

After many years as a *plein aire* painter, Frank Gregory now creates large, complex murals and constructions. He works in many mediums, including oils, acrylic and wood. The astonishing realism in his work extends beyond a superb attention to detail to include genuine mood and emotion. The intense, focused vision required to produce such artwork does not hinder his enthusiasm for working with clients and architects to produce the finest work possible for a given space.

RECENT PROJECTS: Art in State Buildings Program, Palm Beach County Health Department, Florida; U.S. Fish and Wildlife Service, Great Falls Discovery Center, Turners Falls, MA

JANE B. GRIMM
Page 276

1895 Pacific Avenue #305
San Francisco, CA 94109
Tel 415-922-2823
Fax 415-563-6926
E-mail jbgrimm2000@yahoo.com
www.janebgrimm.com

Jane Grimm's unique, wall-hung ceramic sculptures are mounted in wood boxes ranging in size from intimate to large-scale. Subtle transformations of form and/or color are the focus of these sculptures. Freestanding ceramic sculptures and handmade tiles are also available.

COMMISSIONS: Lucent Technologies, Inc., San Carlos, CA; Temple Isaiah, Orinda, CA

COLLECTIONS: Nora Eccles Harris Museum, WA; University of California-Berkeley Art Museum, CA

EXHIBITIONS: *Pacific Rim Sculpture Group Invitational*, 2003, Oakland Museum Sculpture Court, CA; *Cool, Calm and Collected*, 2003, Richmond Art Center, Richmond, CA

AWARDS: Association of Clay and Glass Artists of California Award, 1999, California State Fair; Jack and Gertrude Murphy Fellowship, 1991, San Francisco Foundation

MARK ERIC GULSRUD
Page 58

Architectural Glass/Sculpture
3309 Tahoma Place West
Tacoma, WA 98466
Tel 253-566-1720
Fax 253-565-5981
E-mail markgulsrud@attbi.com
www.markericgulsrud.com

Primarily site-specific, Mark Eric Gulsrud's commissions range internationally and include public, private, corporate and liturgical settings. Media include custom hand-blown leaded glass; sand-carved, laminated and cast glass; handmade ceramic; stone; and carved wood. Encouraging professional collaboration, the artist is personally involved in all phases of design, fabrication and installation, and is primarily concerned with a sympathetic integration of artwork with environment.

GUILD SOURCEBOOKS: *GUILD 3, 4; Architect's 7, 8, 9, 10, 11, 12, 13, 14, 15; Architectural & Interior Art 16, 17*

ARTIST LISTINGS

JOAN ROTHCHILD HARDIN
Page 27

Joan Rothchild Hardin Ceramics
393 West Broadway #4
New York, NY 10012
Tel 212 966-9433
Fax 212 431-9196
E-mail joan@HardinTiles.com
www.HardinTiles.com

Joan Hardin's award-winning art tiles, whether installed or hung as paintings, add richness and interest to residential, corporate and public settings. Layered glazes create jewel-like surfaces depicting abstract and representational subjects.

COMMISSIONS: Private residences across the country; three veterinary hospitals, New York, NY

COLLECTIONS: American Art Clay Company, Indianapolis, IN

EXHIBITIONS: *21st-Century Tiles*, 2002, Minnesota Crafts Council; *Tiles in America*, 2002, Clay Fine Arts Gallery, Cheyenne, WY

AWARDS: Architecture Award, Fourth Silverhawk Competition

PUBLICATIONS: *Ceramic Art Tile for the Home*, 2001

GUILD SOURCEBOOKS: *Designer's 14, 15; Architectural & Interior Art 16, 17*

MICHELE HARDY
Pages 280, 289

147 Acadian Lane
Mandeville, LA 70471
Tel 985-845-0792
E-mail mhardy@michelehardy.com
www.michelehardy.com

Michele Hardy is a full-time mixed-media artist. Her work incorporates surface design, quilting and embroidery in a personalized approach to textile assembly. Vibrant color, energy, texture and graphic appeal are all important aspects of her images. A lifelong love of geology and nature is the inspiration for current work.

COLLECTIONS: Claiborne Collection, State of Louisiana; Salem International University, Salem, WV

EXHIBITIONS: Solo exhibitions, 2000, 2002, 2003, Thirteen Moons Gallery, Santa Fe, NM; *Art Quilts at the Sedgwick*, 2001-2003, Philadelphia, PA; *Contemporary Crafts*, 2002, Mesa Arts Center, AZ; *Crafts National*, 2002, State College, PA

GUILD SOURCEBOOKS: *Artful Home 1*

MARK YALE HARRIS
Page 93

ARTwork
1701 Suite A Lena Street
Santa Fe, NM 87505
Tel 505-982-7447
Fax 505-982-7447
E-mail ARTworkSFE@aol.com
www.markyaleharris.com

Harris's figurative works combine soft lines with geometric shapes and a disproportion which suggests the duality of humanity. In a distinctly different vein, Harris's animal sculptures capture moments in time and the whimsy of nature. The artist eschews excessive detail, allowing line, form and the qualities of the stone to take precedence. Selected works are available in limited-edition bronze.

COMMISSIONS: Edward Peace, Congressman, IN

COLLECTIONS: Arnold and Barbara Stream, Santa Fe, NM; Rosemarie Francis, Gaithersburg, MD; Bernie and Honey Drucker, New York, NY

EXHIBITIONS: *Animals in the Atrium*, 2001, National Sculpture Society, New York, NY; national juried exhibition, 2002, Holter Museum, Helena, MT

PUBLICATIONS: *Sculpture in the Park* catalog, 2002; *Flash of Spirit* catalog, 2002; "News Bulletin," National Sculpture Society, 2002

309

O.K. HARRIS
Page 99

O.K. Harris Studio
4417 11th Street NW
Albuquerque, NM 87107
Tel 505-344-1604
Fax 505-880-8839
E-mail oksculptor@artisok.com
www.artisok.com

O.K. Harris has welded his way into the hearts of thousands, welding steel into non-traditional, unexpectedly animated, often kinetic and always charismatic creatures and designs. Harris's creations are at home in any environment. Unusual textures used to create hair, fur or other interesting surfaces defy the expectations of steel as a sculptural element. Harris combines the durable strength of steel with atomized metallic particles, which produce metal finishes of copper, nickel, pewter, brass and bronze. All of these surfaces can be chemically altered to create completely unique finishes. Harris is available to interpret commission pieces or provide a vast selection of his own ideas.

YOSHI HAYASHI
Page 237

255 Kansas Street
San Francisco, CA 94103
Tel 415-552-0755/415-924-9224
Fax 415-552-0755
E-mail yoshihayashi@att.net
www.yoshihayashi.com

Yoshi Hayashi was born in Japan and learned the rigorous techniques of Japanese lacquer art from his father. Hayashi carries the spirit, history and inspiration of this process with him today as he reinterprets the ancient lacquer traditions for his screens and wall panels. Hayashi's designs range from delicate traditional 17th-century Japanese lacquer art themes to bold, contemporary geometric designs. By skillfully applying metallic leaf and bronzing powders, he adds both illumination and contrast to the network of color, pattern and texture. Recent commissions include works for private residences in the United States and Japan.

RECENT PROJECTS: Lobby, Marriott Desert Ridge; Library, Tokyo, Japan; private residence, Hawaii

GUILD SOURCEBOOKS: *THE GUILD 3, 4, 5; Designer's 6, 7, 8, 9, 10, 11, 12, 13, 14, 15; Architectural & Interior Art 16, 17; Artful Home 1*

MICHAEL HAYDEN & KRISTINA LUCAS
Page 164

Thinking Lightly, Inc.
5076 Hall Road
Santa Rosa, CA 95401-5511
Tel 707-546-0664
Fax 707-546-0661
E-mail thinklt@sonnic.net
www.thinkinglightly.com

Michael Hayden and Kristina Lucas, as Thinking Lightly, Inc., have created architectonic multi-media, site-specific artworks for four decades for museums, public galleries, airports, train stations, schools, civic centers and libraries, as well as corporate and private collections worldwide.

RECENT PROJECTS: For the Charles M. Schulz Museum, Santa Rosa, CA: *Lucy's Baseball Cap*, 2002, fiberglass-reinforced plastic painted with color shifting ChromaFlair® pigments, 14' × 23' × 6'; *Woodstock's Birdbath*, 2002, fiberglass reinforced plastic with five imaging holograms, 44" × 32"; *Charlie Brown's Kite in Kite-Eating Tree*, 2002, heat-formed Implex® with holographic deposition and 1000' florescent electro-luminescent wire, 66"H × 44"W; *Liquid Light* drinking fountains, 2002, polycarbonate basins with holographic features and stainless steel hardware.

GUILD SOURCEBOOKS: *Architect's 8, 13*

ARTIST LISTINGS

RENEÉ HEADINGS
Page 163

PO Box 73
Skytop, PA 18357
Tel 570-992-1754
Fax 570-402-1921
E-mail reneeheadings@yahoo.com
www.sculpturesgallery.com

The intricate attention to detail in Renee Headings's fine-art bronzes creates a feeling of realism that reveals the breath of life within each sculpture. She has significant experience collaborating with committees, architects and designers to create site-specific sculptures in the public and private sectors.

RECENT PROJECTS: Public commission, 2002, Mather Air Force Base, Mather, CA; National War Dog Memorial finalist, 2002, Washington, DC

COMMISSIONS: Shands Arts in Medicine, 1998, Gainsville, FL; Texas A&M Alumni, 1998, College Station, TX; Veteran's Administration Medical Center, 1993, Riviera Beach, FL (all public art projects)

COLLECTIONS: Hiram Blauvelt Art Museum, Oradell, NJ; Sultanate of Oman

AWARDS: Medal of Honor, 1999, American Artist Professional League; Best in Show, Pen and Brush

PUBLICATIONS: *The Spirit of Sculpture*, 1996

HELAMAN FERGUSON, SCULPTOR
Page 146

10512 Pilla Terra Court
Laurel, MD 20723
Tel 301-604-4270
Fax 301-776-0499
E-mail helamanf@helasculpt.com
www.helasculpt.com

Helaman Ferguson's sculpture celebrates science in stone and bronze and is available in sizes ranging from handheld to monumental. Tools include everything from mathematics and computers to chisels and diamond saws.

COLLECTIONS: Maryland Science and Technology Center, Bowie, MD; Merck Pharmaceutical, Upper Gwynedd, PA; Princeton University, Princeton, NJ; Clay Mathematics Institute, Cambridge, MA; Mathematical Sciences Research Center, Berkeley, CA; University of St. Thomas, St. Paul, MN; Smith College, Northampton, MA; Institute for Defense Analyses, Alexandria, VA; Weisman Art Museum, Minneapolis, MN; American Mathematical Society, Providence, RI

PUBLICATIONS: *Fragments of Infinity*, 2002; *Nature*, 2001; *Science*, 1999; *Eightfold Way*, 1998

ARCHIE HELD
Page 165

Archie Held Studio
5-18th Street
Richmond, CA 94801
Tel 510-235-8700
Fax 510-234-4828
E-mail archieheldstudio@attbi.com

Archie Held works mainly in bronze and stainless steel. Many of his works incorporate water. He enjoys using contrasting materials, surfaces and textures in his sculptures.

RECENT PROJECTS: City of Sunnyvale, CA; Alliant Energy World Headquarters, Madison, WI; Chevron Texaco, San Ramon, CA; Four Seasons Resort, Kona, HI

EXHIBITIONS: Triangle Gallery, 2002, San Francisco, CA; Sculpture, *Objects & Functional Art*, 2002, Chicago, IL, and New York, NY

PUBLICATIONS: *Architectural Digest*, January 2003; *Robb Report*, July 2002; Veranda, May 2002

SALLY HEPLER
Page 137

PO Box 2607
Santa Fe, NM 87504
Tel 505-471-7611
Fax 505-983-1118
E-mail hepler3@earthlink.net
www.sallyhepler.com

Sally Hepler's graceful sculptures are divine enigmas —mazes that seem to be not the end of a journey, but the making of one. Her bronze and steel sculptures, constructed from metal plate, are hand fabricated, not cast. Every sculpture—monumental, large and small—is handmade.

RECENT COMMISSIONS: Los Alamos County AIPP, 2002, Los Alamos, NM; Seagate Technologies International, 2001, Singapore

COLLECTIONS: Mayo Clinic, Scottsdale, AZ; College of Santa Fe, NM; Trust Investments, Palm Beach, FL

PUBLICATIONS: *The Collector's Guide*, 2002; *New Mexico Magazine*, 2001; *Southwest Art Magazine*, 2000; *Art Book Arizona*, 2000; *Sedona Magazine*, 1999

HETLAND LTD.
Pages 174, 177

David J. Hetland
1704 Main Avenue, Suite 3
Fargo, ND 58103
Tel 701-293-3066
Fax 701-293-0780
E-mail djhetland@aol.com
www.hetland.com

Sometimes described as "visual parables," David Hetland's liturgical works enhance worship spaces and inform spirituality for people of faith around the world. Whether in stained glass, mosaic or mixed media, his two- and three-dimensional art is divinely inspired and skillfully crafted.

RECENT PROJECTS: Transfiguration Catholic Church, Oakdale, MN; Christ Lutheran Church, San Diego, CA; King Edward Memorial Hospital, Bermuda; United Lutheran Church, Grand Forks, ND

AWARDS: Alumni Achievement Award, 2000, Concordia College; Doctor of Fine Arts (honorary), 1994, Concordia College

PUBLICATIONS: Artwork published in numerous books and periodicals; author of *On Our Way Rejoicing*, a full-color book chronicling the first 75 years of the Concordia College Christmas Concerts

GUILD SOURCEBOOKS: *Architect's 15*

KAREN HEYL
Page 28

1310 Pendleton Street, ML# 2
Cincinnati, Ohio 45202
Tel 513-421-9791/760-489-7106
E-mail heylstone2@aol.com
www.karenheyl.com

Karen Heyl's award-winning mural relief sculpture combines Old World stone carving techniques with contemporary design, lending itself to a variety of architectural applications, both monumental and small. Using varied textural surfaces, Heyl creates aesthetic sophistication with simplified sensual forms.

RECENT PROJECTS: *Ecological Sampler*, six limestone panels, each 5' x 3.5' x 3" mounted on 30' tall steel easel, Orange County Convention Center, Orlando, FL; *Nature's Guardians*, two limestone panels, each 4'x 8'x 10", flanking entryway into housing development, privately funded public art project for the city of Brea, CA

COMMISSIONS: *Organic Life Forms*, courtyard sculpture, 2002, private residence, Ft. Thomas, KY; *Parrots*, 2002, garden sculpture, private residence, Mason, OH; *Cellular Micrographs*, 2000, Vanderbilt University Medical Research Center, Nashville, TN

ARTIST LISTINGS

ARMANDO HINOJOSA
Page 112

ASD Art, Inc.
2702 Gustavus Street
Laredo, TX 78043
Tel 956-722-6678
Fax 956-722-4120
E-mail asd_art_inc@yahoo.com
www.armandohinojosa.com

Armando Hinojosa's work is recognized for its brilliance and realism. His paintings and sculptures are considered among the finest pieces of art being produced today. The beauty and uniqueness of his work are recognized by people in all walks of life, from the everyday collector to the White House.

RECENT PROJECTS: Texas A&M University, Kingsville; St. Agustine Cathedral, Laredo, TX; Sea World of Texas, San Antonio; Mercy Regional Medical Center, Laredo, TX

COMMISSIONS: *Tejano Sculpture*, Texas State Capitol, Austin; *Congressional Medal of Honor*, Veteran's Memorial, Laredo, TX

AWARDS: Official State Artist of Texas, 1982; gold medal for watercolor, Texas Ranger Hall of Fame, 1985, 1986, 1987

CLAUDIA HOLLISTER
Page 29

PMB 158, 333 South State Street, Suite V
Lake Oswego, OR 97034-3691
Tel/Fax 503-636-6684

Using handbuilt colored porcelain, Claudia Hollister creates site-specific architectural wall pieces for public, corporate and residential environments. Highly textured and richly colored, Hollister's work is set apart by the combination of such intricate techniques as inlaying, embossing and hand-carving three-dimensional elements on tiles.

RECENT PROJECTS: Spa at Reynolds Plantation, the Ritz-Carlton, Greensboro, GA; Farmers Insurance, Portland, OR

GUILD SOURCEBOOKS: *Designer's 8, 10, 11, 13, 14, 15; Architectural & Interior Art 16, 17*

CHERYL HOLZ
Pages 206, 256

50 East Galena #202
Aurora, IL 60505
Tel/Fax 630-898-2530
E-mail cheryl@cherylholz.com
www.cherylholz.com

Cheryl Holz creates mixed-media collage works on dimensional wood panel constructions. Woven into her masterful abstract compositions are poignant narratives about nature, the environment and the spirit of the human condition. Varying layers of acrylic paint, plaster, copper, organic materials and found objects coalesce in her stunning works of art. Embracing a myriad of artistic techniques and mediums, she builds a textured surface that emulates the natural processes of accumulation and deterioration.

EXHIBITIONS: National Museum of Women in the Arts; Carnegie Museum of Art; Elmhurst Art Museum; Davenport Museum of Art; Wright Museum of Art; Illinois State Museum; Rockford Art Museum

DAR HORN
Page 243

Union Art Works
402 West 5th Street
San Pedro, CA 90731
Tel 310-833-1282
Fax 310-833-1592
E-mail dar@darhorn.com
www.darhorn.com

Dar Horn's images are uniquely beautiful. The intensely saturated colors and richly detailed forms combine to engage viewers and draw them into the image—and seemingly into vistas and worlds not even imagined. These Ilfochrome™ prints are mounted on aluminum panels and have a purported archival life of 200 years. Various sizes are available.

DAVID L. HOSTETLER
Page 105

Hostetler Gallery
#2 Old South Wharf
PO Box 2222
Nantucket, MA 02584
Tel 508-228-3117/508-228-5152
E-mail susan@davidhostetler.com
www.davidhostetler.com

David L. Hostetler draws his inspiration from mythological, folk and pop culture sources. He has become a wholly original creator of female figures carved directly from American hardwoods and exotic woods such as ziricote, zebrawood and purpleheart. Hostetler's bronzes are cast from the woodcarvings, thereby developing the imagery with painterly patinas, brilliant coloring and polished surfaces. *David L. Hostetler: The Carver*, published by Ohio University Press, chronicles his life and work. Recent large-scale commissions are at Trump International Hotel and Tower, New York, NY; and Grounds for Sculpture, Hamilton, NJ. His sculptures can also be found in over 25 museums. "I love to carve wood. I am passionate about the tactile quality of wood, its color and its connection to humanity. Wood is a living material, never static."

PAUL HOUSBERG
Page 59

Glass Project, Inc.
875 North Main Road
Jamestown, RI 02835
Tel 401-560-0880
E-mail housberg@glassproject.com
www.glassproject.com

Paul Housberg creates site-specific works in glass. Central to his work is the use of light, color and texture to shape and define a space.

The artist welcomes inquiries regarding any planned or contemplated project.

RECENT PROJECTS: International Gateway Facility, Logan Airport, Boston, MA; William J. Nealon Federal Building, Scranton, PA; Le Meridien Hotel, Minneapolis, MN; Peninsula Hotel, Chicago, IL; BankRI, Providence, RI; Dreyfus Corporation, New York, NY; Pfizer Inc., Groton, CT

PUBLICATIONS: *Stained Glass Quarterly*, 2000; *The Art of Glass: Integrating Architecture and Glass*, 1998; *Glass Art Magazine*, 1996

GUILD SOURCEBOOKS: *Architect's 6, 7, 8, 9, 10, 11, 13, 15; Architectural & Interior Art 16, 17*

ARTIST LISTINGS

HOWDLE STUDIO INC.
Page 30

Bruce Howdle
225 Commerce Street
Mineral Point, WI 53565
Tel 608-987-3590
E-mail bhowdle@chorus.net
www.brucehowdle.cjb.net

Bruce Howdle has been a ceramic sculptor since 1976. He has produced work ranging from thrown forms up to 6 feet in height to 30-foot relief murals utilizing 9 tons of clay. He fires with a sodium process that melts the clay surface, preserving the integrity of the media and creating a very durable piece. His work is suitable for freestanding or installed wall locations; pieces are in large public institutions, banks, corporations, private offices and homes. Prices range from $1,500 to $150,000. Howdle collaborates closely with his clients and provides detailed drawings of his proposed projects.

GUILD SOURCEBOOKS: Architect's 7, 9, 10, 11, 12, 13, 14, 15; Architectural & Interior Art 16, 17

312

VICTOR ISSA
Page 118

Victor Issa Studios
3950 North County Road 27
Loveland, CO 80538
Tel 970-663-4805
Fax 970-962-6780
E-mail info@victorissa.com
www.victorissa.com

"Creating living bronze®," "incredible sensitivity," "classical beauty," "wonderfully expressive," "engaging" and "interactive" are some of the descriptions of Victor Issa's work. His 17-year career includes many public and private commissions across the country. Issa's work is internationally collected, with public and private placements across the U.S.

COMMISSIONS: Private collections; City of San Dimas, CA; PCAHS, Denver, CO; Seventh-Day Adventist Headquarters, MD

GUILD SOURCEBOOKS: Architect's 13, 14; Architectural & Interior Art 16

MARGIE HUGHTO
Page 31

Margie Hughto Studio
6970 Henderson Road
Jamesville, NY 13078
Tel 315-469-8775

Margie Hughto is nationally recognized for her ceramic paintings, collages and tiles. These elegant wall reliefs and tiles are made of stoneware, clays, slips and glazes, and are constructed of beautifully colored and textured elements. The works range in size from small pieces to installations of architectural scale suitable for public, corporate and residential environments. Commissions are welcome. Prices, slides and further information upon request. Works are represented in numerous museum, corporate and private collections, including the Museum of Fine Arts, Boston, MA; Everson Museum, Syracuse, NY; IBM; Kodak; Mayo Clinic; Summerlin Casino, Las Vegas, NV; National Association of Secondary School Principals, Washington, DC; and the Cortland Street and 81st Street MTA subway stations, New York, NY.

EXHIBITIONS: Sushi Visual & Performing Arts Gallery, 2003, San Diego, CA; Loveed Fine Arts, 2002, New York, NY; SOFA, 2002, New York, NY

AWARDS: Louis Comfort Tiffany Foundation Award, 2003

JACOB JONES MOSAICS
Page 36

Cindy D. Jones
Louis G. Weiner
229 Third Street
Waveland, MS 39576
Tel 888-365-4008
Fax 228-466-0016
E-mail cindy@jacobjones.com
www.jacobjones.com

Jacob Jones Mosaics creates a full line of glass mosaic architectural elements and furnishings for home and garden. From classical to whimsical, their line includes free-hanging wall art, murals, mirrors, tables, clocks, architectural elements and more. Jacob Jones Mosaics accepts commercial and residential commissions, and enjoys traveling for site-specific installations. Jacob Jones is a partnership of Cindy Jones and Louis Weiner. Jones and Weiner collaborate with their clients on each project, usually beginning with an extensive consultation and/or site inspection.

COMMISSIONS: Chevy's Fresh Mex Restaurants, New Orleans, LA; Moondance Villas, Jamaica; poolside mural, Key West, FL

HARRIET HYAMS
Pages 18, 60, 252

PO Box 178
Palisades, NY 10964
Tel 845-359-0061
Fax 845-359-0062
E-mail harriart@rockland.net
www.harriethyams.com

Harriet Hyams has been creatively designing stained glass for over 30 years. A sculptor of wood, stone and steel in her early career, Hyams, with a love for form and space, incorporated light and color into her work with stained glass.

"Harriet involved us throughout the entire process of design, fabrication and installation. We cannot praise her highly enough. She was wonderful to work with and we recommend her without reservation to anyone seeking an artist who produces work of the highest artistic quality."

—Dominican Sisters

RECENT PROJECTS: Dominican Chapel, Sparkill, NY; Jewish Chapel, West Point, NY

AWARDS: Two Bene awards (Dominican Chapel), 2002, Liturgy & Ministry magazine

GUILD SOURCEBOOKS: GUILD 1, 2, 3; Architect's 12

KATHRYN JACOBI
Page 216

654 Copeland Court
Santa Monica, CA 90405
Tel 310-399-8423
E-mail kathrynjacobi@adelphia.net
www.kathrynjacobi.com

Kathryn Jacobi creates oil portraits from life, still lifes and editioned prints. She is a classically trained realist painter who has been working professionally for over 35 years. She has exhibited in galleries and museums throughout the United States, Canada and Europe, with over 50 solo shows to her credit. Jacobi accepts only six portrait commissions per year, working from sittings or, in the case of children or the deceased, from photographs. For further information and to see a comprehensive overview of her work, please visit her website at www.kathrynjacobi.com.

ARTIST LISTINGS

RUSSELL JACQUES
Pages 156, 166

Russell Jacques Studio
2621 Crestview Drive
Newport Beach, CA 92663
Tel/Fax 949-645-8206
Tel/Fax 760-674-0470
E-mail treartgallery@aol.com

Russell Jacques works in a diverse range of materials, including stainless steel, bronze, brass, painted steel and aluminum. He describes his sculpture as "elegant in appearance, delicate in character and soothing in response—with an almost ethereal contrast to the environments they occupy." He believes that art, as it involves and delights the senses, should, in the end, lift the spirit.

RECENT PROJECTS: Stainless steel sculpture, City of Palm Desert, CA; bronze and stainless steel sculpture, Trè Contemporary, Palm Desert, CA

COMMISSIONS: The National Ballet of Canada, Toronto; Pueblo Bonito Rose, Cabo San Lucas, Mexico

COLLECTIONS: National Gallery of Nova Scotia, Halifax, Canada; Boston University, MA; Amherst College, MA

EXHIBITIONS: Muskegon Museum of Art, 2001, MI

EILEEN JAGER
Page 184

Lighthunter
One Cottage Street
Easthampton, MA 01027
Tel/Fax 413-527-2090
E-mail eileen@eileenjager.com
www.eileenjager.com

"I'm endlessly fascinated by the dance of glass and light. This has been my passion since a magical moment at Chartres Cathedral when I was struck by the power of light and color to transform space." Eileen Jager is inspired by world travels, the cycles of nature and the balance of form and function. Each piece she creates is a journey revealed through vision, trust and perseverance. Her luscious glass mosaic furniture and aquatiture are multidimensional sculptures, a sensory delight to see, hear, touch and experience. Iridescent glass shimmers while water gently flows, creating a subtly soothing and energizing ambiance. Ms. Jager is moved by the power of art to enhance our lives. She welcomes commissions for site-specific projects for the home and garden in private and public collections. Prices range from $2,500 to $18,000.

JERRY MCKELLAR, SCULPTOR
Page 100

Jerry McKellar
195 May Road
Colville, WA 99114
Tel 509-684-2148
Fax 509-685-9114
E-mail jdmckellar@plix.com
www.jerrymckellar.com

Jerry McKellar's sculptures vary widely in style and subject matter, and range in size from miniature to monumental. Strong composition, power and movement are consistent throughout his work. McKellar exhibits widely and accepts commissions for public and corporate sculptures.

COLLECTIONS: Clymer Museum of Art, Ellensburg, WA; Bennington Center for the Arts, VT; Nora Eccles Harrison Museum of Art, Utah State University, Logan, UT

AWARDS: Clymer Museum of Art award, 2002; Best Sculpture and Artists' Choice awards, 1997, C.M. Russell Museum show; purchase award, 1997, Clymer Museum of Art; Best of Show/Bronze 1993, 1995, 1996, 1998, Ellensburg National Art Show.

PUBLICATIONS: *Art of the West* magazine, November/December 2000; *Southwest Art* magazine, July 2001, *InformArt* magazine, Winter 2001

JOEL BERMAN GLASS STUDIOS LTD
Pages 44, 61

Joel Berman
1.1244 Cartwright Street
Vancouver, BC V6H 3R8
Canada
Tel 604-684-8332
Fax 604-684-8373
E-mail info@jbermanglass.com
www.jbermanglass.com

Joel Berman Glass Studios (JBGS) is one of the largest architectural glass art designers and manufacturers in North America. Joel Berman has collaborated with designers and architects to design and fabricate site-specific textured cast glass for corporate, commercial, hospitality and retail environments. He continues to be involved in high-profile projects across Canada and the United States. Most recently, Berman was selected to design and produce the first World Trade Center memorial statue; a rooftop garden windscreen (30'W x 9'H x 9'D) for the Gap headquarters; and lobby sculptures for Nortel headquarters, Princess Cruises and Cadillac (General Motors).

JOHN LEWIS GLASS STUDIO
Page 182

10229 Pearmain Street
Oakland, CA 94603
Tel 510-635-4607
Fax 510-569-5604
E-mail info@johnlewisglass.com
www.johnlewisglass.com

The works of John Lewis Glass Studio include cast glass sculptures, decorative and functional tables, and architectural components. The finished castings often receive additional hand crafting such as cutting, grinding and polishing. Surface treatments such as gold leaf, patinas and tinted epoxies are also applied to enhance the visual impact of the cast glass. John Lewis has been exploring the potential of cast glass since 1969, when he opened his first hot glass studio. His inspiration derives from his ongoing desire to manipulate this material into new shapes and applications.

COLLECTIONS: American Craft Museum, New York, NY; Craft and Folk Art Museum, New York, NY; Corning Museum of Glass, Corning, NY

EXHIBITIONS: The Rachael Collection, 2002, Aspen, CO; Sculpture, Objects and Functional Art, 2002, Chicago, IL

GUILD SOURCEBOOKS: *GUILD 4, 5; Artful Home 1*

BARRY WOODS JOHNSTON
Page 106

2423 Pickwick Road
Baltimore, MD 21207
Tel 410-448-1945
Fax 410-448-2663

Around 9/11, the Evangelical Christian Credit Union (ECCU) in Orange County, CA, commissioned the *Faith, Hope, and Love* sculpture. The city of Le Brea in Orange County locked horns with ECCU over the sculpture, alluding to First Amendment violations, and ultimately forced the ECCU to abandon the commission and select an alternate artist. The sculpture re-creates an arched needle, representing the parable: "It is easier for a camel to pass through the eye of a needle than a rich man to enter the kingdom of heaven." Taking the shape of the eternal flame, the needle illustrates the lack of mortal baggage one can carry into heaven. The three figures of faith, hope and love mirror the positive yearnings of the soul to lead our world in a brighter future through enlightenment and compassion.

ARTIST LISTINGS

JUNO-SKY-STUDIO.COM
Page 259

Juno Sky
Tel 419-422-7777
E-mail junoskyart@aol.com
www.junoskystudio.com

The flow of memories, myths and life experiences, along with the use of rich color, sensual surfaces and innovative techniques, define the mixed-media works of Juno Sky. Media such as handmade papers, acrylic, gold leaf and fabric give her work engaging presence and are, for the artist, spiritually restorative and celebratory. Through the collecting and assembling of life's narratives, the artist continually re-defines herself, and in the process shares an intense record of "resolute visual poems." Available works at www.JunoSkyStudio.com. Price range: $250-$20,000.

COLLECTIONS: Toledo Museum of Art; Mazza Museum of International Art, OH; United States Custom House, Chicago, IL; Hyatt Regency Hotels; Thermos Corporation; Marathon Oil Company; Eli Lilly; U.S. Gypsum; Honda Peace Collection; Long Term Credit of Japan

KEN KALMAN
Page 94

PO Box 147
Canyon, CA 94516
Tel 925-376-0760
E-mail kenkalman@earthlink.net

Ken Kalman's sculptures may be installed outside or inside. They are constructed of aluminum or copper sheet and fastened with solid and blind rivets. There is no welding. Parts of the animals (ears, nose, tail, horns, etc.) are cast of solid copper or aluminum. The aluminum does not weather, but stays shiny and bright and requires no maintenance. The copper pieces will patina to a greenish color naturally and require no ongoing maintenance.

COMMISSIONS: Artech, 2002, Berkeley, CA; public art commission, 2002, Berkeley, CA; Danielle Steele, 2003, Stinson Beach, CA

COLLECTIONS: Nestle Corp.; Abbott Laboratories; Hewlett Packard Corporation; Kaiser Permanente Corporation; Tiffany & Co.; Intergroup Corp., Los Angeles, CA; Crawford/Wu Films; Milwaukee Bucks, WI

EXHIBITIONS: *Native,* 2002, Lindsay Wildlife Museum, Walnut Creek, CA; figurative show, 2002, Virginia Breier Gallery, San Francisco, CA; Boritzer/Gray/Hamano Gallery, 1998, Santa Monica, CA

LISA KASLOW
Page 167

Lisa Kaslow, LLC
PO Box 381
Hibernia, NJ 07842
Tel 877-276-3810
Fax 973-586-4393
E-mail lisa@kaslowpublicart.com
www.kaslowpublicart.com

Lisa Kaslow collaborates with design professionals and communities. She conceives public art projects in the context of master planning, urban design, landscape architecture and transportation systems. Projects include kinetic sculptures, urban identity, monuments, site-specific amenities and design team opportunities. Works are fabricated from a variety of durable, low-maintenance materials compatible with surrounding architectural and landscape elements. Kaslow has completed over 50 public art projects across the country.

COMMISSIONS: Denver Capital Leasing Corporation; Florida Art in State Buildings; Giant Food Stores, Washington, DC; New Jersey Transit; North Carolina Arts Council; P.A.R.K. Foundation, AR

GUILD SOURCEBOOKS: *Architect's 7, 8, 11, 13, 14, 15*

BJ KATZ
Page 62

Meltdown Glass Art & Design LLC
PO Box 3850
Chandler, AZ 85244
Tel 480-633-3366
Fax 480-633-3344
E-mail bjkatz@meltdownglass.com
www.meltdownglass.com

Kiln-cast glass is the new frontier in art glass. With this method, glass is molded and, at times, colored and shaped in large industrial kilns at temperatures up to 1600 degrees. Artwork can be fired multiple times until the desired effect is achieved. The creative process of BJ Katz is spontaneous. She begins with an overall concept and design for each work of art, but the nuances of each piece happen at the time of creation. Her artwork is "in process" until it feels fully evolved.

RECENT PROJECTS: QVC Store, Mall of America, Minneapolis, MN; Phelps Dodge Corporate Headquarters, Phoenix, AZ; Desert Ridge Marketplace, Phoenix, AZ; Texas Children's Hospital, Houston; public art project, Phoenix Children's Hospital, AZ

GUILD SOURCEBOOKS: *Architect's 14, 15; Designer's 14, 15; Architectural & Interior Art 16, 17; Artful Home 1*

GUY KEMPER
Page 63

Kemper Studio
190 North Broadway
Lexington, KY 40507
Tel/Fax 859-254-3507
E-mail kemperstudio@juno.com
www.kemperstudio.com

Guy Kemper's work is distinctive for its emotional and painterly expressiveness. Freeing stained glass from the constraints of traditional technique, he designs windows unlike any others in the world. Kemper's strength lies in listening: to the client, the architect and the space itself. The right questions must be asked with a quiet mind to hear the right answers. Using only the finest materials, he strives for a design of harmonious essentials that will outlast fashion. He guarantees his work for his lifetime.

RECENT PROJECTS: 100' x 14' glass wall for the Greater Orlando International Airport, Congregation of St. Agnes Chapel, Fond du Lac, WI

GUILD SOURCEBOOKS: *Architect's 9, 10, 11, 14, 15; Architectural & Interior Art 16, 17*

TOM KENDALL
Page 32

Oak Leaf Pottery
10936 Three Mile Road
Plainwell, MI 49080
Tel/Fax 269-664-5430
E-mail oakleafpottery@mei.net
www.mei.net/~oakleafpottery

Tom Kendall creates one-of-a-kind wall sculptures and limited-series vessels in porcelain, metal and wood. The surfaces are decorated with durable glazes in leaf patterns and intricate light-and-dark tones, evoking peaceful, intimate scenes. His tiles are created for installations of any size or shape.

RECENT PROJECTS: Sundial, Bronson Hospital, MI; tile installation, Richland Community Library, MI

COLLECTIONS: Kalamazoo Institute of Arts, MI; Carnegie Mansion, Smithsonian Institute, New York, NY; Pfizer corporate collection, Kalamazoo, MI; City Bank corporate collection, New York, NY

EXHIBITIONS: Functional Ceramics National, 1999, Ephrata, PA; Krasl Art Center, 1999, St. Joseph, MI; Craft Alliance, 1989, St. Louis, MO

AWARDS: Second place, 1999, Kalamazoo Institute of Arts; People's Choice, 1999, Functional Ceramics National

GUILD SOURCEBOOKS: *Artful Home 1*

ARTIST LISTINGS

RAIN KIERNAN
Page 131

94 Birch Hill Road
Weston, CT 06883
Tel 203-226-5045
Fax 203-227-3187
E-mail rain@rainkiernan.com
www.rainkiernan.com

Rain Kiernan creates sculpture in marble, bronze, stainless steel and alternative media, including fiberglass and cement. Her abstracts include both large-scale outdoor works and smaller interior sculpture. Kiernan's forms are both free-form and derivative and are characterized by her unique style, which features powerful but sensuous curves, relieved by supporting planes. The artist has won several awards of merit for sculpture and is represented in various U.S. galleries. Kiernan, who has been showing her sculpture professionally since 1990, works with architects, designers and art consultants to create work for public parks, commercial property and private residences.

COMMISSIONS: Bristol Community College, Fall River, MA; Waveny Public Park, New Canaan, CT; private homes and businesses in New York City, Atlanta, Palm Beach, Greenwich, CT, and Southampton, NY

GUILD SOURCEBOOKS: *Artful Home 1*

STEPHEN KNAPP
Page 64

74 Commodore Road
Worcester, MA 01602-2792
Tel 508-757-2507
Fax 508-797-3228
E-mail sk@stephenknapp.com
www.stephenknapp.com

Stephen Knapp has gained an international reputation for large-scale works of art placed in public, corporate and private collections, created in media as diverse as kiln-formed, dichroic and cast glass, metal, stone, mosaic, ceramic and light. His art testifies to a strong direction in contemporary work—an artistic response to technical advancements that encourage new forms. Knapp frequently writes and lectures on architectural art glass, the collaborative process and the integration of art and architecture. Knapp's work has appeared in many international publications including *Art and Antiques, Architectural Record, ARTnews, Ceramics Monthly, Honoho Geijutsu, Identity, Interior Design, Interiors, Nikkei Architecture, Progressive Architecture* and *The New York Times.*

ELLEN KOCHANSKY
Page 173

EKO
1237 Mile Creek Road
Pickens, SC 29671
Tel 864-868-9749
Fax 864-868-4250
E-mail ekochansky@aol.com

Historically, the creation of the friendship quilt involved many people and usually commemorated some major event. Ellen Kochansky's recent work updates this tradition, speaking to public and private events in our time through the collective efforts of the village. Using materials commonly discarded, she reflects on the cycle of deterioration and renewal, our "cultural compost."

RECENT PROJECTS: Chicago Marathon 25th anniversary banner, 2002, IL; hanging sculptures of contributed textiles and debris from 9/11, 2001

COMMISSIONS: Bank of America, Charlotte, NC; Hines Partnership, Cincinnati, OH; Portman Hotels, San Francisco, CA

COLLECTIONS: American Craft Museum, New York, NY; White House, Washington, DC; Mint Museum of Craft + Design, Charlotte, NC

EXHIBITIONS: *Six Continents of Quilts,* 2002, and *Objects for Use,* 2001, American Craft Museum, New York, NY

JOAN KOPCHIK
Page 261

1335 Stephen Way
Southampton, PA 18966-4349
Tel 215-322-1862
Fax 215-322-5031
E-mail jkopchik@voicenet.com

Vat-formed sheets of handmade paper are cast into plaster forms to create sculptural wall pieces. Mixed-media elements are incorporated within the design, developing a rich, complex iconography. Multiple layers of pigments protect the work, making it suitable for hanging without framing.

COMMISSIONS: Private residence, 2002, East Hampton, NY

COLLECTIONS: Rosenwald Collection, National Gallery of Art, Washington, DC; James A. Michener Art Museum, Doylestown, PA

AWARDS: Gallery Award, Artsbridge at Prallsville Mill, National Juried Art Exhibit; James A Michener Purchase Prize, 2002

PUBLICATIONS: Juried Portfolio: "Old Ways, New Views: Photographic Processes on Handmade Paper, Hand Papermaking," 1999, Washington, DC

GUILD SOURCEBOOKS: *Architect's 6; Designer's 6, 7, 8, 11, 15; Architectural & Interior Art 16*

KORYN ROLSTAD STUDIOS
Page 84

Bannerworks, Inc.
2610 Western Avenue
Seattle, WA 98121
Tel 206-448-1003
Fax 206-448-1204
E-mail koryn@krstudios.com
www.krstudios.com

Koryn Rolstad established her internationally recognized business in Seattle in 1975. Working with architects and designers, she creates projects to soften hard architectural lines, diffuse light in various settings, and incorporate color and form to fill large spaces. Her studio facilitates design, engineering and fabrication, as well as construction installation.

COMMISSIONS: Hope & Healing Health Center, 2000, Nashville, TN; East High School, 2003, Anchorage, AK; Nunaka Valley Elementary School, 1999, Anchorage, AK;

COLLECTIONS: Glaxo Smith Kline, Pittsburgh, PA; PNC Bank, Pittsburgh, PA; World Wildlife Fund, Washington, DC

AWARDS: ASID Artistic & Cultural Achievement Award, 2002, WA; "Merit" SEGD Design Awards, 2000; Print's Regional Design Annual Award, 1999

PUBLICATIONS: *This Way: Signage Design for Public Spaces, 2000*

ANDRE N. KOUZNETSOV
Page 201

Buon Fresco Wall Artistry
6442 Overlook Drive
Alexandria, VA 22312
Tel 888-637-3726
Fax 703-914-5605
E-mail wallart@bfresco.com
www.bfresco.com

Andre Kouznetsov has been heralded since his arrival in the United States ten years ago. as a fine arts painter, a portrait painter, trompe l'oeil artist and muralist. A review of his portfolio reveals an artist who has not found his limitations. Mediums include oil, gouache, acrylic and fresco applications, as well as gold and metal leaf.

RECENT PROJECTS: Background mural for Dreamworks film *Head of State;* Landscape mural, private residence, Annapolis, MD; mural, Baltimore Symphony Orchestra Decorator Show House, MD; mural for BET restaurant and Le Lavandou restaurant, Washington, DC; mural, Da Vinci's restaurant, Falls Church, VA

COLLECTIONS: private collections in the U.K., Eastern Europe, the U.S. and the former Soviet Union

PUBLICATIONS: *Paint Pro Magazine,* March-April 2003, July-August 2002, January-February 2002; *Washington Home & Design Magazine,* Spring 2001

315

ARTIST LISTINGS

ALEXANDER KUBAISKI
Pages 210, 221

Alexander Kubaiski Studio
3646 Fredonia Drive
Hollywood, CA 90068
Tel/Fax 323-876-8828
E-mail kubaiski@sbcglobal.net
www.kubaiski.com

"The essentials of art stand outside the doctrine of any single school. The art is timeless; what is right once is right always. We may outgrow ideas or emotions, but our enduring pleasure in pure forms—expressive and balanced—will remain constant." Alexander Kubaiski, internationally acclaimed artist, sculptor and designer, has resided in and operated his studio from Los Angeles, CA, since 1984. Drawing portraits since the age of seven, Kubaiski created his first oil painting at the age of nine. He has studied and exhibited in France, Italy, Yugoslavia, Sweden and Denmark, where his work is not only well received, but also the subject of numerous sold-out exhibitions. Originals are currently sold out, but commissions are accepted. Archival reproductions of any size can be created on canvas and paper. Please visit his website for more information.

316

SILJA TALIKKA LAHTINEN
Pages 222, 294

Silja's Fine Art Studio
5220 Sunset Trail
Marietta, GA 30068
Tel 770-993-3409
Fax 770-992-0350
E-mail pentec02@bellsouth.net
www.wardnasse.org/3000p.htm

Silja Lahtinen's work draws from the myths, landscape, folk songs and textiles of her native Finland. She is especially inspired by Lapland Shamanism in her paintings, collages, wall panels, prints and drums.

RECENT PROJECTS: Creating a series based on Eino Leino's poem "Elegia." Paintings exhibited at Nuutti Galleria, Virrat, Finland

COLLECTIONS: Schacknow Museum of Fine Arts, Plantation, FL; Chattahoochee Valley Museum of Art, La Grange, GA; Mukkulan Koulu, Lahti, Finland; Santa Barbara Museum of Art, CA

EXHIBITIONS: *Thrive,* 2002, Perimeter College, Clarkston, GA

PUBLICATIONS: *PrintWorld Directory,* 2002; *Encyclopedia of Living Artists* (all editions); *Who's Who of American Artists; Who's Who of Women Artists*

GUILD SOURCEBOOKS: *Gallery 1, 2, 3; Designer's 9, 10, 11; Architectural & Interior Art 17*

TUCK LANGLAND
Page 119

12632 Anderson
Granger, IN 46530
Tel/Fax 574-272-2708
E-mail tuckandjan@aol.com

Tuck Langland specializes in figurative bronze sculptures for public and private spaces. Each figure has movement, gesture and a unique personality. Through figurative work, he interprets the message his sculpture is asked to convey.

RECENT PROJECTS: Portrait sculptures of the Mayo brothers; The Mayo Clinic, Rochester, MN; five heroic figures, Hillman Cancer Center, University of Pittsburgh, PA; two monumental figures, Mishawaka, IN; fountain with figures, Indiana University, South Bend; four allegorical figures, Bronson Hospital, Kalamazoo, MI; Herman B Wells portrait sculpture; Indiana University, Bloomington.

GUILD SOURCEBOOKS: *Architect's 8, 9, 10, 11, 12, 13, 14; Architectural & Interior Art 16, 17*

GREG LEAVITT / CAMILLE LEAVITT
Page 43

914 Powder Mill Hollow Road
Boyerton, PA 19512
Tel 610-367-8867
Fax 610-473-8861
E-mail gregoryaleavitt@netscape.net
www.gregleavitt.com

In the 31 years that Greg Leavitt and Camille Leavitt have been exploring the limitless possibilities of forged metal as sculpture, they have turned steel into flocks of birds, clouds of butterflies and gardens bursting with flowers. They are interested in the dualities inherent in sculptural form: masculine and feminine, hard and soft, cold and hot, mass and space. When the integration of these oppositional forces is achieved, it leads to a successful work of art.

RECENT PROJECTS: Lincoln Park Zoo, Chicago, IL; Governor's Mansion, Harrisburg, PA: Mt. Cuba Estate, DE; Hyatt Hotel, Philadelphia, PA; Upper Chesapeake Medical Center, MD

COMMISSIONS: Le Bec-Fin and Brasserie Restaurants; Westminster and Swarthmore Presbyterian Churches; Oaklands Corporate Center; Philadelphia Park System; Waterloo Gardens; Swarthmore College and many private estates

GUILD SOURCEBOOKS: *THE GUILD 2; Architect's 9, 10, 11, 14, 15*

RON LEEP
Page 95

PO Box 294
Redmond, OR 97756
Tel 541-548-8644
Fax 541-548-4744
E-mail ronleep@bendnet.com
www.ronleep.com

Referencing numerous photos and animal anatomy books, Ron Leep creates bronze wildlife sculptures with detail and motion that bring the works to life. The artist brings a fluidity to his sculptures that continues as the viewer observes the bronze from all angles. An avid outdoorsman, Leep emphasizes the importance of studying the source of his work in process—the anatomy, the habits and the habitat. Wildlife commissions welcomed. Self-employment for the past 30 years has instilled in the artist the importance of a quality product delivered in a timely fashion and at a fair price.

ALAN LeQUIRE
Page 114

Alan LeQuire, Sculptor
4304 Charlotte Avenue Suite C
Nashville, TN 37209
Tel/Fax 615-298-4611
E-mail lequire@mindspring.com
www.alanlequire.com

Alan LeQuire is a figurative sculptor, well known in his native Southeast for his public commissions and sensitive portraiture. LeQuire works in a variety of sculptural materials, including wood, stone and cast bronze. He has completed a number of architectural, collaborative and site-specific projects since he began accepting commissions in 1981. Recent projects: Musica, monumental figurative sculpture, Nashville, TN; Dr. Frist portrait group, three life-size bronze figures, Columbia/Hospital Corporation of America, Nashville, TN and Hudson, FL; Nashville Public Library doors, 24 relief panels in bronze, TN; Jack Daniels, life-size bronze portrait, Jack Daniels Distillery, Lynchburg, TN and Louisville, KY; Teacher and Student, life-size bronze, Montgomery Bell Academy, Nashville, TN.

GUILD SOURCEBOOKS: *Architect's 9, 10, 12, 14; Architectural & Interior Art 16; Artful Home 1*

ARTIST LISTINGS

LINDA LEVITON
Pages 7, 254, 273

Linda Leviton Sculpture
1011 Colony Way
Columbus, OH 43235
Tel 614-433-7486
E-mail guild@LindaLeviton.com
www.lindaleviton.com

Linda Leviton's dimensional, modular wall sculptures evoke the colors and textures of nature. Her designs can be combined as one large piece or mounted separtely, creating flexibility for large installations and changing interior spaces. Leviton uses etching, dyes, patinas and oils to create subtle or vibrantly colored designs. Her work is displayed in private and corporate collections across the country.

RECENT PROJECTS: Northeast Utilities, Berlin, CT; St. Vincent's Children's Hospital, Indianapolis, IN; University of Southern California, Los Angeles; Northwest Airlines, Detroit, MI

EXHIBITIONS: SOFA, 2002, New York, NY, and Chicago, IL; Del Mano Gallery, Sangre de Christo Center, Pueblo, CO; Cheongju International Craft Biennale, Cheongju, Korea

PUBLICATIONS: *Color on Metal,* 2001; profiled on HGTV's "Modern Masters"

GUILD SOURCEBOOKS: *Designer's 15; Architectural & Interior Art 16, 17; Artful Home 1*

NORMA LEWIS
Page 144

Norma Lewis Studios
30500 Aurora del Mar
Carmel, CA 93923
Tel 831-625-1046
Fax 831-625-9733
E-mail norma@dlewis.com

Norma Lewis has been a painter and sculptor for 50 years. She works primarily in bronze, but also in stone and aluminum on occasion. She creates both pedestal and monumental pieces. Her sculptures are not sentimental. They embody integrity of material, grace of weight and simplicity of form. She doesn't force the dialog, but waits for the shapes to introduce themselves, then embraces and builds on what they suggest. The forms are complete in themselves without explanations or justification for being. Lewis' works can be found in private and corporate collections worldwide.

GUILD SOURCEBOOKS: *Architect's 14, 15; Designer's 13, 14, 15; Architectural & Interior Art 16*

MICHELLE LINDBLOM
Page 223

MickArt Studio
3316 Hackberry Street
Bismarck, ND 58503
Tel/Fax 701-258-2992
E-mail mickart@bis.midco.net
www.mick-art.com

Michelle Lindblom's work is a challenging and psychological examination of her internal conflicts, thoughts and perceptions. These internal dialogues have their basis in the spontaneous reactions and personal relationships she experiences daily. This is where her most passionate and mystifying dialogues exist. Her work has become the visually tangible result of these examinations and ultimate revelations. Michelle received her undergraduate degree from the University of New Orleans and her M.F.A. from the University of North Dakota. In addition to working as a professional artist, she teaches full-time at Bismarck State College in the Visual Arts department and directs the campus galleries. Her work has been exhibited in the U.S., England and Norway, and has received numerous awards. Prices range from $650-$2,500.

317

LISA KESLER FINE ART
Page 220

Lisa Kesler
12015 Third Avenue NW
Seattle, WA 98177
Tel 206-782-3730
Fax 206-784-3304
E-mail Lisa@lkesler.com
www.lkesler.com

Lisa Kesler's works on paper and canvas integrate printmaking, collage and painting. She finds inspiration by experimenting with materials and techniques and is intrigued by the repetition of pattern. In her art, she stylizes forms into simpler geometric shapes and juxtaposes bold colors into fanciful compositions. Contrasts between light and dark remain central to her art. Kesler's work can be found in private and corporate collections throughout the U.S. and abroad. Commissions welcome. Slides and catalog available upon request.

COMMISSIONS: Zax Restaurant at the Golden Nugget, 2002, Las Vegas, NV; Best Western, San Francisco, CA; Alexis Hotel, Seattle, WA

COLLECTIONS: Evergreen Medical Center, Kirkland, WA; Riversoft Corporation, San Francisco, CA; Microcrafts, Redmond, WA; Eli Lilly, Indianapolis, IN

PUBLICATIONS: *Florida Design Magazine; Art World News*

THOMAS W. LOLLAR
Page 33

41 Central Park West, Suite 8E
New York, NY 10023
Tel 212-362-9117
Fax 212-875-5584

Tom Lollar hand builds clay murals that depict architectural and geographical themes. Subjects include landmarks in both frontal bas-relief and aerial views. The unique surface color results from applying copper, bronze and platinum metallic paints and glazes. Each rectangular clay construction is approximately 20" × 20" × 4" and may be placed in combinations of unlimited numbers suitable to wall size. Lollar has a master's degree in ceramic sculpture from Western Michigan University and has been creating clay murals professionally for over 20 years. His murals are in the collections of Hyatt Hotels, Revlon and Steelcase. His work has also been featured in the store windows of Tiffany and Co., Fifth Avenue, New York City.

GUILD SOURCEBOOKS: *THE GUILD 4; Architect's 15; Designer's 7, 8, 11*

JOYCE P. LOPEZ
Page 290

Joyce Lopez Studio
1147 West Ohio Street #304
Chicago, IL 60622
Tel 312-243-5033
Fax 312-243-7566
E-mail joycelopez@sbcglobal.net
www.joycelopez.com

Photography: multiple series of "in camera" double exposure prints in black-and-white or color. Sculpture: interior, wall-hung works, hand-wrapped with French thread on chromed steel tubes.

COLLECTIONS: City of Chicago; Nokia Collection; Health South; Sony Corporation; State of Illinois; State of Washington; private collections

EXHIBITIONS: SOHO Photo, 2002, New York, NY; Texas Photographic Society, 2002, San Antonio, TX; Riga, Latvia, 2001; Washington State (public art); Art in Architecture, IL; International Tapestry Exhibition, 2000, Beijing, China; San Diego Art Institute, 2000, CA

PUBLICATIONS: Book covers: *Pearson Education College Math Book, The College Math Book Series (4),* and *GUILD Designer's Sourcebook 7*

GUILD SOURCEBOOKS: *THE GUILD 1, 2, 3, 4, 5; Designer's 6, 7, 8, 9, 10, 11, 12, 13, 14, 15; Architectural & Interior Art 16, 17*

ELIZABETH MacDONALD

Box 186
Bridgewater, CT 06752
Tel 860-354-0594
Fax 860-350-4052
E-mail epmacd@earthlink.net
www.elizabethmacdonald.net

Elizabeth MacDonald produces tile paintings that suggest the patinas of age. These compositions are suitable for indoor or outdoor settings, and take the form of freestanding columns, wall panels or architectural installations. Public art commissions include: Wilbur Cross High School, New Haven, CT; and the Department of Environmental Protection, Hartford, CT.

COMMISSIONS: Conrad International Hotel, Hong Kong; St. Luke's Hospital, Denver, CO; Chapel at Mayo Clinic, Scottsdale, AZ;

AWARDS: State of Connecticut Governor's Arts Award

GUILD SOURCEBOOKS: *THE GUILD 1, 2, 3, 4, 5; Architect's: 6, 7, 8, 9, 10, 11, 12, 13, 14, 15; Designer's: 6, 8, 9, 10, 11, 12, 13, 14, 15; Architectural & Interior Art 16, 17; Artful Home 1*

ELIZABETH MacQUEEN

Elizabeth MacQueen Sculpture & Fine Art
58 Fairwood Boulevard
Fairhope, AL 36532
Tel 251-990-5995
Fax 805-543-8154
E-mail macqueensculptor@aol.com
www.macqueenfineart.com

"My passion as an artist is to translate the language of the body into a three-dimensional reality that symbolizes the real essence of movement, expression and human dignity."

RECENT PROJECTS: *The Past Present and Future,* the Women's Basketball Hall of Fame, Knoxville, TN, bronze sculpture, 34'H

RICKY MALDONADO

Maldonado Ceramics
2331 Holgate Square
Los Angeles, CA 90031
Tel 323-225-2668
Fax 323-441-8456
E-mail ram5553@aol.com
www.rickymaldonado.com

Ricky Maldonado's terra cotta pieces are inspired by nature and architecture, and are created with coil, slab and throwing techniques. Using the ancient process of terra sigillata, Maldonado applies glazes one dot at a time using a sable brush.

COMMISSIONS: Nomi Castle, Castle Law, 2002, Century City, CA; Bruce Berman, Warner Brothers, 1997, Burbank, CA; Fort Hill Construction, 1993-2002, Los Angeles, CA

COLLECTIONS: Sonny Kamm, Encino, CA;

EXHIBITIONS: SOFA, 2002, Chicago, IL; Palm Springs Museum of Art, 2002, Palm Springs, CA; Del Mano Gallery, 2002, Los Angeles, CA

AWARDS: Best of Show, 2002, American Ceramics Society; Best of Show, 2002, Palm Springs Desert Museum; Best of Show, 2002, Burbank Municipal Gallery

MARSHA LEGA STUDIO, INC.

Marsha Lega
28 West Crowley Avenue
Joliet, IL 60432
Tel 815-727-5255
Fax 815-727-5424
E-mail marshalega@cs.com
www.marshalega.com

Marsha Lega strives to create abstract metal sculptures that appear to float across the wall and representational public artworks that become touchstones for their communities. The sculptures' clean lines make them appear effortless in execution, denying the real difficulty in cutting and forming metal. Changing and controlling industrial material to bring out its beauty and humanity excites Lega. As she works with public and private projects, ideas continue to evolve. The sizes, shapes and materials change, but the basic concepts of good design remain constant.

RECENT PROJECTS: City of Joliet public art program, IL; Illinois and Michigan Canal Corridor; SAS Institute, Inc., Cary, NC; Embossed Graphics, Aurora, IL

GUILD SOURCEBOOKS: *Designer's 8, 12*

JD MARSTON

JD Marston Photography
13 Baca Grant Way
PO Box 294
Crestone, CO 81131
Tel/Fax 719-256-4162
E-mail jd@jdmarston.com
www.jdmarston.com

JD Marston uses black-and-white silver gelatin photography, color photography, archival digital giclee printmaking, and a meditative approach to capture outdoor scenes that are charged with spiritual and healing archetypes.

RECENT PROJECTS: "This Land Is Sacred," DVD project

COMMISSIONS: Mural installations, Sisters of the Holy Redeemer Hospital, Malvern, PA

COLLECTIONS: Texaco, White Plains, NY; Lucent Technologies, KS; Bear-Stearns, New York, NY

EXHIBITIONS: *An Intimate Vastness,* 1993, the New England School of Photography, Boston, MA; *L'Art Fixe en Mouvement,* 2001, Arles, France

AWARDS: Ansel Adams Award, 1992, Sierra Club; Who's Who In American Art, 2002

PUBLICATIONS: *Baby Shakespeare,* 2002, Disney, Inc.; *Denver Post,* 1992, CO

MASAOKA GLASS DESIGN

Alan Masaoka
13766 Center Street, Suite G-2
Carmel Valley, CA 93924
Tel 831-659-4953
Fax 831-659-3156
E-mail masaoka@mbay.net
www.alanmasaoka.com

Exquisite, distinctive brilliance in stained glass. Masaoka Glass Design has been on the forefront of designing contemporary windows for 27 years. Each project is individually designed and crafted using the finest materials available to produce windows of unparalleled quality. They have installed their glass in private homes, as well as public, commercial, and liturgical buildings throughout the country. It is important to Masaoka Glass Design to work closely with the client to understand their vision so that the art represents a successful aesthetic collaboration.

ARTIST LISTINGS

BARBARA MASLEN
Page 202

Maslen Studio
55 Bayview Avenue
Sag Harbor, NY 11963
Tel 631-725-3121
Fax 631-725-4608
E-mail maslen@optonline.net
www.barbaramaslen.com

Artist Barbara Maslen has expanded her work of over 20 years as an illustrator to produce site-specific, hand-painted murals and large-scale paintings. Her versatile work reflects her dedication to craftsmanship and professionalism. Working with architects and designers to incorporate existing architectural elements and newly specified materials, she provides preliminary scale drawings, color palette and sample boards. Commissions are painted with acrylics on site, or in the studio on canvas or wood panels for installation.

COMMISSIONS: Martinique, Gulf Shores, AL; Bath & Tennis Hotel, Westhampton Beach, NY; East End Pediatrics, East Hampton, NY; waterfront pool house, Hampton Bays, NY

JOHN B. MAY
Page 196

Three60 Studio
141 Norton Road
Kittery, ME 03904
Tel 207-439-8267
E-mail three60studio@attbi.com
www.three60studio.com

For over 15 years, John May has created both decorative vessels and functional objects on the lathe. Since acquiring a love for wood from his father (one of the pioneers of studio woodturning in the U.S.), May has continued to refine his craft, even while exhibiting at some of the most prestigious craft shows in the country. Every piece is turned by hand, using the limitations of the lathe-turning process to refine and carefully control the balance, form and proportion of the design. The results are works that are elegant and contemporary.

EXHIBITIONS: *Objects for Use*, 2001, American Craft Museum, New York, NY

PUBLICATIONS: *Home* magazine, July/August 1996

SUSAN McGEHEE
Page 270

Metallic Strands
540 23rd Street
Manhattan Beach, CA 90266
Tel 310-545-4112
Fax 310-546-7152
E-mail susan@metalstrands.com
www.metalstrands.com

Instead of fiber, Susan McGehee weaves with wire and metal on a 16-harness computerized floor loom to create unique, contemporary wall sculptures that seem to float on the wall. McGehee warps her loom with anodized aluminum wire, which comes in a range of deep colors, including shades of copper that will not tarnish. She then weaves with anodized wire; copper and aluminum pieces are often added as accents. These lightweight, easily installed and maintained pieces complement both residential and commercial settings.

GUILD SOURCEBOOKS: *Designer's 12, 13, 14, 15; Architectural & Interior Art 16, 17; Artful Home 1*

CAMEY McGILVRAY
Page 277

Stairway Studio
670 Radcliffe Avenue
Pacific Palisades, CA 90272
Tel 310-459-3287
Fax 310-459-0891
E-mail sstairway@aol.com
www.cameymcgilvray.com

Camey McGilvray creates colorful free standing sculptures and wall sculptures that appeal to both residential and commercial audiences. The artist uses wood and/or metal to construct these unique three-dimensional pieces, combining forms and color to create sculptures that are suitable for both interior and exterior applications. The artwork is created in an imaginative and contemporary style that is either non-objective/geometric in nature, or abstract, with themes derived from the environment and the human form. Visit the website to view a wide range of images and associated information.

TRENA McNABB
Page 203

McNabb Studio, Inc.
PO Box 327
Bethania, NC 27010
Tel 336-924-6053
Fax 336-924-4854
E-mail trena@tmcnabb.com
www.tmcnabb.com

Applying her unique brand of storytelling through colorful, transparent painted montages, Trena McNabb takes the art of portraiture to a new level. The near-life-size graphite representations of her subjects dominate the paintings, contrasting starkly with the multicolored transparent images that tell the "life stories" of those depicted. This colorful kaleidoscope of images depicts objects associated with the subject's work, interests and passions to convey a complete picture of the individual. Existing portraits are available; new commissions are accepted. McNabb's works are represented in permanent collections in government buildings, major corporations, hospitals, banks and museums. Her international commissions include works for corporate facilities in China, Japan and Germany.

GUILD SOURCEBOOKS: *Architect's: 6, 7, 8, 9, 10, 11, 12, 13, 14, 15; Designer's: 8, 14; Architectural & Interior Art 16, 17*

LIBBY AND JIM MIJANOVICH
Page 291

Mija
651 Long Branch Road
Marshall, NC 28753
Tel 828-649-0200
E-mail contact@mijaartquilts.com
www.mijaartquilts.com

Mija is founded on a philosophy of using the earth's resources conscientiously by recycling vintage cotton clothing to create beautiful, one-of-a-kind quilted fabric art. Libby and Jim Mijanovich combine colors and patterns of a range of fabrics, exploring contrast, value and texture to create the illusion of form, depth and motion. As a result, their quilts often have the appearance of radiant light accompanied by subtle shading of color and value. Each piece is quilted with threads and patterns to accentuate and complement its individual character. Hung in an original unglazed walnut shadowbox frame, creating a stunning focus for home or business.

ARTIST LISTINGS

AMOS MILLER
Pages 224-225

5741 SW 84 Street
Miami, FL 33143
Tel 305-668-3536
E-mail amiller1307@earthlink.net

A professional painter for 20 years, Amos Miller has successfully completed numerous commissioned portraits for families and individuals throughout the United States and in France. Using dynamic brush-work and strong color, Miller captures the personality and unique qualities of each subject he depicts. Amos Miller works primarily with oil and acrylic paint on canvas. He has also worked extensively in bas-relief wood sculpture.

COMMISSIONS: Private collections in Asheville, NC; Atlanta, GA; Cleveland, OH; Miami, FL; and Vence, France.

COLLECTIONS: Masur Museum of Art, Monroe, LA; Constitutional Court of South Africa, Johannesburg; Progressive Corporation, Cleveland, OH

EXHIBITIONS: *New Fauves: Amos Miller and Brian Joiner*, Indianapolis Art Center, 2002-2003, IN; *Amos Miller: Paintings*, Galerie Couleur Figure, 2002, Tourette-sur-Loup, France

320 GUILD SOURCEBOOKS: *Architectural & Interior Art 17, Artful Home 1*

DAVID MILTON
Page 226

4750 Degovia Avenue
Woodland Hills, CA 91364
Tel 818-224-2164
Fax 818-224-2163
E-mail david@davidmilton.com
www.davidmilton.com

David Milton's abstract expressions resonate with the vibrant colors and rhythms of his native South Africa. His art is driven by the exploration of the emotional elements of life, evoking their power. An intuitive use of color gives visual expression to emotion. The use of line creates movement and depth, propelling perception beyond the two-dimensional canvas. Blending, layering and texturing create multiple dimensions.

David's varied styles, along with his collaborative experience, facilitate working with individuals on customized projects. His paintings are in private collections from California to the Caribbean. He accepts commissions in a broad range of sizes. A portfolio of paintings and sculpture is available upon request. Current paintings range from 12" x 12" to 67" x 102".

GUILD SOURCEBOOKS: *Artful Home 1*

MARLENE MILLER
Pages 15, 35

MillerClay Designs
114 Walnut
Washington, IL 61571
Tel 309-444-8608
E-mail millerclay@att.net
www.millerclay.com

Marlene Miller has exhibited figurative ceramics nationally since 1978, and internationally since 1992. Her wall reliefs and freestanding sculpture, ranging in scale from monumental to intimate, evoke human presence, dignity and warmth. She achieves rich variations of texture and color in stoneware suitable for interior and outdoor installations. Miller welcomes collaborations with architects and interior designers on residential and commercial projects.

COLLECTIONS: Davenport Museum of Art; Lakeview Museum of Arts and Sciences; numerous private collections

AWARDS: Artist Fellowship, 2002, Illinois Arts Council; NICHE award, 2001, Philadelphia, PA

PUBLICATIONS: *Ceramics Monthly*, April 2000 and November 1996 (cover and feature article)

GUILD SOURCEBOOKS: *Architectural & Interior Art 16*

MIRO ART INC.
Page 204

Roman Kujawa
704A Locust Street
Mount Vernon, NY 10552
Tel 914-663-8350/914-237-6306
Fax 914-663-8360
E-mail mromank@earthlink.net

Miro Art specializes in decorative painting—fresco, mural, trompe l'oeil—in acrylic, oil or water-based paints. They also create decorative finishes such as marble, wood, wallpaper and stone work, and will conserve and restore your antique paintings, furniture and sculpture. Their high-quality work can be elegant, opulent, dramatic or whimsical. For a Miro Art company catalog, please call 914-237-6306.

RECENT PROJECTS: Fresco, private residence, Greenwich, CT; decorative painting, hotel, PA

COLLECTIONS: Projects range from trompe l'oeil Pompeian fresco in New York, to restoring and gilding the Blue Room of the White House, Washington, DC

PUBLICATIONS: Historical society magazine, Washington, DC

MILLENNIUM MURALS/ MILLING AROUND
Page 209

Zalucha Studio, LLC
119 South Second Street
Mount Horeb, WI 53572
Tel 866-881-8509 (toll free)
Tel 608-437-7880
Fax 608-437-2250
E-mail info@emill.com
www.emill.com

Custom large format murals and ceiling graphics from Zalucha Studio are created by a team of fine artists. All are displayed in various corporate and museum collections. Whether hand painted or computer generated, these vinyl products are durable, washable and are fire retardant. Millennium Murals can use graphics supplied by the client or create custom images. The Internet allows clients located anywhere to view projects and make decisions without delays. View a complete catalog on the web at www.emill.com.

RECENT PROJECTS: St. Elizabeth Hospital, 2003, Appleton, WI; University of Wisconsin Hospital and Clinics, 2000-2003, Madison; Pleasant Company, 1998-2002, Middleton, WI

DANA MONTLACK
Page 246

Studio Montlack
1204 Emerald Street
San Diego, CA 92109
Tel 858-342-5889
E-mail dana@studiomontlack.com
www.studiomontlack.com

Dana Montlack holds a B.F.A. in sculpture from the University of California at Santa Cruz and an M.F.A. in mixed media from the Otis College of Art and Design in Los Angeles. Her work has been exhibited in galleries and museums nationwide, including the Museum of Art, Downtown Los Angeles Conceptual Evolution, Alexandria Museum of Art, LA; Albright-Knox Art Museum and CEPA Gallery, Buffalo, NY; the California Center for the Arts, Escondido, CA; Monique Goldstrom Gallery, New York, NY; Sylvia White Gallery, Los Angeles, CA; and Flux Gallery, San Diego, CA. Additionally, her work is featured in such private collections as Nokia, San Diego, CA; City National Bank, Manhattan Beach, CA; Scripps Memorial Hospital, San Diego, CA; National University, La Jolla, CA and Crown Plaza Hotel, Atlanta, GA.

GUILD SOURCEBOOKS: *Artful Home 1*

ARTIST LISTINGS

LEN MORRIS
Page 247

Leonard Morris, Inc.
Tel 917-992-3313
Fax 718-636-6021
E-mail lenmorris@earthlink.net
www.lenmorris.net

As an artist, Len Morris feels that part of his job is to create opportunities for people to see and think differently. Morris creates and photographs assemblages of objects that are often viewed as disposable, like classified newspaper ads, dried leaves, flowers, or, as featured in this book, a fragment of a paper plate. These images reveal an extraordinary beauty in what may have been considered the ordinary. His photographs are generic in subject, but specific in concept: ordinary objects viewed with consideration and passion.

RECENT PROJECTS: Corporate and private collectors around the world, including the Boca Raton Museum, LA; the Miyako Osaka Hotel, Japan; and WNYC Radio, New York, NY, have enthusiastically embraced and acquired Morris' work.

GUILD SOURCEBOOKS; *Artful Home I*

JAMES C. NAGLE
Page 227

James C. Nagle Fine Art
1136 East Commonwealth Place
Chandler, AZ 85225-5716
Tel 480-963-8195
Fax 480-857-3188 (call first)
E-mail extraice@msn.com
www.jcnaglefineart.com

Since the mid-1970s, James Nagle has worked as an artist, creating paintings and sculpture in a variety of mediums. His work has been placed in private, corporate and university collections worldwide. In recent years, Nagle has focused on dramatic abstract paintings charged with complexity and sensuous color. Commissions are welcomed.

RECENT PROJECTS: Sculpture garden, private residence, Chandler, AZ

GUILD SOURCEBOOKS: *Architect's 15; Designer's 15; Architectural & Interior Art 16, 17*

KEIKO NELSON
Page 143

Keiko Nelson Art & Design
9 Arlington Lane
Kensington, CA 94707
Tel 510-653-8849/510-524-4393
Fax 510-527-4822
E-mail keiko@keikonelson.com
www.keikonelson.com

Keiko Nelson has collaborated with art foundries and architects on integrated architectural commissions for private, corporate and public projects in the U.S. and abroad. She is in an artist of extraordinary versatility. Varying from very large corporate commissions to intimate garden and indoor pieces, her work has been exhibited internationally in museums and galleries.

COMMISSIONS: Hotel Nikko, San Francisco, CA; Kaiser Permanente, CA; Cairo University Children's Hospital, Egypt; Takara Sake Museum, CA; NTT International, Tokyo, Japan; Epcot Center, FL

COLLECTIONS: Oakland Museum of California; San Jose Museum of Art, CA; Hara Museum of Contemporary Art, Tokyo, Japan; Miho Museum, Shiga, Japan; Cairo Opera House, Egypt

PUBLICATIONS: *Sculpture* magazine, April 2003

GUILD SOURCEBOOKS: *Designer's 10, Architect's 11*

321

NEW AGE ARTWORKS
Page 262

Thomas Matchie
140 Huntington Road
Delafield, WI 53018
Tel 262-646-2945
E-mail newageartworks@hotmail.com

Thomas Matchie uses a unique combination of plaster, drywall compounds and a variety of common and unusual troweling tools to create the texture for his attention-grabbing, three-dimensional wall pieces. With the final fusion of acrylics and proper lighting, the deep shadows and striking relief can be intense. It invites the viewer to reach out and touch. Whether the composition aspires to soothe or excite, Thomas' work includes pieces for private collections and also appears in galleries throughout the Lake Country region of Wisconsin.

BRUCE A. NIEMI
Pages 168

Niemi Sculpture Gallery
13300 116th Street
Kenosha, WI 53142
Tel 262-857-3456
Fax 262-857-4567
E-mail sculpture@bruceniemi.com

Bruce Niemi's sculptures range in size from tabletop interior pieces to site-specific public art. He also creates wall sculptures suitable for both interior and exterior locations. Niemi's welded stainless steel and bronze sculptures convey aesthetics, balance, energy and structural integrity.

RECENT PROJECTS: Inter-National Bank, McAllen, TX; Synopsys Inc. Sunnyvale, CA

COMMISSIONS: Wausau Hospital, 2001, Wausau, WI

COLLECTIONS: North American Group, Chicago, IL; Carlisle Companies, Inc., Charlotte, NC

EXHIBITIONS: Skokie Sculpture Park, 2003-2005, IL; Frankfort Public Library, 2003, IL

GUILD SOURCEBOOKS: *Architect's 9, 10, 11, 14, 15; Architectural & Interior Art 16, 17*

MICHAEL-BRIAN NORRIS
Pages 228, 278

PO Box 160
Grimsley, TN 38565
Tel 1-888-510-3758 (toll free)
mbnorris@mbnorris.com
www.mbnorris.com

Michael-Brian Norris offers the viewer a sophisticated yet innocent view of the world through wonderfully colored mixed-media paintings. Considering each work a collaboration, Norris infuses his artwork with materials and subject matter specific to his clients. With their complex layering, Norris's images appear three dimensional when viewed with 3D glasses. The whimsical quality of his work makes it ideal for children's hospitals, schools, libraries and parks, as well as themed restaurants, hotels and resorts.

RECENT PROJECTS: Polk Museum of Art, Lakeland, FL; Sue Kellogg Library, Stone Mountain, GA: Whitney Young Child Development Center, San Francisco, CA

ARTIST LISTINGS

DANIEL OBERTI
Page 141

Daniel Oberti Ceramic Design
3796 Twig Avenue
Sebastopol, CA 95472
Tel 707-829-0584
Fax 707-829-2136
E-mail daniel@danieloberti.com
www. danieloberti.com

Art is a gift that presupposes the dignity of its recipient. Daniel Oberti's work embraces concepts about time, space, light and shadow; they are works that reveal humanity's relationship to symbols, archetypes and forms, and that lift our spirits and instill a tenor of contemplative solace. Oberti is part of a lineage that finds solace in defining oneself by forming works of art that inform and inspire inquiry within. He works to unveil the elusive, and seeks an audience and affinity with others who recognize the value of this pursuit.

COMMISSIONS: *Three Spheres,* 2002, Vineyard Creek Hotel and Conference Center, Santa Rosa, CA; *Time Peace,* 2000, South Carolina Governor's School for the Arts and Humanities; *Spheres,* 1999, Onsala Space Observatory, Goteborg, Sweden; *Sphaera Palermo,* 2000, Osservatorio di Palermo, Palermo, Italy

NORBERT OHNMACHT
Page 108

Norbert Ohnmacht Fine Art
24544 Road 51
Burlington, CO 80807
Tel 719-346-7586
Fax 719-346-5657
E-mail npohnmacht@plains.net

Norbert Ohnmacht's bronze sculptures flow effortlessly between details of high realism and the imagery of interpretive vision. One patron says: "Each sculpture reveals a noble simplicity and reverent quality that adds a special dimension to the mood of each piece." Whether figurative, contemporary, bas-relief, liturgical or fountain, his sculptures range in size from miniature to monumental as limited editions or one of a kind. His goal is to work closely with his clients to co-discover that special something the client would like to see or remember.

RECENT PROJECTS: Life-size wall plaque, Estes Park, CO; portrait, Goodland, KS; bronze bear, Yuma, CO; ballroom dancer monument, Burlington, CO; *15 Mysteries of the Rosary,* St. Charles Catholic Church, Stratton, CO; portrait, Burlington, CO; portrait, Estes Park, CO

KATHRYN PALMER
Page 205

K.P. Murals
19748 Leitersburg Pike
Hagerstown, MD 21742
Tel 866-576-8725 (toll free)
www.d2media.com/kp

Kathryn Palmer paints in many styles, according to the wishes of her clients. She enjoys painting figures, especially using the Baroque style. Palmer also creates full wall murals, ceiling murals, frescoes and framed paintings. She undertakes specialized paintings for individuals and businesses. Mediums include acrylics, oils, watercolors, pastels, charcoals and pen and ink.

RECENT PROJECTS: Italian fresco for garden wall, Harrisburg, PA; landscape scene in private home foyer, Harrisburg, PA; interpretation of *Starry Night* for business office, Harrisburg, PA; ceiling mural for Old Library Building, Hagerstown, MD

COMMISSIONS: Harrisburg City Island Stadium Wall, 2002, PA; Fairhaven Inn, 2003, VT; Castleton State College, 2003, VT

COLLECTIONS: Art Association of Harrisburg, PA; Governor's Row, Harrisburg, PA

322

PAM MORRIS DESIGNS
EXCITING LIGHTING
Pages 192-193

Pam Morris
14 East Sir Francis Drake Boulevard, Studio D
Larkspur, CA 94939
Tel 415-925-0840
Fax 415-925-1305
E-mail lighting@sonic.net

Pam Morris, owner of EXCITING LIGHTING, is a distinguished design innovator. Her clients encompass top restaurants, hotels and private collectors, including Wolfgang Puck, Sugar Ray Leonard, Georgio Armani and the Hong Kong Regent Hotel. "In my work, I create highly original and evocative illuminated pieces. I use light, together with blown, slumped or cast glass and forged or cast metal, to create illuminated art pieces that reflect a special sense of place." Morris has lectured and been published internationally.

GUILD SOURCEBOOKS: *Architect's 12, 13, 15; Designer's 14; Architectural & Interior Art 17; Artful Home 1*

PANTE STUDIO
Page 179

Michael Demetz
Minert 7
Ortisei, Italy 39046
Tel 011-39-0471-796514
Fax 011-39-0471-789854
E-mail info@pantestudio.it
www.pantestudio.it

Pante Studio combines the centennial tradition of wood sculpting with the demands of contemporary design. The studio's goal is to unite the profound beliefs of Christian faith—and/or the demands of public art—with the creativity of architects and artists. The studio develops statues, ornaments, altars, fountains and more, starting from the sketch board. Different woods, bronze, stones and fiberglass are used for liturgical and secular works.

RECENT PROJECTS: Holy Apostles Catholic Church, Meridian, ID; St. Francis Hospital, Milwaukee, WI; St. Conrad Catholic Church, Hohenems, Austria; Plan de Corones-Skiresort, Brunico, Italy

ANNIE PASIKOV
Page 145

360 Lone Star Road
Lyons, CO 80540
Tel 303-823-6757
Fax 303-823-8033
E-mail pasikov@email.com
www.stonesculptures.net

After teaching art for 20 years (including 11 while living at a residential school for troubled teens), Annie Pasikov responded to a health crisis by giving wings to her passion for creating. She began making art instead of just assisting others with their creativity. After lifelong interest, she taught herself to sculpt in stone. Her gracefully flowing forms emerge through a direct carving approach. Pasikov listens to the whisper of intuition that seems to guide her as she considers her design: a unique dance between art sense and sixth sense. Six of her sculptures grace a large healing arts center in Boulder, CO, touching many.

GUILD SOURCEBOOKS: *Artful Home 1*

ARTIST LISTINGS

MELISSA PAXTON
Page 66

Coyote Glass Design
907 Mill Creek Road
Salado, TX 76571
Tel 254-947-0002
Fax 254-947-0402
E-mail m.paxton@coyoteglass.com
www.coyoteglass.com

Melissa Paxton works with a combination of glass, steel, copper, gold, silver and colored light. She sandblast-carves thick glass for a bas-relief effect. Some pieces are tinted or fired, or have metals applied to create a rich surface texture. Lighting may include fiber optics, neon, cold cathode, halogen or low voltage.

RECENT PROJECTS: 2'-30'H plants in steel with faceted acrylic flowers and fiber-optic lighting, Westin Hotel, Scottsdale, AZ

COMMISSIONS: Glendale Public Library, 2000, Glendale, AZ; Gilbert Public Library, 1999, Gilbert, AZ; Marvel Hotel, 1996, Iono, Japan

COLLECTIONS: Miravel Resort, 2002, Scottsdale, AZ; Samaritan Hospital, 2002, Peoria, AZ

PUBLICATIONS: "Modern Masters," 2003, HGTV; *Arizona Republic* magazine, 1999; *Phoenix Home and Garden* magazine, 1997

PEARL RIVER GLASS STUDIO, INC.
Page 67

Andrew Cary Young
42 Millsaps Avenue
Jackson, MS 39202
Tel 601-353-2497
Fax 601-969-9315
E-mail ayoung@netdoor.com
www.prgs.com

Andrew Cary Young believes that the future of art and craft is inextricably mixed up with the future of our world. As creative people, artists and craftsmen have a mission to demonstrate that everything matters: the plates made to eat off of, the clothes woven to wear and the beautiful objects made to inspire. This grounding, taken from the materials artists use, gives their works soul. Creativity is the catalyst that makes this process work.

RECENT PROJECTS: Mills River United Methodist Church, 2003, Mills River, NC

COMMISSIONS: Cross of Christ Lutheran Church, 2002, Bloomfield Hills, MI

EXHIBITIONS: *Made in the U.S.A.: Contemporary Craft,* 2003, Peoria Art Center, IL

AWARDS: Artist's Achievement Award, 2002, Governor's Award for Excellence in the Arts, State of Mississippi

PUBLICATIONS: *Stained Glass Quarterly,* Winter 2002

CHRISTOPHER PETRICH
Page 248

CoolPhoto
3741 North 29th Street
Tacoma, WA 98407
Tel 253-752-4664
Fax 253-276-0116
E-mail cpetrich@CoolPhoto.com
www.CoolPhoto.com

Christopher Petrich's sweeping black-and-white photographs of the Pacific Northwest appear to move like wind on water and feel as though a great struggle were taking place below the surface. This feeling makes his art breathtaking and unforgettable.

COLLECTIONS: James McGowan, Edinborough, Scotland; Alan Ross, Santa Fe NM; Morgan Stanley, Tacoma, WA; Stokes Lawrence, Seattle, WA; Gordon Bowker, Seattle, WA; Kathleen Flynn, AIA, Southport, CT; Franciscan Sisters, Portland, OR; Rick Gottas, Tacoma, WA; James Hauer, San Francisco, CA

EXHIBITIONS: Tahoma Center Gallery, 2003, 2000, 1996, Tacoma, WA; Eastshore Gallery, 2002, Bellevue, WA; Canon USA, 1985, Los Angeles, CA; Tacoma Art Museum, 1983, WA

323

MARTHA PETTIGREW
Book cover, page 88

Pettigrew Sculpture Studio
201 West 21st Street
Kearney, NE 68845
Tel/Fax 308-233-5504
E-mail dpettimar@aol.com
www.marthapettigrew.com

Martha Pettigrew creates figurative bronze sculpture of horses and indigenous people to America's West and Mexico. Monumental to tabletop sizes.

RECENT PROJECTS: Monument for the J.P. Morgan Chase & Co., Bedminster, NJ; sculpture for *"Grounds for Sculpture"* commissioned by Seward Johnson/Johnson Foundation, Hamilton, NJ

COMMISSIONS: City of Kearney, NE; Anheuser-Busch

COLLECTIONS: Benson Park Sculpture Garden, Loveland, CO; University of Nebraska, Kearney; The Irvine Company, Newport Beach, CA

EXHIBITIONS: *Christine of Santa Fe,* 2002; Museum of Nebraska Art, 1998

AWARDS: Best of Show, Cheyenne Frontier Days Museum, WY; silver medal, Knickerbocker Artists Society, New York, NY

PUBLICATIONS: *Southwest Art* magazine, July 1998; *Jumeirah Beach Club* magazine, August 2001

ROBERT PFITZENMEIER
Page 83

111 First Street #1-3A
Jersey City, NJ 07302
Tel 201-659-7629
E-mail repfitz@yahoo.com
www.metalmorphosis.org

Pfitz designs his work with a sparseness and delicacy that transcends the limited space it occupies. These geometric abstractions enliven spaces with an elegant, upbeat spirit. Complex kinetics and a wide use of polychromed or anodized color support this atmosphere. Anodized zirconium responds to light, yielding a full spectrum of colors that vary with changing light conditions. For 25 years, Pfitz has been constructing sculpture and suspended installations for public, private and corporate clients.

RECENT PROJECTS: Astra Zeneca installation, Wilmington, DE

GUILD SOURCEBOOKS: THE GUILD 5; Architect's 6, 9, 11, 12, 13, 14, 15; Architectural & Interior Art 16, 17

BINH PHO
Pages 180, 185

Wonders of Wood
48W175 Pine Tree Drive
Maple Park, IL 60151
Tel 630-365-5462
Fax 630-365-5837
E-mail toriale@msn.com
www.wondersofwood.net

Binh Pho is a Chicago-based artist who works primarily with wood. He combines lathe work, sculpting, airbrush and piercing techniques to create commanding primitive art forms and studio furniture.

COMMISSIONS: Honeywell Corporation, Cupertino, CA; Century 21, San Jose, CA; PreviewProperty.com, Brighton, MI

COLLECTIONS: The White House, Washington, DC; University of Michigan Fine Art Museum, Ann Arbor; Museum of Contemporary Art and Design, New York, NY; Long Beach Fine Art Museum, Long Beach, CA

EXHIBITIONS: SOFA, 2000-2002, New York, NY and Chicago, IL; solo exhibition, del Mano Gallery, 2003, Los Angeles, CA

GUILD SOURCEBOOKS: *Designer's 15; Architectural & Interior Art 16, 17; Artful Home 1*

ARTIST LISTINGS

JUNCO SATO POLLACK
Page 268

11 Polo Drive NE
Atlanta, GA 30309
Tel/Fax 404-892-2155
E-mail junco@juncosatopollack.com
www.juncosatopollack.com

Junco Sato Pollack's light-reflective fabric sculpture is exhibited internationally and housed in the permanent collections of museums, corporate workspaces and private homes. Her work hangs like a scroll, referencing the meditative calm and serendipitous articulation of Eastern ink-and-brush painting. The work's intrinsic kinetic quality is sensuous, dynamic and expressive of both Eastern and Western aesthetics. A native of Japan, Pollack began her training with a silk master weaver in Kyoto. She now uses a digital printer and industrial transfer press to simultaneously color and texturize her fabrics.

COMMISSIONS: Pittsburgh Airport, Pittsburgh, PA; Hotel Mandarin Oriental, Miami, FL; Kiang Gallery, Atlanta, GA; Pinnacle Assurance Headquarters, Scottsdale AZ; McGrath & Braun, Denver, CO

COLLECTIONS: American Craft Museum, New York, NY; Wallace Memorial Library, Rochester Institute of Technology, Rochester, NY; Arimatsu Shibori Kaikan Museum, Japan

MARV POULSON
Page 249

Imagedancer Photography
3631 South Carolyn Street
Salt Lake City, UT 84106
Tel 801-558-0875
E-mail marv@imagedancer.net
www.imagedancer.net

Photography represents both work and joy in life for Marv Poulson. "I strive to engage the emotions evoked by the natural realm, especially the mystery or magical essence of light-play in the world. My pictures emerge through imagination and experience with the interaction between light and subject." Poulson works in natural light using 35mm and 4" x 5" color transparency film scanned at high resolution to create a digital file. He then edits his digital files in the virtual darkroom of Adobe Photoshop and Corel PhotoPaint to match the natural image. Poulson uses museum-quality giclee printing techniques and archival materials to create luminous prints with full color and tonal depth. Recent work includes expansive images of wild landscapes and intimate studies of the natural realm. Poulson's photographs are exhibited widely and included in the finest nature publications.

COLLECTIONS: Phillips Gallery, Salt Lake City, UT; Hogan Gallery, Moab, UT

BEV PRECIOUS
Pages 14, 171

Precious Design Studios, Inc.
950 North Alabama Street
Indianapolis, IN 46202
Tel/Fax 317-631-6560
E-mail bbprec@aol.com

Dichroic glass is kinetic, exciting and unequalled when creating intense color. When combined with stainless steel, aluminum, bronze and limestone, dichroic glass enlivens a sculpture with transmitted and reflected color.

RECENT PROJECTS: University of Indianapolis, IN; University of Wisconsin, Madison; Miami University, Middletown, OH; Charlotte County Courthouse, Punta Gorda, FL; Lansing Community College, MI

COMMISSIONS: Merrill Lynch, Pennington, NJ, and Denver, CO; Nestle Research & Development, New Milford, CT, and Marysville, OH

AWARDS: Design award, 1998, AIA Georgia

GUILD SOURCEBOOKS: *Architect's 8, 9, 10, 11, 12, 13, 14, 15; Architectural & Interior Art 17*

GARY LEE PRICE
Page 113

Gary Lee Price Studios, Inc.
38 West 200 South
Springville, UT 84663
Tel 877-457-7423
Fax 801-489-9588
E-mail info@garyleeprice.com
www.garyleeprice.com

"Lifting the human spirit" is the mission of sculptor Gary Lee Price. For over 20 years, this exceptional artist has graced the world with his interpretation of this mission. Price says: "Although my work is constantly evolving, with each creation, my goal is to end up with a piece of art that is somehow inspirational in nature, something that lifts us to a higher plane or level."

COLLECTIONS: American Community Schools, Surrey, England; Westmann Islands, Iceland; Hong Kong Central Library; Brentwood United Methodist Church, Brentwood, TN; Olen Properties, Newport Beach, CA; Our Lady of Fatima Catholic School, Lafayette, LA; Culver Academy, Culver, IN; NuSkin International, Provo, UT; City of Decatur, GA; Cessna Corporation, Wichita, KS; New Hartford Memorial Library, CT, and hundreds of others.

JOHN PUGH
Page 208

PO Box 1332
Los Gatos, CA 95031
Tel 408-353-3370
Fax 408-353-1223
E-mail artofjohnpugh.com
www.artofjohnpugh.com

John Pugh's trompe l'oeil murals transform flat walls into other "spaces." He has been awarded an array of national public art projects, and articles about John's work have appeared throughout the world. For all murals, indoor or outdoor, large or small, projects may be painted in Pugh's studio on canvas or non-woven media (outdoor material) and then site-specifically integrated. Prints are also available.

COMMISSIONS: Cities of Anchorage, Boise, Den-ver, Dublin, Miami, Palm Desert, Phoenix, Sacramento, San Jose, South San Francisco; University of Alaska; California State University, Chico; University of Northern Florida; Stanford University

PUBLICATIONS: *Time, Focus, Artweek, Via, Art Business News, Southwest Art, L.A. Times, New York Times, San Francisco Examiner*

MAYA RADOCZY
Page 69

Contemporary Art Glass
PO Box 31422
Seattle, WA 98103
Tel 206-527-5022
Fax 206-524-9226
E-mail maya@serv.net
www.mayaglass.com

Maya Radoczy is known for creating cast glass collages, bas-relief images and sculpture for corporate, public and residential projects. She exhibits internationally and is included in numerous collections.

COMMISSIONS: Elliot Hotel, 2001, Seattle, WA; REI Flagship Stores, 2000, Tokyo, Japan, and Denver, CO; King St. Center, 1999, Seattle, WA; Deschutes County Library, 1999, Bend, OR. Exhibitions: International Sculpture Invitational, 2001, Seadrift, TX; Sculpture show, 2000, Erlangen, Germany; Northwest Women in Glass, 1999, Tacoma, WA; Focus on Fire: Fine Art in Architecture, Seattle, WA, 1994. Publications: Glass House, 2002; Seattle Homes & Lifestyles magazine, 2001, "Modern Masters" HGTV, 1999.

ARTIST LISTINGS

JOHN RAIMONDI
Page 142

John Raimondi, Sculptor, Inc.
1120 Gator Trail
West Palm Beach, FL 33409
Tel 561-687-1585
Fax 561-687-3854

8 Inkberry Street
East Hampton, NY 11937
Tel 631-329-4040

E-mail jrsculptor@aol.com
www.jrsculptor.com

John Raimondi has specialized in site-specific monumental sculptures since 1971. His themes include great jazz musicians, endangered species, political figures and other abstractions. His works are romantic, inspiring and exquisitely fabricated. He is regarded as an innovator for the use of color in his patinas. Raimondi typically produces smaller editions of each monumental sculpture: tabletop and garden-scale works are available immediately.

JANE RANKIN
Page 109

19335 Greenwood Drive
Monument, CO 80132
Tel 719-488-9223
Fax 719-488-1650
E-mail jrankin@magpiehill.com

Jane Rankin creates limited-edition bronze sculpture specializing in life-size and tabletop figures, mostly of children and child-related things.

COMMISSIONS: Harvest Community, 2002, Ft. Collins, CO; Town Hall, 1999, Cary, NC; Morse Park, 1998, Lakewood, CO

COLLECTIONS: Dogwood Festival Center, Jackson, MS; Waukegan Public Library, IL; Colorado Springs Fine Art Center, CO; Buell Children's Museum, Pueblo, CO; Lincoln Children's Museum, NE; Creative Artist Agency, Beverly Hills, CA

EXHIBITIONS: Pueblo Street Gallery, 2001-2002, Pueblo, CO; American Numismatic Association, 2002, Colorado Springs, CO

GUILD SOURCEBOOKS: *Architect's 14, 15; Architectural & Interior Art 16, 17*

VICKI REED
Page 250

Vicki Reed Photography
N66 W5594 Columbia Road
Cedarburg, WI 53012
Tel 262-377-1197
Fax 262-377-9273
E-mail tinter8x10@aol.com
www.vickireed.com

Vicki Reed's subtly hand-colored black-and-white photographs capture the stillness of a moment. The images can transport the viewer from his or her harried world to a more contemplative, quiet place. Reed's subjects, drawn from travels in Africa, America, the Caribbean and Europe, reflect a fascination with windows, doorways and the simple play of light. Her native state of Maine is a favorite photographic study.

EXHIBITIONS: Solo shows: Bank One Plaza, 2000, Milwaukee, WI; Boerner Botanical Gardens, 2000, Hales Corners, WI; Bradley Gallery, Lakeland College, 2002, Sheboygan, WI

PUBLICATIONS: Reed is currently an art editor and photographer for *Porcupine Literary Arts Magazine.*

REUBEN SINHA STAINED GLASS STUDIO
Page 68

Reuben Sinha
104 West 119th Street
New York, NY 10026-1306
Tel 212-316-3519
Fax 212-316-3602
E-mail reusinha@yahoo.com
www.reubensinha.com

New York artist Reuben Sinha, whose large-scale oil paintings tend toward figurative compositions with vivid, often unexpected colors, has also been creating stained glass pieces for several years. His most recent piece, a large commission for a private client in New York, helps transform a small, interior room into a lush atmospheric space. While serving a functional purpose, the work, which combines hundreds of individual pieces of stained glass in a variety of textures and colors, also draws the viewer into an almost magical, serene landscape.

RECENT PROJECTS: Three private commissions, leaded stained glass panels, New York, NY

COLLECTIONS: United States Education Foundation in India, 1998, New Delhi; numerous private collections, New York, NY

AWARDS: Fulbright Scholarship, 1998; Edward G. MacDowell Traveling Grant, 1992

KEVIN ROBB
Page 152

Kevin Robb Studios
7001 West 35th Avenue
Wheat Ridge, CO 80033-6373
Tel 303-431-4758
Fax 303-425-8802
E-mail 3d@kevinrobb.com
www.kevinrobb.com

Kevin Robb creates individual contemporary sculptures in stainless steel or bronze, as well as limited-edition cast bronze for intimate environments and large-scale public areas. Robb brings a natural curiosity to his work, combined with the knowledge gained from an understanding of how positive and negative spaces, shadow and light work together.

RECENT PROJECTS: Deer Creek Development, Overland Park, KS; Healthpoint, Fort Worth, TX; Austin Ranch, Austin, TX

COMMISSIONS: Rod Mitchell, Granite Bay, CA; Robinson & Shades Design Group, Tuscon, AZ; Keith and Sally Huzyak, yacht sculpture

GUILD SOURCEBOOKS: *Architect's 12, 13, 14, 15; Architectural & Interior Art 17; Artful Home 1*

ROCK COTTAGE GLASSWORKS, INC.
Pages 190, 195

Dierk Van Keppel
6801 Farley
Merriam, KS 66203
Tel 913-262-1763
Fax 913-262-0430
E-mail rcglass@grapevine.net
www.VanKeppelArtGlass.com

Rock Cottage Glassworks, featuring glass artist Dierk Van Keppel, creates blown and cast glass objects and combines them with various materials to produce custom lighting, sculpture and art glass. Rock Cottage clients include public, residential and corporate projects. Collaborating with architects and designers, the artist is involved in all aspects of design, including concept, fabrication and installation of pendant lights, wall sconces and chandeliers.

COMMISSIONS: *Fogo de Chao* Restaurant; Helzberg Diamonds; Carnuba Café; S.C. Johnson Corporate Headquarters; The Lighting Studio, Aspen, CO; Overland Park Convention Center, KS; St. Alexian Medical Center

GUILD SOURCEBOOKS: *Architectural & Interior Art 17, Artful Home 1*

ARTIST LISTINGS

CHRISTINA ROE
Page 260

Fantan Studio
2716 North Adoline Avenue
Fresno, CA 93705
Tel 559-226-1533
Fax 559-226-7490
E-mail fantanstudio@yahoo.com

Christina Roe combines traditional and abstract decorative motifs with original surface finishes and textures in papier-mâché and hand-cast wall sculptures. The paper castings usually begin with a clay original, from which a mold is made and then cast using a paper pulp, which she recycles herself. Using cut fragments of these casts, she assembles designs for her wall reliefs like a mosaic, gluing them to a backing to create a unified appearance. The final piece is then painted with many layers of color and may be cast again. Richly colored and textured, her multilayered relief surfaces are both durable and lightweight. Wires attached to the back enable them to be hung unframed. Prices range from $500-$5,000.

GUILD SOURCEBOOKS: *Designer's 14; Architectural & Interior Art 16; Artful Home 1*

MARTHA ROEDIGER
Pages 218, 292

66 Pearl Street
Portland, ME 04101
Tel 207-828-8771
Fax 207-828-8772
E-mail marthar@ime.net
www.martharoediger.com

Waves of exuberant color undulate across the surface of Martha Roediger's woven and carefully constructed fiber art, while her original use of textures and fibers (primarily wool, cotton, linen and metallics) heightens the tactile and sculptural qualities inherent to the medium.

COMMISSIONS: Case Western Reserve University, 2001, Cleveland, OH; R.M. Davis, Inc., 2000, Portland, ME

COLLECTIONS: Avaya Communications, Inc., Denver, CO; the White House Ornament Collection, Washington, DC

EXHIBITIONS: Holiday exhibition, 2002, Craft Alliance Gallery, St. Louis, MO; three @ 3, Art3 Gallery, 2002, Manchester, NH; the Inaugural Show, the Columbus Museum Uptown, 2001, Columbus, GA; multi-media show, Mercer Island Art Gallery, 2001, Seattle, WA

MARY ROLEY
Page 150

PO Box 3230
Madison, WI 53704
Tel 608-219-3647
E-mail mabroley@hotmail.com

Mary Roley's steel and glass sculptures encapsulate the subtle beauty and character of the Midwestern countryside, while paying homage to its agricultural history. Sculptures range from monumental to small and intimate. Roley's talents include welding, metal fabrication, glass blowing and casting, and neon fabrication. She maintains a fully equipped metal-working studio and participates in shows across the nation.

COMMISSIONS: Ross Horrall Memorial, 2003, Fitchburg, WI; Bluephie's Restaurant Madison, WI

EXHIBITIONS: *Sustenance*, 2001, Sinsinawa Mound Gallery, Sinsinawa, WI; *Culture and Agriculture*, 2001, New Vision's Gallery, Marshfield, WI; *Mid by Midwest*, 2000, Millenic Glass, Kansas City, MO; *Landmarks and Rural Routes*, 1999, Tobacco Junction Gallery, Stoughton, WI; *Women's Caucus for Art*, 1995, UN/NGO World Women's Conference, Hauirou, China; *Redefining Power*, 1995, Esperanza Peace and Justice Center, San Antonio, TX

PUBLICATIONS: "Glass and Steel," *Telegraph Herald*, 2001; "New Visions' Culture and Agriculture," 2001

ROSENFELD
Page 232

16 East 96th Street #4B
New York, NY 10128
Tel 212-996-5013
Fax 212-360-1774
E-mail info@rosenfeldart.com
www.rosenfeldart.com

To discover Rosenfeld's luminous landscapes in the midst of the concrete reality of New York City is an unexpected pleasure. In her urban studio, Rosenfeld paints from memory and photographs—dramatic junctures of land, sky and sea discovered in Florida, the Caribbean, Hawaii and Martha's Vineyard. Carefully removing most evidence of civilization from her compositions, Rosenfeld restores the landscape as carefully as an environmentalist. Through her eyes, one can savor the beauty of nature in its primordial state.

COLLECTIONS: Purdue University, Hammond, IN; Hofstra Museum, Hempstead, NY; Pepperdine University, Malibu, CA

EXHIBITIONS: Hofstra Museum, 2000, Hempstead, NY; Purdue University, 2000, Hammond, IN; Gallery Leuenberger, Zurich, Switzerland

AWARDS: Ford Foundation, Studio Art Award

TALLI ROSNER-KOZUCH
Page 244

Pho-Tal Inc.
15 North Summit Street
Tenafly, NJ 07670
Tel 201-569-3199
Fax 201-569-3392
E-mail tal@photal.com
www.photal.com

Talli Rosner-Kozuch works in black and white, sepia tones, color, platinum prints, lithographs and etchings. Her areas of expertise include large-format photography. The images range in size and vary in style from architectural portraiture and documentary to landscape and still life. Using signature techniques, she achieves a unique blend of minimalism and sensuality in her work.

RECENT PROJECTS: Forty exhibitions all over the United States, Europe and Asia; working with designers and galleries on hospitals, hotels, restaurants and companies in commercial buildings.

COMMISSIONS: Restaurants, hotels, banks, corporations, building entrances, stores, Ethan Allen catalog

GUILD SOURCEBOOKS: *Designer's 13, 14, 15; Architectural & Interior Art 16, 17*

BARTON RUBENSTEIN
Page 147

Rubenstein Studios
4819 Dorset Avenue
Chevy Chase, MD 20815
Tel 301-654-5406
Fax 301-654-5496
E-mail bartsher@aol.com
www.rubensteinstudios.com

As a former visual scientist, Barton Rubenstein has always been interested in the various visual forms of nature, especially those related to water, motion and suspension. Rubenstein typically uses bronze, stainless steel, stone and glass to create sculpture, with or without water. He has enjoyed the collaborative process of public art, commercial and residential site-specific commissions.

NATIONAL COMPETITION COMMISSIONS: University of Central Florida, 2003, Orlando; Bridgerland Applied Technology College, 2001, Logan, UT; Florida Turnpike Authority Headquarters, 2001, Orlando; Lopez State Veterans Home, 1998, Land O' Lakes, FL

COMMISSIONS: Weizmann Institute of Science, 2003, Israel; Blue Cross Blue Shield Regional Headquarters, 1998; Brookside Gardens, Wheaton Regional Park, 1998, MD; Crowell & Moring, LLP, 1997, Washington, DC

ARTIST LISTINGS

BRIAN F. RUSSELL
Pages 8, 151

Brian F. Russell Studio
10385 Long Road
Arlington, TN 38002
Tel 901-867-7300
Fax 901-867-7843
E-mail info@brianrusselldesigns.com
www.brianrusselldesigns.com

The transparency and optical nature of colored cast glass has an inherent emotional effect that enables the artist to speak quietly, yet powerfully, about his ideas on the nature of reality and the purity of form. The effect of the metal forgings, synergized by the images presented in vivid glass castings, gives life to his sculptures.

RECENT PROJECTS: Large chandelier, private residence, Berkeley, CA

COLLECTIONS: Rhodes College, 2001, Memphis, TN; Bell South Collection, Tennessee State Museum, Nashville, TN

EXHIBITIONS: Governor's Inaugural Exhibition, Tennessee Arts Commission, Nashville

PUBLICATIONS: *Direct Metal Sculpture*, 2001; *Contemporary Blacksmith*, 2001

JAMES THOMAS RUSSELL
Pages 148-149

James Russell Sculpture
1930 Lomita Boulevard
Lomita, CA 90717
Tel 310-326-0785
Fax 310-326-1470
E-mail james@russellsculpture.com
www.russellsculpture.com

Elegantly crafted and fastidiously polished, James T. Russell's sculptures are ribbons of stainless steel, gracefully arching and twirling in space. His professional career, in its fourth decade, includes worldwide commissions ranging from wall reliefs to gallery editions to fountains and monumental towers of gleaming inspiration.

COMMISSIONS: Princess Cruises, 2000, Italy; Westborough Corridor, 1999, South San Francisco, CA; AT Kearney, Inc., 1999, Chicago, IL; Motorola Corporation, 1998, Beijing, China

COLLECTIONS: *Architectural Digest*, CA; Riverside Art Museum, Riverside, CA; Caesar's World, Century City, CA

PUBLICATIONS: *Landscape Architect*, 2000; *Focus Santa Fe*, 2000; *Art Calendar*, 1999

GUILD SOURCEBOOKS: *Architect's 7, 8, 12, 13, 14, 15; Architectural & Interior Art 16, 17; Artful Home 1*

MATTHEW RYAN
Page 154

Studio M
4340 East Kentucky Avenue #235
Denver, CO 80246
Tel 303-632-3800
E-mail mryanart@earthlink.net
www.artofryan.com

The main goal of Matthew Ryan's artwork is to capture the grace, energy and fluidity of the animals that he encounters underwater. He generally begins a piece by studying the movement of the animal (rather than the anatomy). He then focuses on the relationships between lines in a design.

SABLE STUDIOS
Page 85

Paul Sable
2737 Rosedale Avenue
Soquel, CA 95073
Tel 800-233-7309
E-mail paul@sablestudios.com
www.sablestudios.com

Paul Sable has collaborated successfully with art consultants, architects and designers for over 35 years. His kinetic, acrylic mobiles integrate color, light and movement to create a multidimensional experience. His custom-designed sculptures harmonize with private, corporate and public spaces.

RECENT PROJECTS: Union City Senior Center, CA; Lucent Technologies, CO

COMMISSIONS: Metro Plaza Building, San Jose, CA; Syntex Corporation, Hayward, CA; Berklee Performance Center, Boston, MA; Quantum Corporation; 3 Comm; Cadence Corporation

GUILD SOURCEBOOKS: *Architect's 11, 12, 13, 14, 15; Architectural & Interior Art 16, 17*

SABOROSCH
Page 103

Glenn Saborosch
PO Box 61
Fletcher, MO 63030
Tel 314-974-3546

Energy, strength, grace: these characteristics best describe the sculpture of Glenn Saborosch. The balance of positive and negative space is the basic principle he uses to achieve these characteristics. His figurative works are classical in form, contemporary in design; structural integrity is paramount. Saborosch works primarily with mild steel, Corten® steel and bronze.

COMMISSIONS: Private commissions; Visionworks, 2000, Columbia, MO

EXHIBITIONS: *Sculpture in the Park*, 1999, 2000 and 2002, Loveland, CO

AWARDS: Second Best of Show and First Place in Sculpture, 2001, Art in the Park, Columbia Art League, Columbia, MO; featured artist, 1998, Riverbend Art Festival, Atchison, KS

PUBLICATIONS: Roadway *Express Spotlight* magazine, 2002; *St. Louis Homes & Lifestyles* magazine, March, 2001

JOY SAVILLE
Page 293

244 Dodds Lane
Princeton, NJ 08540
Tel/Fax 609-924-6824
E-mail jsaville@rcn.com
www.joysaville.com

Joy Saville expresses "frozen moments" in her fabric constructions by piecing together cotton, linen and silk in an impressionistic, painterly manner. A colorist, she uses the inherent quality of natural fabrics to absorb or reflect light, producing a constant interplay of light, texture and color.

COMMISSIONS: Johnson & Johnson; Ortho Pharmaceutical; The Jewish Center, Princeton, NJ

COLLECTIONS: American Craft Museum; the Newark Museum; Bristol-Myers Squibb; Time-Warner Inc.; Ropes & Gray, Boston, MA; Wilmington Trust, DE; H.J. Heinz; PepsiCo

EXHIBITIONS: Solo and group exhibitions throughout North America and internationally since 1976

GUILD SOURCEBOOKS: *THE GUILD 3, 4, 5; Architectural & Interior Art 17*

ARTIST LISTINGS

RHONA LK SCHONWALD
Page 230

Historic Savage Mill
8600 Foundry Street
Carding Building #205
Savage, MD 20763
Tel 410-880-4118
www.rhonalkschonwald.com

Life's milestones, miracles, adventures and triumphs are reflected in the award-winning creations of Rhona Schonwald. Relationships among colors in her paintings and forms in her sculpture evoke thought, sensuality and joy. Her paintings celebrate the interaction of colors with drama and delicacy. Sculptures flow and undulate, illuminating nature's rocks, root systems and shriveled leaves. Rhona Schonwald's art unleashes emotion. Whether viewing her sculptures or her paintings, patrons experience exhilaration, inspiration and a sense of peacefulness. Schonwald paints and sculpts because she loves the process, an adventure of the mind expressed through material. When this adventure comes to an end for the artist, another one begins for the viewer.

GUILD SOURCEBOOKS: *Artful Home 1*

MARSH SCOTT
Page 170

3275 Laguna Canyon Road, Studio M1
Laguna Beach, CA 92651
Tel 949-494-8672
Fax 949-494-8671
E-mail marsh@marshscott.com
www.marshscott.com

Marsh Scott works in sculptural and two-dimensional media to create site-specific commissions for public, corporate, medical, residential and hospitality projects.

COMMISSIONS: Public: Brea, CA, 1999, 2000; Laguna Beach, CA, 2000, 2001; Los Angeles, CA. 2001; Private: Associated Television International, CA; Baxter Labs, CA; Canal Plus U.S., CA; Discovery Museum, CA; Edison Co., NV and CA; Four Seasons, NV; Regency Hotel, Guam; Orange County Airport, CA; Torrance Memorial Hospital, CA; Verizon, CA; Viking Components, CA; Waterfront Hilton, CA

SUSAN SCULLEY
Page 231

4731 North Paulina #3N
Chicago, IL 60640
Tel 773-728-6109
Fax 773-728-9305
E-mail susan.sculley@scdchicago.com

Susan Sculley works in both oil sticks and chalk pastels to create compositions of color and form, capturing the essence of peace and beauty found in the landscape. Sculley works with interior designers, art consultants and galleries. Her work is found in both corporate and private settings, and can be contemporary or traditional in style.

COLLECTIONS: Commonwealth Edison Corporate Headquarters, Chicago, IL; Amoco Corporation, Chicago, IL; Hartford Insurance Company, Chicago, IL; Loyola University Medical Center, Maywood, IL; numerous private collections

PUBLICATIONS: *Beautiful Things*, 2000; *Metropolitan Home*, November/December 2000

GUILD SOURCEBOOKS: *Architectural & Interior Art 16; Artful Home 1*

JOHN SEARLES
Page 271

SearlesArt
642 South Lombard Avenue
Oak Park, IL 60304
Tel 708-222-8160
E-mail johnsearles@ameritech.net
www.searlesart.com

The wall sculptures of John Searles reflect his enduring interests in mathematics, visual pleasure, energy and freedom. Working with copper, brass, stainless steel or aluminum (sometimes melting one onto the other), Searles cuts one piece of patinated metal into many pieces, then reassembles them into a more visually stimulating, often large-scale, level of order. His purpose is to delight the brain and visual center in a non-cerebral manner. He calls his work "music for the eyes."

RECENT PROJECTS: Private residences in Flossmoor, IL; Evanston, IL; River Forest, IL; Chicago, IL

COMMISSIONS: Private residences in Deerfield, IL; St. Paul, MN; Des Moines, IA

COLLECTIONS: Rohrer Corporation, Wadsworth, OH; Unico Alloys, Columbus, OH; Richard E. Jacobs Architects, Cleveland, OH

EXHIBITIONS: Don Drumm Gallery, 2000, Akron, OH; Corporate Art Gallery, 1999, Mentor, OH; one-man show, 1998, Gallery Nine, Cleveland, OH

SUSAN SINGLETON
Page 264

AZO
728 Grindstone Harbor
PO Box 39
Orcas, WA 98280
Tel 360-376-5898
Fax 360-376-5519
E-mail azo@rockisland.com
www.azoart.com

Susan Singleton lives on Orcas Island in the San Juan Archipelago, with her husband, Andrew Shewman. Together they collaborate on site-specific installations, but the main focus of Singleton's work are the large paper constructions she calls *Ziggurats*. These pieces reflect her love of tactile surfaces, architectural structure and grand scale. Balance, beauty, reflection, humility, humor and imperfection frame Singleton's work and her life. The power of our natural world, and the love of handmade objects are the basic force behind the work. Two recent favorite projects have been the *Golden Excavation* sculptures for the Mitsubishi Shiodome, Tokyo, Japan, and a stage set for *Camelot*, for the Orcas Community Theater. Materials used are handmade washi papers, metallic leafing, collaged patterns and acrylic stains. The work is universal in its appeal, reflecting ancient artifacts and architecture.

SLEDD/WINGER GLASSWORKS
Page 189

Nancy Sledd
Mary Lu Winger
1912 East Main Street
Richmond, VA 23223
Tel 804-644-2837
Fax 804-644-6821
E-mail sleddwinger@aol.com

Since 1985 Nancy Sledd and Mary Lu Winger have collaborated in a multifaceted stained glass studio, featuring internationally collected commission work as well as limited-production gallery pieces. Known for their meticulous attention to detail, this versatile pair works closely with clients to determine design and color direction. Often combining such divergent elements as fiber optics, water and fusing, Sledd and Winger constantly strive for the unexpected. Projects range from entryways and windows to furniture, lighting and sculpture. Exhibits and awards: American Craft Council (ACC) Spotlight; Baltimore ACC; Philadelphia Furniture Show; Smithsonian Craft Show; numerous Niche magazine awards. Publications: Niche magazine, Stained Glass Basics, Glass Craftsman, Stained Glass for the First Time, Glass Art, Home & Design, Leadlight.

GUILD SOURCEBOOKS: *Artful Home 1*

ARTIST LISTINGS

JEFF G. SMITH
Page 70

Architectural Stained Glass, Inc.
PO Box 1126
Fort Davis, TX 79734-1126
Tel 432-426-3311
Fax 432-426-3366
E-mail info@archstglassinc.com
www.archstglassinc.com

Whether in a courthouse, a place of worship, a restaurant or library, Jeff Smith's stained glass becomes a dynamic, integral part of one's experience of people, light, landscape and sky within an architectural space. Smith has received three Honor Awards from the American Institute of Architects Interfaith Forum on Religion, Art and Architecture.

RECENT PROJECTS: Oncology Center, St. Vincent Hospital, Indianapolis, IN; Quentin N. Burdick Federal Courthouse, Fargo, ND; American Airlines Admirals Club, Dallas/Fort Worth, TX; St. Matthew Catholic Church, Windham, NH; University of Alaska, Fairbanks, AK; Washington Hebrew Congregation, Washington, DC; Salt Lake City Community College Library, UT; Wilcox Memorial Hospital, Lihue, HI

GUILD SOURCEBOOKS: *THE GUILD 4, 5; Architect's 7, 8, 9, 10, 11, 12, 13, 14, 15; Architectural & Interior Art 16, 17*

TREMAIN SMITH
Page 258

4520 Locust Street
Philadelphia, PA 19139
Tel 215-387-1869
Fax 215-387-6337
E-mail look@tremainsmith.com
www.tremainsmith.com

Working with layers of beeswax and rich earth colors, Tremain Smith creates paintings that are mappings of a spiritual nature. Each piece, with its oil glazes, transparent wax and collaged elements, has a richly textured surface that draws the viewer into the layers underneath.

COLLECTIONS: Metropolitan Museum of Art, New York; Visa Corporation, Littleton, CO

EXHIBITIONS: Cervini Haas Gallery, 2003, Scottsdale, AZ; *Cartography of Spirit*, 2002, Lancaster Museum of Art, PA; Phoenix Gallery, 2000, New York, NY; SOFA, 2000, Chicago, IL

PUBLICATIONS: *The Art of Encaustic Painting: Contemporary Expressions in the Ancient Medium of Pigmented Wax*, Watson-Guptill, 2001

DOUG SOELBERG
Page 71

Architectural Art Glass
869 West 2000 North
Provo, UT 84604
Tel 801-224-6646
Fax 801-223-9938
E-mail aag@aagdesign.com
www.aagdesign.com

Doug Soelberg has been producing leaded glass windows for nearly 30 years. He has explored a variety of styles but favors abstract expression and minimalism. He views his work primarily as architectural components to be integrated into site-specific projects to complement the finished space. He attempts to create a stasis in his work—to persuade the viewer to stop moving around the object and instead move into it.

COMMISSIONS: St. Patrick's Hospital, Missoula, MT; St. Vincent de Paul, Salt Lake City, UT; Orem City Library, UT; Latter-day Saints Temple, Campinas, Brazil; Snow College Administration Building, UT

329

EDDIE SOLOWAY
Page 253

Eddie Soloway Photography
PO Box 6745
Santa Fe, NM 87502
Tel/Fax 505-466-6030
E-mail soloway@anaturaleye.com
www.anaturaleye.com

Eddie Soloway's photography captures the essence of our natural world. He creates images—both representational and abstract—using natural light and historic photographic techniques. An established and meticulous printer, Soloway uses archival photographic papers and finishes his pieces to museum standards.

RECENT PROJECTS: *Gentle Edges; Forest Abstracts; Sense of Place; Wilderness Moments*

AWARDS: Excellence in Photographic Teaching, 1999, Santa Fe Center for Visual Arts

PUBLICATIONS: "A Natural Eye," *Camera Arts*, August-September, 2002

CYNTHIA SPARRENBERGER
Page 111

Sparrenberger Studio
5975 East Otero Drive
Englewood, CO 80112
Tel 303-741-3031 (studio)
Tel 303-618-8974 (cell)
E-mail cynthia6@mac.com
www.sparrenbergerstudio.com

Cynthia Sparrenberger's work is figurative, with a loose, impressionistic quality. Because of her dance background, she is passionate about gesture, line and movement, for it is these very elements that bring a sculpture to life.

RECENT PROJECTS: Life-size sculpture for Mynelle Gardens, Jackson, MS

COMMISSIONS: Private portrait, 2003; canine portrait, 2002, Sedalia, CO; private portrait, 2000, Parker, CO

COLLECTIONS: Mynelle Gardens, Jackson, MS; the Washington Ballet, Washington, DC

EXHIBITIONS: Loveland invitational, 2003, 2002; *Renaissance Sale*, 2001, Houston, TX; *American Art Classic*, 2001, Houston, TX; *Sculpture in the Park*, 2000, Loveland, CO

PUBLICATIONS: *Artists of Distinction*, 2003; *The Hilton Head Monthly*, 2001; *The Clarion Ledger*, 2001

DIMITRY "DOMANI" SPIRIDON
Page 91

Domani Studio
PO Box 22717
Santa Fe, NM 87502
Tel/Fax 505-438-8388
E-mail dimitry@domani-studio.com
www.domani-studio.com

Bronze sculpture—abstract to stylized to representational. Domani Spiridon's work is a celebration of life. To view an unbridled spirit, one remembers that freedom often commands a price, one which Spiridon has experienced personally and now chooses to transform into an exhilarating collection.

COMMISSIONS: Public commission, bronze sculpture, Santa Fe, NM; private commission, bronze sculpture, Santa Fe, NM

RECENT PROJECTS: Romanian Embassy, Washington, DC; private collections in Brazil and throughout the United States

EXHIBITIONS: Loveland Sculpture Invitational, CO

ARTIST LISTINGS

ARTHUR STERN
Pages 1, 72

Arthur Stern Studios
1075 Jackson Street
Benicia, CA 94510
Tel/Fax 707-745-8480
E-mail arthur@arthurstern.com
www.arthurstern.com

Arthur Stern Studios creates site-specific architectural glass installations, primarily in leaded glass. Specializing in the collaboration with design professionals and clients, the studio currently has installations in 36 states, as well as Japan. Commissions range from residential work to large public art projects and churches. Arthur Stern has been widely published and has won numerous awards, including several American Institute of Architects design awards, as well as honors from the Interfaith Forum on Religion, Art & Architecture, the Construction Specifications Institute, and *Ministry and Liturgy* magazine's BENE Awards. Each project undertaken receives the same thorough attention to detail and fine craftsmanship. Stern also works in other media, including wood and glass bas-relief sculpture, mixed-media works on canvas, and works on paper.

ROB STERN
Page 155

Rob Stern Art Glass
1510 Baracoa Avenue
Coral Gables, FL 33146
Tel 305-903-8566
Fax 305-661-1109
E-mail rasglass@aol.com
www.robsternartglass.com

Rob Stern combines glass and mixed media to realize work that is both personalized and reflective of his environment. His sculptural works are inventive and seek to engage the viewer with profound energy.

RECENT PROJECTS: *Fountain,* private residence, 2001, Miami, FL; *Bottle Wall,* 2002, Plaza 57, South Miami, FL; *Dancing Vase,* 2001, Sheraton Hotel, Bal Harbor, FL

COMMISSIONS: *Neon Columns,* 2001, private residence, Miami, FL

COLLCECTIONS: Paley collection, Miami, FL; Ajeto collection, Novy Bor, Czech Republic; Cohen collection, Miami, FL

EXHIBITIONS: Ajeto symposium, 2002, Novy Bor, Czech Republic

STUART REID ARCHITECTURAL GLASS
Page 74

Stuart Reid
364 Annette Street
Toronto, ON M6P 1R5
Canada
Tel 416-762-7743
Fax 416-762-8875
E-mail stuartreid@sympatico.ca
www.stuartreid.net

Stuart Reid's large-scale lyrical works use rich color, mouth-blown etched glass and enamel painting on float glass to create environmental works of luminosity and beauty.

RECENT PROJECTS: Junction Redevelopment, an urban design/art/architecture project for West Toronto, Canada (see website); Crowne Plaza Hotel, Toronto, a curved glass wall 'backdrop' for the main lobby reception desk; Salzburg Congress, a curved glass 'floating sail' in the grand foyer of the new convention center, Salzburg, Austria; Mississauga Living Arts Centre, a multi-sectioned glass mural in the three-story height lobby; St. James Cathedral, Toronto, three windows celebrating the 200th anniversary of the cathedral, unveiled by Queen Elizabeth II.

330

MARTIN STURMAN
Page 186

Martin Sturman Sculptures
3201 Bayshore Drive
Westlake Village, CA 91361
Tel 818-707-8087
Fax 818-707-3079
E-mail mlsturman@aol.com
www.steelsculptures.com

Martin Sturman creates original contemporary sculptures and furniture in carbon steel or stainless steel. His work is suitable for indoor or outdoor placement. Stainless steel surfaces are burnished to achieve a beautiful shimmering effect. Carbon steel sculptures are painted with acrylic and coated with polyurethane to preserve color vitality. Sturman encourages site-specific and collaborative efforts.

COMMISSIONS: Tesoro Galleries, Beverly Hills, CA; Hyatt Westlake Plaza Hotel, Westlake Village, CA; Manhattan Beach Car Wash, Manhattan Beach, CA

COLLECTIONS: McGraw-Hill Publishing Company, Columbus, OH; McDonald's Corporate Art Collection, Oakbrook, IL

GUILD SOURCEBOOKS: *Architect's 12, 14; Designer's 7, 8, 9, 10, 11, 12, 13, 14, 15; Architectural & Interior Art 16, 17*

NAOMI TAGINI
Page 274

1902 Comstock Avenue
Los Angeles, CA 90025
Tel 310-552-1877
Fax 310-552-2679
E-mail naomi@naomitagini.com
www.naomitagini.com

Up a stairway, down a hallway, around a corner or center stage, Naomi Tagini's artwork is always fun. Depicting places, emotions and words using color, shape and texture, the pieces of her work are often interchangeable, encouraging owner participation. *Belize,* pictured in this book, is bold and exotic, featuring spectacular coral reefs, parrots, toucans and jungle nights; the crackle finish suggests movement. *Uncut (A Diamond in the Rough)* represents the journey to find one's potential. Tagini opted for three colors: mud (representing the excavation of diamonds), and silver and bronze metallic (representing sparkling faceted diamonds). A textured coating makes the surface rough.

COMMISSIONS: Front entry wall, children's school, 2002, AL

EXHIBITS: *Art in Public Places,* 2003, Florida Keys Council of the Arts, Key West, FL

GUILD SOURCEBOOKS: *Architectural & Interior Art 17; Artful Home 1*

CHARLES BROOKING TAUZER
Page 37

New Mosaics
321 South Main Street #19
Sebastopol, CA 95472
Tel/Fax 707-823-2297
E-mail ctauzer@newmosaics.com
www.newmosaics.com

Although swimming pools are a common site for Charles Brooking Tauzer's tile images, his mosaics need not be limited in their use or placement. Inspired by nature, Tauzer draws upon various techniques to achieve his unique lines. Because all mosaics are a personal interpretation, each work becomes an original unto itself. Porcelain tile is Tauzer's dominant medium; it is both versatile and beautiful, enabling the artist to execute works in a number of styles and patterns.

COMMISSIONS: Pezzi King Vineyards, 1994, Healdsburg, CA; private residences in Woodacre, CA, 2002; Butte County, CA, 2002; Tiburon, CA, 2002; Santa Rosa, CA, 2002

ARTIST LISTINGS

STEVE TEETERS
Page 172

St. Eligius Studio
719 Buddy Holly Avenue
Lubbock, TX 79401
Tel 806-741-1590
Fax 806-744-8507
E-mail steve@steligius-studio.com

From architectural metal installations to small sculptures to large-scale public art, Steve Teeters' forged and welded steel designs are imbued with a sense of magic and mystery, humor and whimsy, myth and fantasy, past and future. Through his art, he comments on and redefines our cultural legacy.

COMMISSIONS: Texas Tech University public art commission, 2002, Lubbock; Albuquerque Zoo public art commission, 2002-2004, NM; City of Lubbock centennial sculpture commission, 2002

COLLECTIONS: Steve Teeters' sculpture is found in numerous public and private collections throughout the U.S.; Philip Bareiss Contemporary, 2003, Taos, NM; LeMeiux Galleries, New Orleans, LA

AWARDS: Excellence in Public Art award, 2002, Texas Tech University; numerous Best of Show and Juror awards

ROBERT S. TOLL
Page 90

3830 Willat Avenue
Culver City, CA 90232
Tel 310-841-5050
Fax 310-217-0859
E-mail robert@tollsculptor.com
www.tollsculptor.com

Robert Toll uses steel strips that have been gas-welded together to create the image he wants to convey. Each steel strip is heated and manipulated until the desired form is attained. Toll's goal is to transform cold, hard steel into a soft, expressive statement of human emotion.

RECENT PROJECTS: *Disconnect,* private collector, Pacific Palisades, CA; *Higher Ground,* Summit View School, Culver City, CA; *11:05,* office building, Century City, CA; *Don't Look Back,* El Paseo, Palm Desert, CA

COMMISSIONS: *Connection,* 1999, school, Sherman Oaks, CA; *Out of Focus,* 1998, office, Beverly Hills, CA

COLLECTIONS: Numerous private collections throughout the U.S. and Europe

AWARDS: Best Figurative Sculptor, 1993, National Sculpture Society

PUBLICATIONS: *Welding Magazine,* August 2002; *Southwest Art* magazine, July 2002

CASSIE TONDRO
Page 233

1348 Grant Street
Santa Monica, CA 90405
Tel 310-452-2964
E-mail cassie@cassietondro.com
www.cassietondro.com

Cassie Tondro uses color, texture and gesture to create unique woven paintings that convey a sense of energy and excitement. She works on two pieces of unstretched canvas at once, cutting them into strips after they have been painted. Finally, she weaves the strips together to form a harmonious whole. These paintings brighten and enliven any space and are meditative as well as lively; they evoke reflection and contemplation and take us somewhere else. Tondro invites commissions, which provide her with an opportunity to explore new color combinations and designs.

331

LUIS TORRUELLA
Page 139

Cond. Tenerife, Apartment 1201
Ashford Avenue 1507
San Juan, PR 00911
Tel/Fax 787-722-8728 (studio)
Tel 787-268-4977 (home)
E-mail luistorruella@aol.com
www.luistorruella.com

Luis Torruella, a Puerto Rican sculptor, designs in a contemporary, abstract context. His Caribbean heritage is reflected in his work's color, rhythm and movement. Torruella collaborates with architects, designers and developers in public and private commissions.

COLLECTIONS: Museo de Arte de Puerto Rico, San Juan; Mead Art Museum, Amherst, MA; Performing Arts Center, San Juan, PR; Skokie Sculpture Park, IL

EXHIBITIONS: Palma de Mallorca, 2001, Spain; Galeria Botello, 2002, 1997, 1994, 1992, San Juan, PR; Theatrical Institute, 1992, Moscow; World Expo, 1992, Seville, Spain; numerous private collections

GUILD SOURCEBOOKS: *Architect's 14, 15; Architectural & Interior Art 16, 17; Artful Home 1*

TRIO DESIGN GLASSWARE
Page 194

Renato Foti
253 Queen Street South
Kitchener, ON N2G 1W4
Tel 519-749-2814
Fax 519-749-6319
E-mail renatofoti@rogers.com
www.triodesignglassware.com

Simple geometric designs and bold colors exemplify Rento Foti's work. He brings structure, balance, color and simplicity to home and work environments. Balance is the key factor in the success of Foti's designs; it reflects his personal philosophy in life. These designs are incorporated in all of his products, from vessels and sinks to wall sculptures and lighting.

RECENT PROJECTS: Hanging lamps, Toronto, ON; glass sink and vanity, Chicago, IL

EXHIBITIONS: *One-of-a-Kind,* Chicago, IL, and Toronto, ON; Rosen Buyers Mart, Philadelphia, PA; New York Gift Show

AWARDS: NICHE Award Finalist for fused glass, 2003

PUBLICATIONS: *Canadian House and Home,* December-January, 2001-2002

GUILD SOURCEBOOKS: *Architectural & Interior Art 17; Artful Home 1*

JEFF TRITEL
Page 104

Tritel Studios
19432 Richmar Lane
Grass Valley, CA 95949
Tel 800-882-8098
Fax 888-796-3776
E-mail tritel@tritelstudios.com
www.tritelstudios.com

A bronze sculptor for over 30 years, Jeff Tritel has artwork in over 800 private and corporate collections. Tritel is appreciated for his formal sensibilities, his sense of whimsy and his keen psychological insight. Sculptures range in size from 3" to 100'.

RECENT PROJECTS: Tritel Sculpture Park, CA

COMMISSIONS: Lobby, Wells Fargo Bank, Salt Lake City, UT; sculpture, San Jose, CA, 22'H

COLLECTIONS: City of Anaheim, CA

EXHIBITIONS: Rosicrucian Museum, San Jose, CA

AWARDS: Best of show, 2000, 1999, 1987, *Art on the Main,* Walnut Creek, CA; first place, 2000, 1991, Art Festival, Hermosa Beach, CA

PUBLICATIONS: *Millionaire* magazine, July 2000; "Arts Alive," PBS TV, 1988-1990; *Easyriders* magazine, May 1995

ARTIST LISTINGS

ELLEN TYKESON
Page 101

Ellen Tykeson Sculpture
1033 Sharon Way
Eugene, OR 97401
Tel 541-687-5731
E-mail etykeson@yahoo.com

Classic form and elegance define the figurative bronze sculpture of Ellen Tykeson. Her work ranges in scale from table top to monumental outdoor pieces for public settings. Tykeson welcomes commissions, bringing to them the strong design, attention to detail, and emotional content demonstrated in each of her works.

RECENT PROJECTS: *Gertrude Bass Warner Memorial*, University of Oregon Art Museum, 2003, Eugene; *Luna*, Norwalk Furniture Design, 2002, Palm Desert, CA; *Treasure*, Southwest Community Church, 2000, Indian Wells, CA

EXHIBITIONS: Silvercreek Gallery, 2002, Silverton, OR; National Sculpture Society Annual Exhibit, 2001; Brookgreen Gardens, 2001, NC; NSS Headquarters, New York, NY; Lane Community College, 2001, Eugene, OR

GUILD SOURCEBOOKS: *Architect's 12, 15; Architectural & Interior Art 16*

KAREN URBANEK
Page 269

314 Blair Avenue
Piedmont, CA 94611-4004
Tel 510-654-0685
Fax 510-654-2790
E-mail KrnUrbanek@aol.com

Karen Urbanek builds painterly images and sculptural forms—both abstract and representational—in luminous layers of complex color and texture. Her extensive palette derives from natural sources and working methodologies that adhere to principles of environmental responsibility. Constructed primarily of compacted tussah silk fiber, her work is finished with a protective coating to add crispness and strength. Surfaces range from smooth and translucent to dense high relief. Works may be double sided or composed of several separate layers or elements, but weigh very little. Framing is usually not necessary. Easy to ship, mount, maintain and clean.

Commissions accepted. Visuals and pricing available upon request.

MURIEL VAUGHN
Page 229

Mood Moments
6745 East Superstition Springs
Mesa, AZ 85206
Tel 602-403-2213
E-mail jztime@cox.net

Muriel Vaughn, a Native American/African-American artist, is originally from Los Angeles, CA, but now resides in Phoenix, AZ. From as far back as she can remember, she has had the ability to create. She worked as a quality assurance engineer for an aerospace company for a number of years before deciding to go back to school in advertising design. She took all the fine art classes available during that time. She notes, "I thought that my artwork was good before I started those classes, but I was quickly humbled." Most of Vaughn's art is created as a result of her mood and emotions. She creates with oil, pen and ink, color prism, watercolor, acrylics and pencil. She also works with computer art applications. Her style varies from abstract to realistic. Vaughn has participated in the Pan African Film & Art Festival; the PaPalnk online exhibit "When They Were Children," and local exhibits in Arizona. She belongs to the WESTAF Artist Registrar.

RECENT PROJECTS: *Will's Blues*, acrylic on canvas, for blues club

SUSAN VENABLE
Page 272

Venable Studio
2323 Foothill Lane
Santa Barbara, CA 93105
Tel 805-884-4963
Fax 805-884-4983
E-mail susan@venablestudio.com
www.venablestudio.com

Susan Venable's work is an exploration of structure and surface. Her reliefs are constructed of steel grids and copper wire. The paintings are encaustic and oil. The physicality of the materials is expressed in the rich, complex surfaces of her wall pieces. Venable's work has been installed in public spaces, homes, corporations and museums in the U.S., Europe, Asia, Mexico and Australia. These expressive and luminous pieces are low maintenance and inspire public as well as private spaces.

GUILD SOURCEBOOKS: *Architect's 12; Designer's 9, 10, 11, 12, 14, 15; Architectural & Interior Art 16, 17*

CHRISTOPHER P. VESPERMANN
Pages 40, 187

Vespex, LLC
10 Scotland Road
Kingston, NH 03848
Tel 603-642-3384
Fax 603-642-6601
E-mail vespermann@vespex.com
www.vespex.com

Christopher Vespermann began working in glass full time with his family at Vespermann Glass Studio in Atlanta, GA, in 1984. From 1986 to 1997, he worked as a technical assistant for internationally known artist Dan Dailey. Vespermann's works include sculpture, furniture, architectural glass and lighting. His pieces often use glass in conjunction with metal, stone and other materials. Because of his technical background, he also does mechanical designs and fabrication for other designers. Vespermann created the chairs for the Oklahoma City Bombing Memorial from a concept by Butzer Design Partnership. Vespermann currently lives and works in New Hampshire, where he creates commissioned designs, as well as design and fabrication for James Carpenter Design Associates, on a contract basis.

SERANDA VESPERMANN
Page 75

Vespermann Glass Gallery & Studio
309 East Paces Ferry Road
Atlanta, GA 30305
Tel 404-266-0102/770-936-0633
Fax 404-266-0190/770-986-9101
E-mail seranda@vespermann.com
www.vespermann.com

Since 1984 Seranda Vespermann has been successful in bringing warmth, wit and organic energy to impressive structures nationwide. The Richmond, Virginia Convention Center commission is an example of this, with 55 glass panels distributed throughout the ballroom and exhibition hall of the newly renovated building. "The intent," says Vespermann, "is to facilitate the convention-goer's ability to find the various rooms, which are normally identified by name or number alone." Hence, each of the panels is individually designed, with its own color scheme. The panels are punctuated with mouth-blown rondels and hand-chipped *dalles de verre* pieces.

COMMISSIONS: Round window, 6'Dia, the Cable Center, Denver, CO; two fireplace screens, private residence; exterior wall, private residence, 4' x 16'

GUILD SOURCEBOOKS: *Architect's 14*

ARTIST LISTINGS

VITRAMAX GROUP, INC.
Page 77

Fred diFrenzi
116 South 10th Street
Louisville, KY 40202
Tel 502-589-3828
Fax 502-589-3830
E-mail fred@vitramax.com
www.vitramax.com

Vitramax Group Inc. works with hot glass and various types of architectural glass. Projects range from national monuments to public art to private residences to commercial building projects. Vitramax Group, Inc. specializes in site-specific commissions and installations.

RECENT PROJECTS: National Monument, Indianapolis, IN; Louisville Water Company, KY; Louisville Medical Center, KY; Indiana State Museum, Indianapolis; Park Meadows Mall, Denver, CO

COLLECTIONS: Butler Institute of Art, Youngstown, OH; Huntington Art Museum, WV

AWARDS: National Endowment for the Arts, Artist in Residence

PUBLICATIONS: *Washington Times; New Glass Review 6, 7, 9, 10; Kentucky Arts and Crafts Survey*

GUILD SOURCEBOOKS: *Architect's 13, 14; Architectural & Interior Art 16*

PAM PRINCE WALKER
Pages 234-235

c/o Image Spirit
137 Ridgewood Place
Marion, VA 24354
Tel 276-783-2887
E-mail images@imagespirit.com
www.imagespirit.com

Specializing in acrylic on canvas, Pam Prince Walker's technique relies on concentration, a vivid awareness of all five senses and "living within the character and the place." She begins her work with free-flowing brush strokes. As the canvas takes shape, she occasionally moves into collage, adding touches of paper, glitter, wood and other materials.

RECENT PROJECTS: Appalachian Spirit Arts Association, Marion, VA

COLLECTIONS: The Gallery, The Art Place, Chilhowie, VA; www.imagespirit.com

EXHIBITIONS: Cave House and Barter Theatre, 1970s, Abingdon, VA; Emory and Henry College, 1982, Emory, VA; James Monroe Gallery, 1980, The Arts Club of Washington, DC

AWARDS: The Governor's Award for the Arts, 1986, VA

PUBLICATIONS: *Bring in the Arts,* 1993

SUSAN WEINBERG
Page 236

1605-1/2 Ocean Front Walk
Santa Monica, CA 90401
Tel/Fax 310-392-5042
E-mail infinitystudio@aol.com
www.glassumbrella.com

Susan Weinberg has been a working artist since 1972. She holds a B.S. in science, home economics /education from Northwestern University and the University of Wisconsin, and a B.F.A. and M.F.A. from Otis Art Institute in Los Angeles, CA. The scientist in Susan has driven her to experiment constantly. She is not only interested in image or subject matter, but in what paint does: how it moves, separates and responds on wet surfaces. "An artist shouldn't be afraid to experiment and make mistakes. Sometimes by putting two mistakes together, you create something new." Weinberg has extensive experience working with designers and architects and creates work in a wide range of sizes, from miniatures to murals.

333

NIKOLAS WEINSTEIN
Page 197

Nikolas Weinstein Studios
1649 Valencia Street
San Francisco, CA 94110
Tel 415-643-5418
Fax 415-643-3723
E-mail info@nikolas.net
www.nikolas.net

Inspired by the essential geometry of nature, and reflecting the influence of gravity, position and scale on the evolution of molten glass, the contours of Nikolas Weinstein's work catalog the fluid potential of a single form. In addition to smaller artworks, Weinstein creates glasswork by commission for large installations, exploring the intersection of sculpture and architecture.

RECENT PROJECTS: DZ Bank Headquarters, Pariser Platz 3, Berlin, architect: Frank O. Gehry; Bonny Doon Vineyards, Santa Cruz, CA, architect: Holt Hinshaw; Sangiacomo residence, Pebble Beach, CA; Miller residence, Carmel, CA; Campton Place Hotel restaurant, San Francisco, CA; Miller residence, San Jose, CA

DANIEL WINTERICH
Pages 12, 76

Studio Winterich
29 Weller Court
Pleasant Hill, CA 94523
Tel 925-943-5755
Fax 925-943-5455
E-mail dw@winterich.com
www.winterich.com

Seeking to create places replete with luminosity, this artist and architect is focused on the design of inspirational glass structures within architectural environments. His Studio Winterich is a multi-disciplined design studio recognized for a range of innovative projects, from small works of glass to large-scale public commissions incorporating glass, concrete, steel, light and water. Shown in this book is the private commission *Structural Mondrian.* Inspired by the paintings of Piet Mondrian, the glowing structural glass wall separates a reception room from the board room. The west-facing wall bathes the reception area in golden light during evening hours.

GUILD SOURCEBOOKS: *Architect's 15; Architectural & Interior Art 16*

LAURIE WOHL
Pages 178, 267

236 West 27th Street Suite 801
New York, NY 10001
Tel 646-486-0586
E-mail lauriewohl@hotmail.com

Laurie Wohl's Unweavings® evoke in a modern idiom the spirit of mystery and celebration of the oldest traditions of narrative textile. The gentle radiance of these pieces complements residential, liturgical and commercial settings. Narratives are conveyed by form, color and texture, with unwoven spaces forming shapes suggestive of ritual garments. The narrative is enhanced by Wohl's own iconographic language, as well as Hebrew, English and Chinese calligraphy. Wohl's Unweavings® are held in the collections of the Museum of Arts and Design, New York, NY; the American Bible Society; the Constitutional Court of South Africa; Catholic Theological Union, Chicago, IL; and U.S. embassies in Tunis, Vienna, Capetown and Praetoria. Fourth Presbyterian Church of Chicago, IL, has commissioned 11 major works for its sanctuary, five of which were installed in 2002-2003.

ARTIST LISTINGS

RED WOLF
Page 265

Red Wolf Fine Art
PO Box 396
Laytonville, CA 95454
Tel 707-984-7003
Fax 07-984-9377
E-mail redwolf@RedWolfFineArt.com
www.RedWolfFineArt.com

Red Wolf incorporates industrial materials in a layering process that enables him to create elements of structural color within his paintings. Structural color is an optical effect, that in nature, is characteristic of surfaces such as hummingbird feathers, tropical fish and opals. These color effects are not possible to produce in traditional pigmented paintings. Artwork is painted upon sandwiched honeycomb aluminum aerospace panels that are lightweight, rigid and nonflammable. Paintings can be shaped to conform to any configuration and any scale.

COMMISSIONS: Fountain Hills, Arizona, 2003; Bahrain Sheraton nightclub, 2002, Manama, Bahrain; Nagoya Marriott Associa Hotel, 2000, Nagoya, Japan; Lockheed Space and Exhibition Center lobby, 1997, Sunnyvale, California

PUBLICATIONS: *Designer's Workshop,* August 2000, Japan

BRUCE WOLFE
Pages 120-121

Bruce Wolfe Ltd.
206 El Cerrito Avenue
Piedmont, CA 94611
Tel 510-655-7871
Fax 510-601-7200
E-mail landbwolfe@earthlink.net
www.brucewolfe.com

Most of the subjects of Bruce Wolfe's portraits are imposing, dynamic personalities. He hopes to portray that energy and presence. "I put my ego aside and make a likeness that reflects the spirit of the subject—not just a mask and body." Recent installations include the monumental bronze of Barbara Jordan at the Austin-Bergstrom Airport, TX. Wolfe was selected to complete this portrait after a comprehensive artist selection process. He has installed two large bronze figures at the Old Mission in Santa Barbara, CA, and will unveil two additional figures, *Christ* and *Mary Magdalene,* on Easter day, 2003. Just unveiled at the gala opening of the New Asian Art Museum, San Francisco, CA, is a bronze bust of major donor Chong-Moon Lee.

WOODLAND STUDIOS
Page 251

Gary Walker
Cindy Lou Hoesly
4378 Jordan Drive #4
McFarland, WI 53558
E-mail gwalker@woodland-studios.com
www.woodland-studios.com

Woodland Studios creates custom original artwork to fit the architectural design of any property. They mix art and photography with digital and natural mediums. Tools include cameras, computers, watercolors, pastels, colored pencils and acrylics. Applying graphic skills, they abstract the photographic images and over-paint each one until the brush strokes takes over and the photo "melts" into the background. Even with a magnifying glass, it is difficult to see where the photo ends and the graphic image begins. Call to request an image catalog of their complete portfolio.

334

LARRY ZGODA
Page 73

Larry Zgoda Studio
2117 West Irving Park Road
Chicago, IL 60618
Tel 773-463-3970
Fax 773-463-3978
E-mail lz@larryzgodastudio.com
www.larryzgodastudio.com

Larry Zgoda embraces color, pattern, texture and light. Working with a sublime cache of stained glass materials, he models these qualitites to create stained glass not simply for our aesthetic drama but for the stage on which the drama unfolds.

RECENT PROJECTS: Five stained glass entries, Sacred Heart of Jesus Chapel, Our Lady of Victory Convent, Lemont, IL

COMMISSIONS: *Lake and Sky Meet the Land,* 2002, Huron Public Library, Huron, OH

PUBLICATIONS: *The Art of Stained Glass,* 1998; *Beautiful Things,* 2000; *Object Lessons,* 2001

GUILD SOURCEBOOKS: *THE GUILD 1, 2, 3, 4, 5; Architect's 6, 7, 8, 9, 10, 11, 12, 13, 14, 15; Architectural & Interior Art 17; Artful Home 1*

RAY ZOVAR
Page 183

Silk Purse Enterprises, Inc.
2499 Keenan Road
McFarland, WI 53558
Tel 608-345-2991
Tel/Fax 608-838-6617
E-mail ray@zovar.com
www.zovar.com

Ray Zovar's years of experience in sculpture, painting and color enliven his current mosaic medium with fascinating interplays of rich colors, textures, and often, three-dimensional effects. He blends chips of porcelain (approximately five pieces per square inch) with inlays of stained glass, exotic woods, metals, marble and granite to form freestanding, hanging or functional art. Painterly effects sparkle and organic lines flow readily from the hard stone and metals, creating contradictions that demand to be touched. Both abstract and representational commission inquiries are welcome.

Location Index

LOCATION INDEX

337

Index of Artists & Companies

INDEX OF ARTISTS & COMPANIES

340

INDEX OF ARTISTS & COMPANIES

342